SPIRIT

Also by Arthur Kornhaber, M.D.

Between Parents and Grandparents

SPIRIT

MIND, BODY, AND THE WILL TO EXISTENCE

ARTHUR KORNHABER, M.D.

ST. MARTIN'S PRESS · NEW YORK

The author is grateful for permission from Martin Stone to use material from *California Business Magazine*, November 1986.

DESIGN BY JUDITH A. STAGNITTO

Library of Congress Cataloging-in-Publication Data

Kornhaber, Arthur.
  Spirit / Arthur Kornhaber.
    p.   cm.
  "A Thomas Dunne book."
  ISBN 0-312-02286-7
  1. Spirit. 2. Mind and body. I. Title.
BD421.K66 1988   88-18235
128'.2—dc19

First Edition

10 9 8 7 6 5 4 3 2 1

For Aunt Rose

For Uncle Louis

For all "naturals"

In a previous work* I noted that there
exist certain people who, as individuals,
parents, and grandparents, place an emotional priority on their lives. Rooted in
emotional attachments to their loved ones,
they possess an altruistic nature, are un-
selfish, are usually involved in helping others in some way, and seem to be immune
to the negative teachings of the culture in
which they live, although they are acutely
aware that these cultural aberrations exist.
I called them "naturals."
At that time I tried to figure out how
they got that way. Were they born that way?
Was it their experience that helped them
achieve the ability to see to the emotional
core of things?
What I didn't realize then, because I
was not considering spiritual "variables,"
was that their emotional abilities did not
arise from mind or body at all. These abilities arose from a third factor, which I now
know to be spirit.
"Naturals" possess what I now know to
be spiritual intelligence.
This book is for all "naturals"—a way
of saying that, more often than not, they
are right and the world is wrong.

*Between Parents and Grandparents, St. Martin's
Press, 1986.

· ACKNOWLEDGMENTS ·

The creative process is similar to the creation of life itself.

A new baby's coming to exist depends on many factors: its ancestors for its genetic beginnings and its mother for its cultivation in the womb. Once born, it depends on its parents for care and nurturing, and on all the people in its world who influence its unique identity, which is shaped by all that it learns from being in the world.

Much the same is true for this work. It represents not only my own efforts as its "carrier," it also contains what I have learned both from observing nature and from every person I have met during my lifetime, either directly through personal contact or indirectly, by reading, hearing, or studying what they have created. They have all contributed. I want especially to thank those who have been instrumental in directly "seeding" and "cultivating" this work.

When *Spirit* was only a "glint in the author's eye," Barry Silverstein was of inestimable help during the early phase of this project. Together we churned ideas while Barry probed and challenged many of the concepts that I formulated, and contributed some of his own. Thus his spirit and mind have touched these pages.

Randall A. Meeks, by his diligent scholarship, played an important role as "cultivator." More than a research assistant, Randy was not only involved in both the clinical and literary research phases of the study, but he brought his own special views to bear on the subject. He substantially contributed to the section entitled "A Short History of Spirit."

All creative works, whether babies or books, need someone to care for their "carrier," to teach, to inspire, to encourage, and to ensure a healthy delivery—sort of "literary prenatal care." Thus I wish to thank two editors at St. Martin's Press, Brian DiFiore and Ruth Cavin, who spent many hours with this manuscript and have contributed much to it.

And my very special thanks to Thomas Dunne, executive editor at St. Martin's Press, friend, coach, teacher, and literary "obstetrician," who guided this work through the literary birth canal.

I cannot thank by name all those who participated in this study of spirit, since their names have been changed here to protect their privacy. I am deeply indebted to all of these fine people. You know who you are.

· CONTENTS ·

· INTRODUCTION ·
A Paradox:
Halfminded People in a
Halfminded Society

> *. . . true aristocracy, devolves not*
> *from edict, nor from rote, but from*
> *the preservation of kinship with the*
> *elemental forces and purposes of life*
> *whose understanding is not farther*
> *beyond the mind of a Native shepherd*
> *than beyond the cultured fumblings*
> *of a mortar board intelligence.*

> —*Beryl Markham,* West with the
> Night

The time has come to talk about spirit. Here's why.
    A disturbing paradox is affecting a great many of us:
    The more that we learn, the less we seem to know.
    The more intellectually "smart" we become, the less we
        seem to be able to handle these "smarts."
    The more natural mysteries that we uncover,
        the more confused we are about ourselves,
        the more frightened we are about juggling the hot po-
    tatoes of new knowledge, and

the more helpless and bewildered we seem to be about what to do with all that we learn.

All this new "know-how" that mankind has acquired just doesn't seem to make people happier.

Why is this?

It's because we have unknowingly made a trade-off. In the course of our singleminded and relentless pursuit of intellectual and technical knowledge, we have become intellectually polarized—a halfminded people who increasingly ignore the part of our minds that provides hopes and dreams, romance and love, altruism and wonder. We voluntarily relinquished the humane and spiritual in favor of the tangible material benefits offered by the immediate everyday world. And in doing so, we have neglected the best part of ourselves. We have become *halfminded*—intellectually knowledgeable but at the same time more spiritually ignorant.

This is the paradox.

Halfminded people are restless and unhappy people.

However great their success as measured by the everyday world, halfminded people are rarely happy, simply because they are out of touch with the part of their minds that experiences happiness. We have lost the capacity for anything more than a temporary "high" perceived by the halfmind. Only wholeminded people, whose intellect *and* spirit are mentally balanced, are able to experience genuine happiness.

The mind has essentially two functions. The first is that of a biochemical computer, storing and processing information from the everyday world. This is the "intellectual," analytic, conscious half of the mind, which is constantly involved in everyday life: learning, monitoring the environment, making decisions.

Some think that this halfmind is all that humans possess,

and that it encompasses all of the senses. But I believe the mind has another part to it, one generally ignored in today's society. Its nature is qualitative and responds to different stimuli than input from the everyday world. It contains knowledge from a source beyond the five senses and is linked to spirit. I call this the *seventh sense* (the sixth sense is intuition, a mixture of inspiration and what is learned from the everyday world).

The wholemind is one that has access to all of its senses. The halfmind has an executive function: It governs the "how" of things. The seventh sense formulates policies for the halfmind to carry out—it controls the "why" of things. The halfmind "computer" supplies the nuts and bolts necessary for function, the seventh sense informs the way the nuts and bolts are to be used. It is the architect of human experience and the philosopher within.

The halfmind supplies the form of life, the seventh sense, the substance.

The wholemind, with access to all of its seven senses, is rooted both in the everyday world and in the world beyond the five senses. When the mind has access to all of its senses, the self is integrated, fulfilled, has the capacity for happiness and the ability to create, with others, a humane and responsive society.

If the halfmind predominates, chaos often results within the self because, like a computer, the halfmind has no inherent values, meaning, or purpose for its existence. Cut off from the seventh sense, it is no more than de-spirited matter, a biochemical computer.

This condition of halfmindedness is what has become insidiously entrenched during mankind's quest for intellectual and technological "progress." Too many of us have banished our seventh sense from our private and public consciousness. We have allowed the halfmind to become as anarchic as a child let loose in a candy store and are increasingly unable even to observe how halfminded we have become. If you have any doubts about this statement, just look around to see how insecure, dissatisfied, frustrated, disgruntled, or plain unhappy so many people are, without really knowing why.

Why isn't the world better off? Why are love, peace, happiness, and personal self-satisfaction in such short supply? Why do so many destructive things continue to happen in the world? Why as people are we becoming increasingly isolated and alienated from one another? Why has love, romance, and wonder given way to contractual relationships, conditional attachments, cynicism, and skepticism? Why have so many people lost the dreams of their childhood? Why do we continue to promote a narcissistic culture of mind and a technology that roars ahead ignoring the emotional and spiritual destruction that follows in its wake?

Why are so many people so *miserable*?

Why? Because we have ignored our seventh sense, our conduit to spirit. By "spirit" I mean that quality that every human being has within. It is an attribute of both mind and body, and the source of the meaning and purpose of life. We have allowed our halfmind to overrun its borders and expand into the areas where it does not belong. We "think" instead of feel, "explain" instead of wonder, "measure" and "judge" people instead of empathize with them, and "use" others instead of loving them. This is the ethic of the halfmind.

The halfmind is devoid of spirit.

The qualities of love, caring, and altruism are part of the seventh sense, the locus of spirit within the self. And spirit is what makes human beings . . . human.

What I am increasingly concerned about, both as a psychiatrist and a citizen, is the disproportionate amount of energy and attention we are devoting to cultivating our halfminds. Our intellectually polarized culture has, in effect, relinquished its spirit, producing abundant numbers of de-spirited people, many of whom are self-serving, self-centered, and concerned about little beyond their local material world. Yet these same people can't understand why they are bitter, angry, and full of anguish, why they lose their will to existence and often just drop out.

Our society ignores anything beyond the halfmind, except for an occasional token mention. "Spirit" is rarely discussed outside of a religious setting. For to acknowledge the existence of spirit and to act upon this knowledge would disrupt business-as-usual—the entrenched ethic of the times. It would reveal the futility of the halfminded pursuit of "self-realization" through work and materialism. Because of this silence, we perpetuate the system; we see to it that our children are raised in the ethic of halfmindedness, sacrificing them on the altar of narcissism and materialism by cultivating their intellectual growth while neglecting to encourage, or even recognize, the spiritual in them.

In my clinical experience I have found that halfminded-ness is the key to the existential despair and unhappiness of many—especially those who otherwise "have it all." I have encountered them all: the depressed executive out of touch with his family, the overworked, disgruntled housewife, the confused and angry adolescent, the drunk, the addict, the lonely career woman, the "workaholic," the philanderer, the gambler, the clergyman who loses his calling, the attorney suffering a "mid-life crisis" . . . What these people have in common is that somewhere along the way they lost complete touch with their seventh sense. They have become, in varying degrees, de-spir-ited.

And there are others who have relinquished the dreams they once had and who suffer from a sort of spiritual "anemia":

professionals who achieved their glorious career and became disillusioned; old people who have "retired" from family life; men and women who have chosen careers over closeness to their children; businesspeople, lawyers, doctors, teachers, people who hurt others, who lie, cheat, and abandon integrity for advancement; those who flee from close emotional relationships—all of them are halfminded.

Halfminded people construct a negative life philosophy to rationalize their loveless existence in order to be able to live with that bleak reality. Thus in a halfminded society, love is replaced by a social contract that supplies different justifications for becoming involved with others: status justifies a "good" but passionless marriage; physical need a loveless sexual liaison; personal advantage a "friendship."

The halfminded society deals with spirit by ignoring it, drowning it out in a maelstrom of action, movement, noise, stimulation, frenzied acquiring of the latest fashion, and an inordinate emphasis on work, work, work, and more work—all to keep the halfmind full so there is no time for mystery, no time to reflect, no time for subversive spiritual questions to sneak in. No wonder so many people are miserable.

Halfmindedness is a plague. I have become more and more convinced over the years that varying degrees of diverse syndromes categorized as mental illnesses that are physically and psychologically manifested are also *spiritually* related. And that the spiritual origins of these conditions are ignored not only by halfminded therapists who give halfminded treatments, but by gifted and effective therapists, as well, who unknowingly help people with such conditions but don't really recognize that their successful results had anything to do with spirit.

For myself, I was certainly unaware of any influence of spirit when I first started practicing medicine. As a neophyte I began with a basic nuts-and-bolts, technical, halfminded attitude. It didn't take me long to learn that "bedside manner"—caring and paying real attention to my patients—was a potent, if intangible, medicine. Like other doctors, I found that the ability to lift the patient's spirits was often medically beneficial.

It is time now for medicine, psychiatry, and psychology to state openly that they have been involved with the human spirit since the first patient ever arrived for treatment. Therapists must acknowledge that they have been reluctant to deal with spirit because they lacked knowledge and were afraid of trespassing in the area of religion. They must begin a systematic exploration of matters of the spirit and call it what it is.

Psychiatry of the spirit is compatible with religious teachings as far as, in the words of William James, "Religion . . . shall mean for us the feelings, acts, and experiences of individual men in their solitude."[1] The difference is that I am considering spirit as part of a biological, psychological, physical, and social whole. I am concerned with spirit from the inside out—spirit's relationship to the self. Religion is concerned with spirit from the outside in—spirit's relationship to a person or an institution *outside* of the self.

In this work I refer to your personal spirit. My primary concern is what you, the reader, can do for yourself, from the inside out, to learn about your own spirit, to increase your spiritedness, and to enhance your existence.

I hope to help you to augment your own seventh sense, for surely you have been personally affected, as most of us have in some degree or another, by halfmindedness. If you have felt confusion, despair, a sense of meaninglessness in life, a lack of direction, a feeling of just "going through the motions" of existence, this could well signal that your life has become unbalanced—that you have lost touch with your seventh sense, that you have become de-spirited to some degree.

Fortunately this is not an incurable condition. In order to be strong and purposeful, and to live a happy and meaningful life, one must learn to proceed beyond the halfmind and become wholeminded, spirited. Learning about spirit will immeasurably enrich one's personal life, for spirit offers a bottomless well of love and patience in dealing with others.

Some wonderful things can happen. By attending to spirit

you will find yourself marching to the sound of your own drummer. You may achieve a greater order and greater control in life and a greater immunity from the foibles of the everyday world. Knowing that you are primarily accountable to spiritual imperatives for the way you live your life can supply you with an inner strength and a powerful internal agenda, an agenda for living that is an exhilarating alternative to what you learn from society's "trendy" teachings.

By tending to your spirit, you can establish not only a sanctuary within the self but a communion with the kindred spirits of loved ones. You will have the ability to embellish your community and your world—and to give true meaning to your existence.

By tending to your spirit, you will expand the range of your awareness of what is going on around you, be a more serene person, and join the ranks of those to whom the infinite possibilities of life may be more nearly realized.

·1·

SOMETHING MORE

Socrates asks Alcibiades:
"What are we and what is talking
with what?"

This work rests on the premise that spirit indeed exists and that it communicates with and makes the mind whole through a seventh sense.

Must the existence of spirit be scientifically "proven" for this work to be useful and credible?

Not necessarily.

Lack of *scientific* proof doesn't mean lack of existence. There are other "proofs."

Science can teach us about form but not always about substance. Science can describe a human body but not a person. Your own "proof" is in your experience.

How aware are you of spirit?

Do you believe that there is such a thing as a human spirit?

Your answer to this question should be illuminating.

Agreed, it's not an easy question to answer with "yes" or "no," because of the elusive nature of "spirit" itself. Reflect for a moment. Have you ever wondered, when you enjoy something, what part of you does the enjoying? Have you ever wondered, when you are crestfallen, what part of you experiences unhappiness? What part of you marvels at the beauty of foliage in the fall, swells with joy at becoming a parent or a grandparent, mourns when a beloved person dies? What part of you savors and suffers life? Longs to love or be loved?

What part of you sighs? Ponders the mysterious?

Is it only your mind or your body that does this?

You may answer that your "self" does this. But what is your self? Isn't it only a mental idea that encompasses the intertwined "parts" that make up the perception of "I"? Not a tangible thing.

Then what "parts" of your self can you identify? A mind. A body. Anything else?

Do you feel that there is perhaps something more to you than body and mind, something whose existence you can't prove, but that you feel, or intuit, or know? Can you relate this undefined part of yourself to unexplainable experiences you may have had—or sudden feelings of connection with another person? Can you associate it with the part of you that loves, or that gets "high" when an infant smiles at you? To what makes you happy? And unhappy?

Is it present in the part of you that muses at the stars?

Do you think that these experiences arise from your mind and body alone, or could you consider the possibility that there is something else operating here—another "part" of yourself that perhaps affects and uses your mind and body to express it? A thing so many people describe as something "way inside"?

Look at a seed. What do you see? Only a tiny piece of substance, matter, right? But is that all that is there? Is not something more than substance contained in that seed? Is there not an indescribable force contained within that seed that will, one day, bring forth something larger and more beautiful than the seed itself?

Is it possible that we all contain "something more" within ourselves? What do you believe? If you believe that there is indeed more to you than mind and body, reflect for a moment. What is it like? How does it operate within you? How is it different from the part of your mind that copes with everyday life? If you are aware of "something more" within you, you are aware of spirit.

Perhaps these suggestions have you snickering, or thinking, "This is absurd. This psychiatrist has gone off the deep end. Next he'll be bringing up ghosts, and auras, some kind of cult talk, or maybe the stuff that belongs in horror movies."

It's not surprising if it strikes you that way. These are understandable reflex ideas instilled in you by a culture that pokes fun at spirit. I had thoughts like this when I first began to think seriously about spiritual issues. But they only clutter up your mind and get in the way of seeing clearly. Put them aside whenever they pop into your mind, since what's at issue here does not involve the external or the occult.

Have you been halfmindedly ignoring the "something more" within you most of your life? Can you now free yourself from prejudices long enough to acknowledge the *possibility* that spirit is omnipresent; that you were unaware of it just because you haven't been paying attention to its presence?

Think about the important people in your life and what is unique about each of them. Have you noticed how some "sparkle" with life energy, how they, like most babies, emanate a force that seems to pull you to them and makes you feel good? Surely you've seen people like this who can walk into a room and electrify it with their presence? There are others who, seemingly serene and quiet, can nevertheless profoundly influence a multitude. There are lovers who actually soften and "glow" in each other's company. We have all seen these things.

Would you now consider that these phenomena, vague

and subjective as they are, are manifestations of the presence of "something more," something beyond the realm of mind and body, like the force within a seed—something we may call spirit, present in all of us?

I believe so, and I am not alone in this belief. Surprisingly to some, Sigmund Freud himself would agree if he were alive today. In a private conversation he was known to have said, "Humanity has always known that it possesses a spirit; it was my task to show that it had instincts as well."[1]

In studying this subject, I found that the overwhelming majority of people of whom I asked "Do you believe that there is such a thing as a human spirit?" responded in the affirmative. They agreed that there was something more to life than that which meets the senses.

To the minority who said: "Prove it to me," I answered, "I can't." I am convinced of its presence, but (at least for the moment) I find it impossible to irrevocably "prove" using such an inadequate tool as a human mind.

Can one page describe a book? Can an eye see itself?

• THE ANNIE PHENOMENON •

My serious interest in the subject of spirit began to stir in 1975, while I was researching the relationship between grandparents and grandchildren. Interviewing a large number of children and elders, I noticed things taking place that could not be adequately explained by psychological theory. I became aware that "something more" beyond what I understood as emotion was operating between the generations, something I couldn't fit into my previous ideas.

For example, one day I had brought several elementary school children to visit a nursing home as part of an intergenerational program linking the two institutions. One of the youngsters who accompanied me was Annie, a perky seven-year-old. When she entered the sitting room of the nursing home where the frail residents were talking with one another or just sitting alone, she spied a lifeless old woman in a far corner of the room. The woman sat listing over the side of her wheelchair, held in place by a belt tightly secured around her waist. Her bright red dress and white lace collar were neatly starched but disheveled. She appeared oblivious to her surroundings.

"Look at that cute little granny over there," Annie said to me. "She looks so lonely."

"See if you can talk to her," a nurse said. "That's Mrs. Boyce." I went over with Annie. She squatted in front of Mrs. Boyce, and tilted her head sideways so she could look up into the old woman's dim gray eyes.

"Hi!" Annie said, smiling.

Mrs. Boyce's body shifted. "Hello, child," she whispered hoarsely.

"I like your dress," said Annie. "It's cute." She straightened Mrs. Boyce's collar. "And this is pretty . . ."

At this point, I wandered away to see how the other children were doing. After an hour I returned to check up on Annie. She was nowhere to be found. "She wheeled Mrs. Boyce back to her room," the nurse told me. "It's 112."

When I entered the room, I found Mrs. Boyce sitting up straight in her chair and combing Annie's long blond hair. The two of them were chatting away. Annie was radiant. "She knew my grandpa!" she announced.

I couldn't believe my eyes. Mrs. Boyce was not the same woman that I had seen a short while before. She was transformed. She was sitting up straight, there was life in her movements, and her eyes were bright. Something amazing had happened! Something within her had been energized, illuminated, by this child. Annie had released a force within her—I had no idea what it was. What could perform such a miracle? *What was that something?* I wondered. *What changed Mrs. Boyce?*

What I now call my halfmind went to work on it. Reflex medical, psychological thoughts raced through my brain, frantically trying to give "reason" to this occurrence. Did Annie remind Mrs. Boyce of someone or something in her past that activated her memory? Was it just that Annie's presence simply engaged Mrs. Boyce's interest because usually she had no such stimulation? And then did these phenomena cause her body to react by pumping adrenaline into her bloodstream, which would explain her "activation"?

Although these explanations were plausible, they didn't "feel" right; they were not sufficient, in my view, to explain the extent of Mrs. Boyce's sudden and unexplained vitality. So it came to mind that perhaps Mrs. Boyce wasn't revitalized because her thyroid or adrenal glands pumped hormones into her bloodstream, but that the opposite was true: Her glands were pumping because she was vitalized—spirited—by some close interaction with the little girl. At this point I stopped myself short. "Wait a minute," I said to myself. "This idea is off the wall." I asked Annie. "What did you do, Annie? You sure perked up Mrs. Boyce."

"I didn't do anything," she answered. "She just combed my hair."

It was at times like these that I came to realize that the nature of the attachment between the old and the young is not primarily physical or psychological. It is spiritual.

Since then I have seen the Annie phenomenon repeated over and over again and not only between the old and the young, but between parents and children, friends, colleagues, and in myriad other ways.

It's frustrating to try to describe this phenomenon. Words literally fail me. Terms like "energy," "life force," "human transformation" come to my mind, but they relate only feebly to what I have witnessed. The inadequacy of my effort became so aggravating at one point that I decided to ignore the whole topic. I felt, at that time, since it was too enormous in scope and too frustrating to deal with it was better left to theologians and mystics. So many people I spoke with had told me that a quest for a definition of spirit was an impossible task—that it was something one could only feel but not express, that the subject was better left alone.

But I couldn't ignore the topic for long. It came back to mind every time I saw the Annie phenomenon repeated. The human spirit was there all right—elusive, intangible. The Annie phenomenon, although unexplainable by current medico-psychological theories, was nevertheless real. Finally I asked myself if Spirit was a figment of my imagination, or was spirit an entity beyond the mind and body, present in every human being?

And I wondered, is spirit, if it exists, not just a noun, but a verb? Not a passive thing beyond personal control, as some religions claim, but an active, changing, living force, rooted in something beyond imagination that is manifested within the self through both the mind and the body?

Is the individual human spirit a private and personal portion of a universal life force that is present in each human being? If so, where does this force come from? Does it originate in what some call God, others nature, the cosmos, or some other name? Is it all around us? Is spirit life itself or something separate from life? Does it manifest itself in a person at a specific point of development, or does it enter each of us with our first breath and leave us with our last? Could this intangible thing called spirit ever be given substance—even a little—so a person could consciously use its power within the self?

✳   ✳   ✳

I decided to get the opinion of others. I asked several people: "Do you believe that there is such a thing as a human spirit?" Often people would respond to my question with another question. "What do you mean by spirit?" I usually told them it meant whatever they thought it did.

I quickly learned that most people do believe that a human spirit exists—95 percent of those I interviewed either intuited or clearly acknowledged the existence of spirit. The majority said that they "knew" it existed but that they rarely talked about it spontaneously, even with friends or relatives. A sixty-five-year-old physician summed up the feelings of this group when he said, "It's there but I never think about it," and "People keep their 'spirits' very private." Another group acknowledged the presence of spirit, but were out of touch with it and found no room for it in their everyday lives. As a young working mother said, "Out of sight, out of mind—no time for that kind of thing. Too busy."

The fact that most of the people I talked with did believe in a human spirit piqued my interest. I knew then that I wasn't making something up because I wanted it to be true. Here was a consensus.

Now what? How could I learn more? Before I went any further I knew it would be necessary to fine-tune my definition of "spirit." In fact, was "spirit" the right word to use at all? Most of the people I spoke with, like Sally, a thirty-seven-year-old mother of four, had difficulty in pinning down what they understood by "spirit."

Sure, I have a spirit, a something, I've always known it. But it's not a word thing—something to talk about. It's a special secret deep within me—private. It's hard to get to it. In fact, when I talk about it, even try to think too much about it, then I lose it. I can't grab it. In fact, when I am feeling it—sort of a communion—and then I try to pay attention to it . . . to think about it . . . I lose touch with it, it's confusing. It's like trying to see a special star on a very dark night. If I look straight at it, I lose it. I can only see it if I look away from it, and there it is at the edge of my view. If I look back quickly—it's gone. Things of the spirit are like that. At least, mine is.

In seeking to define spirit, I wondered whether the dictionary definition of "an animating or vital principle" was a good place to start. At first this didn't seem to be right. In common usage, "spirit" is a nebulous term at best and for most, it is a word laden with baggage of diverse and personalized meaning. So, for myself, I defined "spirit" in the following way: a universal and omnipresent force present both within the universe and within the self. Within the self it is joined to mind and body. It is at once the universal "spirit," the "one," and "human spirit"—a personal part of our selves. I use the term "spiritual" to describe things relating to or consisting of the spirit. These terms have no other associations here except as I have defined them.

While reading this book, try to shed your previous stereotypes and associations to the words "spirit" and "spiritual."

If you agree that the possibility of an individual spirit exists, many questions arise that seem unanswerable or too awesome to contemplate. Questions like: What is the nature of spirit? Where does it come from? How does it operate within the person? Do some people have more spirit than others? Do spirits affect one another or resonate with one another? Does the human spirit think and feel? Can it make the self sick? How? Can such an illness be healed? Does spirit evolve through life or does it stay the same from birth to death? Indeed, can it be altered, deadened, killed, exalted during the life of the person? What is its relation to other aspects of the individual's mind and body? What is its relation to the "life force"?

These are just some of the questions I asked people in the study. I am certain that you, too, have plenty of your own. Certainly I still do. The workings of spirit are not easily learned.

·2·

EXPLORING
SPIRIT

*I am not my mind nor my body.
There is something more within me
that coexists with the two. What is
possible is either its demise, its
persistence after death, or its existence
before me.*

—*Barry Silverstein*

It's one thing to believe that spirit exists. It's another to try to find out how it works. Before I got involved in the study, I asked myself if it was possible (1) to study spirit in a realistic, natural, and rational way and (2) to reasonably and practically communicate what is learned to others. Did any credible authorities on the subject exist?

Indeed there is no dearth of literature on the subject, but as far as I know most of what has been written about spirit is theoretical rather than practical. Furthermore, although man has been fascinated with this issue since the beginning of time and has created diverse conceptual systems and institutions in testimony to the unknown, no one, to my knowledge, has ever "proved" the existence of spirit. Many brilliant, speculative thinkers have ventured into this cosmological netherland only to return with tales that sounded like science fiction. Other investigators of spirit produced an abundance of brilliantly formulated theories that were unfortunately so convoluted and incomprehensible that they were practically useless to the average person. I was struck by how some "far-out" cosmic theoreticians were unfairly ridiculed by their colleagues. It seems that for anyone except those with religious credentials of some sort (or members of the subculture of mystics, whom many people regard as "weird" anyway), to investigate spirit means to venture out on a precarious limb of credibility. Anyone who talks about spirit and is not a member of the clergy seems to invite public ridicule, especially in a spiritually deficient, halfminded culture. This is understandable, because the boundaries between what many people call "spirit" and parapsychological phenomena can be truly fuzzy. And it is always audacious to claim credibility in these matters, since so much is unknown.

But common sense told me that anything learned about the workings of spirit is better than nothing at all. I encouraged myself with the thought that temples of knowledge are, after all, built of small stones. For example, in medicine not everything must be known about a disease in order to deal with its effects or limit its ravages. Even though much about the common cold still puzzles scientists, empirical measures—keeping away from those infected; taking aspirin, vitamin C, and plenty of fluids; getting lots of rest—help to avoid complications and hasten recovery. The same holds for investigating spirit: Something is better than nothing.

Good. Now, was there a method of study that could produce enough down-to-earth information to stimulate those thinking about the issue of spirit and seeking to know and, hopefully, to cultivate their own?

One thing was clear from the outset: Traditional scientific methods weren't applicable to the subject. Furthermore, I had no illusions that the work would be given any credence by academic reductionists, those whom Carl Jung deservedly casti-

gated when he wrote: "Rationalism and doctrinairism are the
diseases of our time; they pretend to have all the answers."[1]
Jung knew well that rationalism, by its very halfminded nature,
is a technique incapable of addressing matters of spirit. Ra-
tionalists give no credence to a seventh sense; they believe (as
Gertrude Stein reputedly said about California) that "there is no
there there." The idea of exploring the workings of the human
spirit would be ludicrous to them. The accepted credo of science, "if it can't be proved, it ain't so," reduces the believable
world of such people to a very narrow tunnel of "hard" knowledge.

But that's their problem.

Science can describe "how" things work but not "why."
For example, the chemical compounds called endorphins are
secreted by the brain and produce a feeling of well-being. Science can describe their function and location but is helpless to
explain "why" these chemicals are secreted, how they got to be
there in the first place, and why their activity makes us feel
good. Scientific tools can't measure "gossamer" things like feelings, emotions—or the human spirit. They can't reduce to
numbers and symbols an intangible like "goodness" as described
by a distinguished clergyman whom I interviewed. Speaking of
some survivors of the Holocaust and the people who shielded
them from death at their own peril, he said,

> How do you see this—the goodness—that emanates
> from them? There are these people who have a kind
> of energy that comes from them. They light up a
> room when they enter. It's physical and spiritual.
> After the hell that they have endured they still shine
> their light on those around them.
>
> How do you explain the incredible human
> beings—non-Jews—who risked everything to save the
> lives of Jews in the Nazi-occupied countries? More

than a few and at enormous personal risk and risk to
their families. What is the *Neshamah*—the spirit—
within them?

Contrary to commonly held views, useful scientific findings need not be limited to "hard" data. Reality courses across a
broad spectrum that includes both "hard" and "soft" information. In fact, this "hard" view of science is being chipped away
by scientists involved in the New Physics movement; they are
redefining the nature of "scientific" evidence.

Convinced that traditional scientific methodology was not
appropriate for my study of spirit, I considered a method I had
used in a previous study.

In investigating the relationship between grandparents and
grandchildren, I used a combination of listening, talking with
people, intuition, professional expertise, life experience, consultation with colleagues and "experts," concept formation and
categorization, and speculation. Some academicians regarded
this as highly unscientific, but what emerged from it was down-
to-earth information that was very useful for many people. And
usefulness is, after all, the goal.

To my knowledge, no one had ever asked a large number
of people what they thought about the nature and workings of
their own spirits. But first, as in any traditional scientific endeavor, I searched the literature in order to find out what was
already known on the subject. (The results of this search, "A
Short History of Spirit," are presented in Appendix A.)

One of the most interesting things I noted in reading about
spirit is how the influence of society's acknowledged spiritual
"experts" has waxed and waned over time. New "experts" come
upon the scene while the old take a back seat: from the shaman
and healer in early times, to the clergy and the psychologist in
the very recent past.

Psychology's spiritual influence, however, was short-lived.

Although the discipline deals intimately with spirit, it has backed off the subject and relegated itself to the domain of the intellectual halfmind—at least in public. This is surprising, since most people are aware that what heals people in psychotherapy is, more than the method used, the quality of the relationship between patient and therapist—a clearly spiritual factor. Early in the century when Freud's great discoveries opened a psychological floodgate, a new psychological clergy eagerly but clumsily stepped into religious turf, proclaiming that psychology had answers to the eternal questions of man. This initial enthusiasm waned as soon as some outspoken practitioners, among them Ernest Becker, recognizing the limitations of the new discipline pulled the profession up short. Becker wrote: "All the analysis in the world doesn't allow the person to find out who he is and why he is here on earth, why he has to die and how he can make his life a triumph."[2] Otto Rank, Viktor Frankl, and others agreed. In the latter half of this century, psychiatrists and psychologists like Jung, Fromm, Erikson, and others have considered the relationship between psychology and spirit by drawing attention to the limitations of viewing the mind in isolation.

Currently a new "expert" is on the scene. Physical scientists, with their eyes on the cosmos, have staked their claim to this area. Contemporary mathematicians are saying publicly that, in fact, they are not discovering anything "new" but are merely rediscovering what one called the "Creator's elegant equations"—things that have always been there.[3]

There is a consensus that spirit exists, but even among the most brilliant minds that have written on the subject, there is little agreement on what or how it *is*. And no one person or academic discipline has a monopoly on the answers—or even on the questions. Religion, philosophy, science, medicine, psychology, physics, academics, clergymen, witch doctors, philosophers, mystics, and physicists are all holding hands on this subject.

YOU, THE EXPERT

Whatever you may learn by reading acknowledged experts, it is only truly useful if you yourself can use this knowledge to change your life for the better. Anything less and you have half-mindedly fooled yourself, and a lot of people do.

Remember, whatever you have read—you are the final authority concerning your own spirit.

Everyone has a spirit, thus everyone is an expert, of sorts, on the subject. You have only to look inside yourself to find yours. Of course, people differ in their spiritual understanding. Individual spiritedness has nothing to do with any sociological factors like economic status, race, gender, religion, or education. It wasn't the "expert" intellectual knowledge of the noted anthropologist I interviewed that I learned the most from . . . it was from the man himself—from what he shared with me about his spirit while telling me the story of his life. And the same was true for the others in my study: the neighborhood gas station attendant, the grocer, the mayor, the student, the housewife, and the local travel agent . . .

I found that talking with people about spirit was not only informative but extremely enjoyable. Try it! During these interviews, I attempted to elicit an "emotional history" of their ideas, awareness, concepts, relationships, and unique experience with the individual's own spirit as well as his or her interaction with the spirits of others. I also sought to elicit their spontaneous statements about spirit in general. In a history of this kind, what is most important is how things (events, perceptions, and so on) "feel"—how they are immediately experienced by the person.

I originally used this technique to investigate the nature of the complex bond between grandparents and grandchildren. By this method, I learned of the immense power of the biologically rooted "vital connection" between the young and the old. And I did it by asking the real "experts" on the subject—grandchildren, parents, grandparents, and great-grandparents. There, within the emotional sanctuary of the grandparent-grandchild relationship, I learned how two spirits can play and dance and love together—be "crazy in love" with one another—in a secret way, hidden from the outside world. A clergyman I talked this over with had seen the same thing. "I have seen grandparents who have been so ordinary, so inhibited in their expression of affection and ordinary virtues . . . and when they relate to their grandchildren, there is a miraculous transformation."

This was the experience that taught me about spiritual bonds and that kindred spirits relate to one another. I had witnessed it with my own eyes.

• THE ORACLE WITHIN •

How is spirit perceived within yourself? What is it like? How does it relate to mind and body? These are questions that can't easily be answered by the halfmind. But the people I interviewed tried. The majority were less skeptical than I had anticipated, agreeing that humans have a spirit. But, except from the children, the answers were given hesitantly. After all, imagine someone coming up to you and asking about your spirit—it's not one of the things we talk about easily in our culture—it's even considered "weird."

The first young person—a depressed eighteen-year-old who was having scholastic difficulties—whom I asked, "Do you think that your spirit has a personality?" answered, "What? How can a spirit have personality?"

"Well, if it did," I said, "what would it be like?"

"Don't tell anyone I said this, but I think that it would be yellow, happy, funny, and well, pretty nice." He thought for a moment. "But it doesn't get much of a chance to be that way."

"What would it say, in one sentence, if it could?"

"Life sucks."

*   *   *

Children are not as reticent as adults to talk about spirit. I routinely asked young children to "draw a spirit." Then I talked with them about their drawings, hoping to gain access to their clear view of reality, their brilliant intuition and organic knowledge. Kids are naturally spirited, wholeminded, seeing the big picture and the broad brush of reality quite clearly. That's why halfminded people have so much trouble with kids, and vice versa.

I asked Pete, a ten-year-old, to draw his spirit. He drew a smiling, legless phantom ascending into heaven "to meet God." The phantom was wearing a tuxedo. "Why a tuxedo?" I asked.

"He is happy because he is going back where he came from."

I was surprised. "How do you know that?" I asked.

"I just know it," he said, smiling.

I thought about that for a while.

At the beginning of the interviews, people were usually intrigued by the subject of spirit, but found themselves at a loss for words. After they realized that all they needed to do was just be themselves and answer the questions naturally, they relaxed. Soon they were freely airing deep thoughts and feelings that, under other circumstances, they would have kept to themselves. They were allowing themselves to enjoy the experience of the interview. I urged them to say anything that came to mind, the more "far out" the better.

I asked Shamus, a well-known cartoon animator and a wise and good friend, if he thought that spirit had a "personality." To him, God and spirit were one and the same. He told me that they both had a sense of humor.

I was sitting in my garden one afternoon particularly
down in the dumps. I just lost a good job that I was
counting on, things weren't going well at home, and
life looked pretty bleak. Suddenly this cat jumped over
the fence and landed in my garden. It was a cat with a
pink nose. I looked at it closely. The nose was so
artfully done and according to such a pattern that
someone had to have done it. It was a gag. I laughed.
A gray and white cat with a pink nose. God couldn't
be that bad if he gave that cat a pink nose.

Not all of the people I spoke with were as humorous and
articulate as Shamus. With some, I had to pay close attention
in order to hear their other, more personal and intimate voices,
which were often almost obscured by that of their socially programmed "party line."

Although the halfmind is programmable, spirit is not. But
we can't be aware of spirit if the halfmind blocks it out.

An eight-year-old youngster named Jamie learned that his
beloved grandmother and grandfather, who lived next door to
him, had decided to retire to sunnier climes, one thousand
miles away. His grandfather, James Paulsen, had worked hard
all of his life as a railroad engineer in Ohio. Like so many of his
friends, he had looked forward all of his life to "takin' it easy."
His grandmother, Claudia Paulsen, didn't want to leave her
family but agreed to follow her husband. Jamie's parents, who
both worked full time, were happy for Mr. and Mrs. Paulsen
because they were devoted and hard-working people who "de-
served a rest." Jamie was very close to his grandparents and especially to Mr. Paulsen who, as Jamie enthusiastically said, "lets
me drive the locomotive" (unbeknownst to the railroad company)—great stuff for a child.

The family had a going-away party for the Paulsens on the
eve of their leaving. At the party Jamie appeared, at first, to be

enjoying the festivities. But after a while, looking dejected, he cornered his grandfather and asked him, "When will you be back?"

His grandfather replied that he didn't know but he would return as soon as he could. "But Halloween is in two weeks," Jamie cried out, his eyes filling with tears, "and we always make costumes together. You promised that we would make a big TV set out of wood for a costume."

His grandfather, embarrassed, changed the subject. "But you can visit me and we can have fun . . ."

Jamie shouted, "I don't want to visit you, Grandpa, I want you next door!"

His mother, noticing something was wrong, walked over. "What's going on here?" she asked.

"Grandpa's going away, I won't see him any more. Grandpa, don't you want to be with me?" Jamie started crying. His mother looked around at the guests. People were starting to notice.

"Jamie, go to your room until you feel better. Don't spoil Grandma's and Grandpa's party." Jamie left.

Later, when we discussed what happened, Mr. Paulsen told me, "When Jamie asked me that question I was thunderstruck, deep in the pit of my stomach. A cold chill came over me. I almost got sick."

That night Jamie's parents chastised him for being "selfish," "making a scene," and not understanding that his grandparents would be happy in "retirement." In addition, he was made to feel guilty because he upset his grandparents and "Grandpa even said that if you felt that strongly maybe he shouldn't go." Jamie's mother explained to me that after the party, the senior Mr. and Mrs. Paulsen had a "big fight because my mother-in-law didn't want to leave in the first place and when she saw how Jamie reacted she knew that they were doing the wrong thing." She shook her head slowly. "To tell the truth, Jamie's right. I don't want them to go, either."

In a previous work I've said that children have an "oracular" function. Tuned into their spirit and true perceptions, they are able to report reality very well, no matter who likes what they say. What they say out loud depends on who is "policing" them. As they grow they see that there is a difference between their truthful perceptions and how the world wants them to handle those perceptions. The world trains children to adhere to the cultural "party line" of the times. The older children grow, the more they experience these incongruities and desire to announce them publicly. But they are not allowed to do this. Their fate is to be silenced by the powerful adults who live by the rules, regulations, and myths of society.

Most healthy children are fun-loving, impulsive, and, in varying degrees, are distractible and have a poor frustration tolerance, poor concentration, and a short attention span. They are "spirited." There lives a permanent child within us all, full of life, enthusiastic, glowing, "out there"—radiant. Children have an immediate (an imperative *now*) view of life. Because youngsters are unaware of how their truthful reportage of reality can affect others, they can get in trouble when they allow their spirits to show. A prim and proper mother of a bright six-year-old girl complained to me that she couldn't take her "high-spirited" precocious daughter anywhere. "I can't take Lori out anymore. I took her to the supermarket and when a large woman passed her she said out loud, 'Mother, look at that big fat lady.' We passed someone in a wheelchair and she asked them why God forgot to give them legs."

All children think these things, but when a child is especially "high-spirited," thoughts can spontaneously blurt out of his or her mouth, bypassing the "censor" of the socially trained conscience. Children are often as surprised at what they say as those who hear it. "I say a lot of things that I don't want to," Lori said. "The words just pop out."

This "oracular" function is linked not to the mind and body but to a deeper source of wisdom that assesses things as they really "are" and opposes the cultural party line. This is the seventh sense. When Jamie said "When will you be back?" to his grandfather, it was his spirit that spoke, that's why his grandfather was "thunderstruck" (I will show in a later chapter how powerful feelings are a signal from spirit) with the realization of the consequences of following a social imperative. Jamie's question flooded over his grandfather's halfmind. For the first time Mr. Paulsen was alerted that a basic spiritual wound was about to be inflicted . . . separating their kindred spirits. Jamie, in touch with his seventh sense, knew this would happen.

Jamie was saying "We've got a great thing going. Why leave? In spite of your friends leaving. In spite of society saying that's what people do at your age. In spite of the million things that are pushing you to leave. Why go? What about me? Don't you love me?"

Mr. Paulsen's emotional reaction to Jamie's "input" alerted him, but he didn't act on it. After all, for Mr. Paulsen, going away to retire was a natural, logical, and accepted thing to do. He never thought to question the emotional and spiritual implications of his decision. So he left anyway. "Oracles" are hard to hear, especially if what they are saying goes against the party line. So, like Jamie, they are chastised (You are selfish!) or made to feel guilty (How dare you spoil your grandparents' party!) and worse. When Jamie said "I don't want to visit you, Grandpa, I want you next door" it was the oracle in him speaking.

AN INTERVIEW WITH JEFF

The interviews were carried to elicit not only reflex halfminded party-line responses, but to help those questioned relate their thoughts, feelings, intuition, and behavior to the subject at hand. A portion of one interview—with Jeff, a thirty-eight-year-old world champion athlete from Maine—will show how a typical one unfolded.

When I asked Jeff if he believed that such a thing as a human spirit existed, he answered: "Sure, but you don't have to bother with it. It's not important to understand your spirit. I have never given it a lot of thought and I was brought up understanding that I would get the answer someday . . . it's not a concern right now. Don't question it and you'll find out someday. That's how I feel."

He continued. "I was raised Irish Catholic and being raised that way, you're brought up to believe that your spirit comes and your spirit goes. The body is your shell and that's it. I don't think that there is a distinction between the human being and the spirit. You are the spirit and the spirit is you."

Jeff also stated that the spirit is "a form of energy" that comes from "a place we've never been before. A place that we are going back to. This is our final chance to make good at what we'll be for eternity." He could not give me a reason for his comment.

I asked him if he felt that the mind, body, and spirit were related. "The mind is part of the body," he answered. "The spirit generates the mind and allows it to act independently." I asked him if the mind and body can affect the spirit. "No, the mind and the body are the mechanical means for the spirit to express itself totally."

"What about feelings?" I asked. "Does the spirit have feelings?"

Jeff didn't think so. "I believe that the spirit isn't affected by things . . . that it is not of this dimension—earth."

I remembered that before the interview began, Jeff had commented on the beautiful foliage that covered the countryside. I wanted to see how he fit "beauty" into his perceptions.

"What part of you enjoys the autumn colors?" I asked. "The part that can experience stimulation—the receptive ability of the eyes. The colors are pleasant to the eyes . . ." He continued, describing a behaviorist-computer model of perception. "The mind is like a computer and the body is the mechanical carrier of the mind . . ." But suddenly his description took on a "romantic" tone. "Fall meant it was time to wear warm clothes and be in a warm house . . ." When I asked him where those thoughts came from, he answered, "Memory . . . the computer remembers."

"If the spirit is on earth to do a job, as you said," I asked, "then doesn't it make sense that it would have some authority, some direction over the mind and body?"

"No, I think your mind directs your spirit. At first your body is the carrier of the spirit, but then as you get older, the mind and the body respond to society. If it wants something it gets it. Without the body the spirit would be dead."

Because Jeff was a world-champion athlete, I wanted to explore the possibility of a connection between his spirit and his achievements. I asked him if he thought that some people had stronger spirits than others.

"Probably," he answered, "but I don't know if it can be measured."

"Jeff, there are probably thousands of people in the world with the same physical talent as you but yet you were the best. How did that happen?"

"Motivation." He thought for a moment. "Psychologically I wanted to prove something to my father . . ."

I interrupted. "Was that a 'mind' thing?"

"Totally. Mind and physical training—patterning."

I decided to be adventurous. "What if I said to you that maybe your spirit needed—"

He interrupted. "To express itself?"

I decided to hint at possibilities. "Possibly, or something to do with the spirit of your father, to validate something in your-self, and that your spirit went into overdrive to help you do something incredible, transforming your body and your mind. Or that you had an exceptional spirit that had to express itself somehow in the world."

"I wouldn't begin to understand that. It's difficult for me to speak in terms of spirituality, I am so mechanically ori-ented . . ."

"Jeff," I said, "since you agree that there is such a thing as a spirit, do you think that spirits can relate to one another?"

He pondered for a while. "I guess if everything is driven by this energy, somehow there is communication in the deepest sense." He became frustrated. "Look, the spirit is there. It ex-ists, you can't measure it, you can't feel it, you can't touch it. It's best to let it go. Worry about things that you can do some-thing about." At the same time that he agreed to the existence of his spirit, he professed helplessness at it being a living, palpa-ble part of his everyday life. He was intellectually disassociated from his spirit.

Jeff was getting a bit uncomfortable, because he began to realize that his way of dealing with the spirit issue (by ignoring it) was being challenged by his own reflections. This was evi-dent in the following interchange. He was talking about after-life. "I believe that the people who died are someplace and that there will be a reunion of those spirits in the future. I hope it will be wonderful. The closest people in my life are dead."

I asked if he ever spoke to them in his mind, like so many children do with grandparents who have died.

"Sure, in my thoughts."

"*What* do you talk to?"

"I don't talk to anything, I ramble."

"Do you visualize something?"

"No, I visualize their faces but I don't see their spirits in their faces. A face is only a memory to let me know who I am talking to. I don't see a little heart running around with wings or a white ghost at the pearly gates."

"Is the spirit the personality of the person?"

"I don't think so. I think the personality of the person was here [on earth]."

"So what's left for the reunion?"

"A recognition, there has got to be. A memory of that energy. You asked me earlier if spirits recognized one another and I said probably not. But if that is true then my pipe dream is wrong. Maybe we'll get to this place and there will be massive energy and we won't know who is who. Okay. What I hope and what I truly believe may be totally different. If my spirit is my mind, the only thing allowing me memory is my mind and memory will die with the body. If it doesn't then my mind is fooling me that my spirit will be happy when it reunites with other spirits."

He said that he had experienced premonitions. Several years prior to the interview he had a dream in which an older woman was killed in an auto accident. Three days later a friend of his killed an older woman in an auto accident under remarkably similar circumstances. "How does this fit into your mind-body computer model?" I asked.

"Absolutely unexplainable. If somebody has that talent, it is a true gift of the spirit. Then it is not mechanical."

"So there are fuzzy borders."

Understand that I wasn't trying to give Jeff the "third degree," or differ with his opinions. I was attempting, in a respectful manner, to push his logic as far as it would go so I could learn from him.

He admitted to the inevitable fuzzy areas of the subject. "Definitely. That's one of them. You want another fuzzy area? I want tradition in my life, family . . ."

"Your 'computer' wants tradition, family, lots of kids . . ."

At this point the interview took a radical turn. Jeff placed his "computer model" aside. "It's not the computer. The same thing that wants it is the same thing that recognizes it. No, it's not the computer. If I knew I would tell you. Maybe it is the spirit—something between the energy of the spirit and the mechanical. I never thought about it, but maybe there is that link. There has to be that link. I don't know what that is, though."

Since he agreed to the possibility of some actual "now" function of the spirit, I wanted to know if he thought there was any possibility that the spirit had its own thoughts, feelings, or behavior. "What about memories?" I asked.

"Feelings attached to memories are perhaps the area of the spirit. That might be the interlink. The mind may be able to hold the memory, but it's the feeling that counts. The body perceives, the mind remembers the perception, and the emotion or the feeling might be [in the realm of] the spirit. The mind is the interlink between the spirit and the body."

The interview ended with a question from Jeff. "If the mind breaks down, does the spirit, too? Or just the body? Hmm. Interesting question. . . ."

This interview not only taught me a great deal about Jeff's views of the spirit, but it was instrumental in leading him to confront his halfmindedness and to exhume and reexamine his old, entrenched attitudes toward issues of the spirit—issues that had lain dormant since his early days. The view of himself as a passive receptacle of a spirit that arose from an unknown source and for which he bore no responsibility and derived no pleasure was to be further examined. He began to question the perception that he had no conscious connection to his acknowledged spirit. He recognized that his interaction with the world was not entirely through the channels of his mind-body computer because his need for tradition and his experience with premonition could not be accounted for in this way of understanding total human experience. The interview broke through the barricade of silence concerning how Jeff's spirit lived and operated within him. He had opened a door to a new dimension of self-knowledge.

· 3 ·

THE WORKINGS
OF SPIRIT

Again, in the air, there are and always have been vulgar and not so vulgar theories about bodies, minds and souls and their several natures, destinies and relations, with no guarantee that these theories can be harmonized with the meanings of such terms as "minds" or "soul" as actually determined by whatever is the accepted correct usage of the culture concerned.

The consequence of this is that the issues tend to be presented not as a matter of first giving some suitable sense to the word "soul" or "mind" and asking whether in that sense the term would in fact have any application but, rather, as an inquiry which presupposes that we have souls or minds, asks what is in the nature of the soul or mind. Such a presentation is bound to constitute a

temptation to prejudge the question
whether, in the sense eventually
chosen, we have or are such things.

—Plato

SPIRIT—THE VITAL PRINCIPLE

With all due respect to the above admonition, I would like to describe what I have learned to date of how spirit operates within the self. But first it is important to, in Plato's words, "give suitable sense to the word"—to define more precisely what I mean by "spirit." In *Webster's*, spirit is defined as "breath, an animating or vital principle held to give life to a physical organism."

I use the word "spirit" to describe the "nature and operation" of the individual's *personal* portion (in quality and quantity) of this mysterious and unknown force. Within the self, spirit is dynamic, energetic, radiated outward, and is sensed and received by others. In searching for definitions, spirit must be differentiated from life. Life itself is a quantitative factor— something is alive or it isn't. Life is a continual cyclic process: birth, death, and renewal. Human life, for example, just doesn't begin—in effect it is a continuation of the life carried within egg and sperm and evolves into a more complex physical form. Life is something passed on from generation to generation, like a baton in a relay race.

Spirit is a qualitative factor and therefore is to my mind more than just life. Although it contains a distinct energy— "spiritedness"—it is a separate entity from the "on-off" switch of life itself that activates the body and is necessary to be "on" for spirit to be present.

The relationship between spirit and life has always intrigued mankind, raising some tough questions. For example, is there a temporal relationship between life and spirit? Does life and spirit enter the body at birth and depart at death?

It is a common observation that when someone dies both life and spirit seem to leave the body. Simultaneously. But what happens when a person is in a long-term coma? The body is alive. But is spirit still present? People who have had "near-death" experiences say yes. They report that at a moment near death, they found themselves hovering above their dying bodies until they reentered and "came back to life." Have you ever experienced any glimmerings of insight, thought, or emotion that gives credence to these views?

Another intriguing question is if spirit and life aren't one and the same, is there a special moment when spirit enters the physical body?

To my surprise, a lot of people have opinions about this. A practitioner of an Eastern religion said. "Life and spirit permeate each other. When I was born . . . my spirit . . . was not a baby spirit. It was more mature than spirit in the infant form. Spirit watches and observes the person for a time, then enters. There was a time in my youth when I awoke and realized that there was a spirit within me."

An obstetrician of my acquaintance, an expert in fertility and a pioneer in the field of in-vitro fertilization, related that he "was amazed to watch the two cells unite and to know that everything, all that the person would be was there, under the microscope." For him: "Spirit enters the fetus at about the time when it is formed and starts to look like a person. When I visualize fetuses with ultrasound and other methods, there is a time in my own soul when I see them as 'human' and as having a self . . . that's around four, maybe five, months . . . of course this is subjective and don't tell anyone I said this . . . but you may quote me anonymously."

Many expectant mothers said that they experienced the first movement of the child they were carrying as a miracle, a truly spiritual experience. "When I feel that first stirring I know that my child has been touched with something," a mother of six told me.

Further, some people believe that spirit enters the child in the womb. Others say that it is possible that spirit enters the body with its first breath, at birth. This view has a surprisingly consistent historical thread. The early Greeks connected the spirit with breathing and believed it was a dynamic entity—the generator of movement. During the Middle Ages it was felt that the surest way to keep the soul from leaving the body when one sneezed was to say "God bless you." One primitive cultural belief is that inhaling the last breath of a dying person confers "power" to the inhaler.

What is your own experience in these matters? Have you ever seen someone die? Do you think that it is possible that spirit exits the body with the last breath? What do you think about the possibility that spirit vitalizes and devitalizes the body as it enters and leaves?

More unanswerable questions? Not unanswerable to everyone. A young man, prefacing his remark by saying that what he was going to say would sound crazy but he would say it anyway, told me: "When I was little, about three years old, I was thinking about before I was born . . . before I was on the earth. I thought that being born was like opening a door and walking into a new room. Well! I said to myself. Here I am on earth. Things are supposed to be new. But I really felt that I had been kept in a waiting room . . . a nice darkness . . . but light, too . . . like I was an energy. I knew I was but I have no way of expressing it. My body was alive but I . . . *me* . . . was like a visitor." He went on. "I knew when I was four that my breath was important, too . . . like that was the life in me . . . and I got life from my breath and the air around me."

Ella, a thirty-two-year-old teacher, said she saw her father's spirit leave his body. "I watched my father die. He stopped breathing while I was sitting with him, looking into his eyes. I held my breath, too, and stared at him, then I started to cry. But suddenly he took a deep breath, opened his eyes, and looked at me. 'Not yet,' he said. I almost jumped out of my chair. Then he smiled, took a deep, deep breath, and let out a long, long exhale that seemed to go on forever. Then he grunted and was dead. His body was there but my dad was gone. A crazy thought went through my mind. I remembered the old movies when they put a mirror in front of the mouth of someone who died to see if they were breathing. I wanted to do that, to make sure. But I knew that *he* wasn't there anymore. There was no one at home in his body."

What Ella said "was gone" from her father is what she later called his spirit. "Giving up the ghost" is a folk saying confirming the universal observation that so many people have made: "Something goes somewhere when a person dies."

Is spirit peripatetic? Does it come *from* somewhere and go *to* somewhere? What do we know that may shed some light on these questions? Well, we do know that birth and death really happen—they are observable events. Next, it is not too far-fetched to assume that what we call "life" is a switch that turns the body on and off. People are "alive" even in a coma or vegetative state. (The mother of an adolescent in a long-term coma told me, "My Pete is breathing, all right, but he's not *there* anymore." The young man eventually died.) But there is a difference between people in a vegetative state and others going about their daily lives, those truly "alive"—and "spirited." Further, we may say that since the body exists in two states, "alive" and "dead," and that the "live" body also exists in two states, "spirited" and "de-spirited" (vegetative), it follows that there may be mysterious factors responsible for these states. Is it beyond possibility that if these factors come and go, they could come *from* somewhere and go *to* somewhere? And where could that possibly be?

Now let's get back to experience which at least for me is more credible. Another obstetrician I spoke with, who has delivered over four thousand babies, "knew" that "Life is there at birth. It is going on in the womb. But it's the first breath—the first breath is critical. Maybe it's the human spirit entering the body—and don't ask me to explain it any further. I can't. When I see the babies inside, with the sonogram [an instrument that visualizes the fetus inside the mother] it's not the same as when they breathe their first breath—it's the difference between a mannequin and a person."

Even without objective proof, most of the people I have questioned believe that spirit exists. I suspect it is highly probable that the majority of humanity holds a similar belief. I say this with the same confidence that I can state that most people are aware of the fact that stars are always present in the sky even though they can be seen only at night.

Many eminent thinkers have attempted to identify aspects of spirit.

In 1901 Dr. R. M. Bucke, a Canadian psychiatrist, recognized that to "know" (not just hope or believe) that spirit exists, the mind must have access to spirit via the seventh sense. For him, what I call the seventh sense is "cosmic consciousness." He wrote: "[it] is not simply an expansion or extension of the self-conscious mind with which we are all familiar, but the superaddition of a function as distinct as any possessed by the average man as self-consciousness is distinct from any function possessed by one of the higher animals."[1]

In pursuit of spirit, Wilhelm Reich, an outstanding (though controversial) mid-twentieth-century psychiatrist, spent a good part of his life trying to identify and materialize what he called the "life force." He named it "orgone energy" and founded the science of "orgonomy" to study it. He claimed to have demonstrated the presence of orgone energy as a blue spark in an apparatus that he devised. In addition, he was among the first to develop a psychotherapeutic technique that deals with not only the mind but its intricate relationship with the body. He called this "vegetotherapy."[2]

Most people believe that spirit is in us and all around us.

Like Ella, when I have witnessed people die it seemed to me, too, that life was "expired" out of the body with the last breath. What remained seemed to be only an inanimate object—a husk—a discarded shell.

For what it's worth, I would like to share an additional observation, which I made at a time when I was delivering babies, that suggests a ubiquitous, although mysterious, life-spirit-air connection. Babies who have a rough time being born emerge from the womb floppy and inanimate, like a rag doll, when they are finally delivered. When a birth like this takes place, the doctors and nurses in the delivery room (while doing everything they can to help) are naturally quite apprehensive. They anxiously wait for the baby to take its first breath, to cry—for an unknown "something more" to happen (something more than life because the baby is already alive). When the baby cries, there is, for a flash of a moment, something special, powerful, and radiant in the room.

I always wondered if it was at that magic moment that a spiritual switch was turned on . . . that "spirit" connected with the baby and superimposed itself upon life already present. I could chalk up this observation to my own subjectivity (the observer and the observed can never be fully separated) except for the following: The other people present in the delivery room on those occasions were as affected as I was. I have seen even the oldest, most crabby, battle-weary, and wizened doctor or nurse light up when babies let out their first cry. Then, as soon as the baby's cries became regular and the crisis is over, this "magic" slowly dissipates. Things return to normal, the obstetrical team "comes down" from the experience.

Viewing such a scene, an outsider could easily think that this ecstatic communal feeling is easily explained by the elation everyone feels because the baby started to breathe for itself. That's surely part of it. But there is "something more." And it is related to more than life itself—it is spiritual. Could it really be that spirit connects with the baby at that time?

This spiritual event happens every time a baby is born. Ask

most people who are involved in delivering babies and they will agree (as one doctor said, "Sure, what else is new?").

Although life and spirit are different entities many of the people I spoke with see them as joined, as the "something more" that connects with body to form the self. As Ella put it: "When someone dies, something goes somewhere." When a person dies the "something" is lost. The two components of a living person (spirit and body) become reduced to inanimate matter—a dead body. That's evident.

The connection among life, spirit, and newborn is more complex. First, the baby has always been alive, because sperm and egg were alive when the child was conceived. So when does the baby become "spirited"?

Find out for yourself. Here's the way to do it. First talk to a pregnant woman about her pregnancy. Ask her about the child inside of her, what the child is like. Ask her if it has a spirit. Listen carefully to what she says.

Then attend a birth. Observe a baby being born and see how you react—what thoughts and feelings you experience. You will learn a lot. Challenge your halfmind to figure out this miracle, not the mechanical nuts and bolts of two cells uniting and growing, and so on, but why this came to be in the first place . . . that a being comes out of the body of another.

THE TRIPLE HELIX OF THE SELF

In the adult the mind, body and spirit interact as one, intertwined, as strands in a braid. These three components make up the triple helix of the self.

To learn how each of these components work, it's necessary to examine them individually. Spirit (energy and consciousness) is connected and "one" with the universe. The brain and body is "stuff"—matter—through which the spirit has issue into the everyday world.

It is necessary to examine mind, body, and spirit separately, to obtain even the smallest glimpse of some of the workings of spirit.

Furthermore, in order to get any degree of precision in defining the limits of spirit, factors rooted in the halfmind like personality, character, temperament, talents, and physical, emotional, social, and psychological traits will not be considered for the moment.

Also, I ask that you bear with me as I arbitrarily divide the cosmos into two parts: the universal whole and the local everyday world—the "part of the whole." The halfmind interacts with the latter.

Thus the self is made up of three components: One is a body that "acts," "thinks" on a reflexive level, and "feels" with its substance. A complex (biochemically driven) brain that is part of the body, the material representation of the mind and the seat of the halfmind.

And a third, nonmaterial, component: an animating, vitalizing spirit that "thinks," "feels," and "governs" behavior through the seventh sense, the spirit's "ambassador" to the mind.

Halfmind and spirit form the wholemind.

The relationship between mind, body, and spirit is not fixed and rigid. It changes throughout life.

For the newborn a spirit quest is unnecessary. Spirit is present in the newborn child. All dimensions of the self are united and in harmony. (See figure 3.1.)

Look at a happy, loved baby (and its loving relatives) and you will probably agree. Within its intrauterine environment, the infant's existence is loving and peaceful. Its wholemind is filled with spirit, its halfmind doesn't yet exist. Within the womb of a happy and healthy mother, its needs ideally are continually satisfied. The idea and the reality of its prospective "being" radiates into the world, bringing joy to its prospective parents and family. By doing nothing, a baby does something—

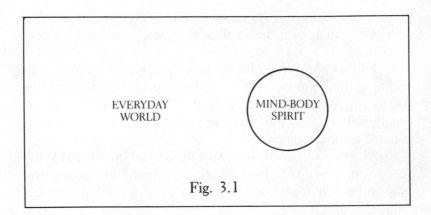

Fig. 3.1

just by existing. It is a spiritual symbol, a testament to family continuity, joy, happiness, naturalness, spontaneity, living evidence of the basic stuff of existence. The baby is love personified.

Within the uterus, spirit permeates the child. The infant self is inwardly focused. It is in the perfect contemplative state—the blissful condition sought after by practitioners of many, especially the Eastern, religions. This state has been described as dharma, megha, samadhi, the "highest" form of consciousness, Gurjieff vibration level 3, satori, and so on.

Birth, the first great trauma of life, ends the solitary and idyllic state of the baby. If you could remember your own birth, you would recollect being ejected from a warm, dark, and cozy womb into a cold, bright, and boundless universe, having burning medication poured into your eyes, being plopped into a hard bassinet, so different from your mother's womb, and then, for some, dreaded circumcision.

At birth the "outside" suddenly and overwhelmingly floods over the infant's mind and body. All at once outside "information" enters the mind-space and the halfmind is born. The mental computer becomes "plugged in." As this happens, spirit has to accede to the primacy of the flood of external information

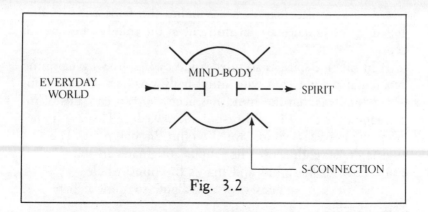

Fig. 3.2

bombarding the child's senses. The brain computer begins to accumulate "input" from the outside world at a startling rate.

The attention of the self starts to become more focused "outside" of itself. Then, very slowly, spirit recedes, making room for the growing halfmind. (See figure 3.2.)

As spirit recedes, a point of contact is formed where spirit meets the mind-body. I call this juncture the S-Connection. It is a point where the halfmind has access to spirit and the whole-mind is formed. This S-Connection may be opened, hypo-thetically allowing spirit to "illuminate" the self, or it may be closed down, thus de-spiriting the self. For purposes of illustration, I have likened this portion of the S-Connection to a rheo-stat, a gadget that is used to brighten or lower the intensity of light given off by a light fixture. The seventh sense, spirit's path-way to the mind, reaches it through the S-Connection.

The evolution of the S-Connection is remarkably similar to what physically happens to the ovum during intrauterine growth. As the single fertilized egg divides and becomes dif-ferentiated, an umbilical is formed between the fetus and the placenta, which is attached to the mother's uterus. This assures the passage of vital nutrients from mother to baby. Similarly, like the primary egg, the self is "one" in the uterus.

Like the placenta, which supplies the fetus with its life-blood, spirit supplies a vital nutrient to the mind—the seventh sense.

In infants, spirit is shunted aside by the growing halfmind but remains connected with mind-body via the S-Connection. What results is that the mind has access to two conduits of information. The first I call first-order knowledge. This is "input," from the everyday world, stored within the halfmind. The second is the seventh sense. Its "input" originates in spirit and is transmitted to the mind and makes the mind whole.

As the sun radiates heat and light, so spirit radiates the seventh sense. (See figure 3.3.)

When a child is born, it is wholeminded. It's first-order mind is *tabula rasa*—an empty slate containing no knowledge of the everyday world. The newborn's self is comprised of spirit and rudimentary mind-body.

Newborns are spiritually powerful beings. Isn't it surprising what power they possess, especially since they are without worldly experience or practical knowledge, and since they really don't do too much more than eat, eliminate, sleep . . . and smile? Consider how quickly being in the presence of a small

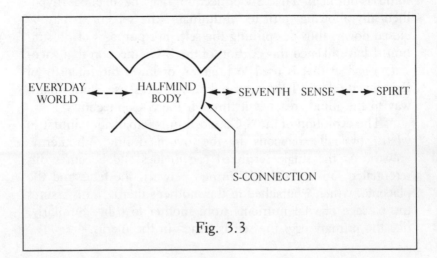

Fig. 3.3

child can reduce even the most austere and reserved people to joyful silliness. Few adults are immune to this force in children.

No matter how we try to explain the physical workings of such phenomena in the limited terms of socialization, instinct, or the "wiring" of the nervous system, it does not satisfactorily explain things like intense love, the joy of people when the baby smiles (indeed, the goofy things people will do to get a baby to smile in the first place), and the "holiness" (as one mother described it) of a mother nursing a baby.

As the child's self strives to maintain a harmonious balance between spirit and the mind-body, it seeks pleasure from "need satisfaction." First of the body: food, elimination, health. The mind, driven by an intellectual imperative, seeks its pleasure in the form of learning; children are the most curious creatures on the face of the earth. Spirit seeks illumination: affection, love, being cared for. Children "feed back" love to those who love them.

As the child moves into the universe of its parents, the flood of external information it receives threatens to displace spirit more and more. The child's mind-body is increasingly "trained" to adhere to the ways—expressed as social imperatives—of its culture. The process of training that a child undergoes to learn the rules and regulations of its culture can wreak havoc on its spirit. The only things a newborn really wants is the love and consideration of its caretakers and to be happy. Simple enough. But does this happen?

Imagine how regulations like artificial feeding schedules, sleeping schedules, toilet training, illnesses, and most of all separation from beloved persons confuse a child's mind and pain its spirit. R. D. Laing, the controversial psychiatrist, bemoans the effect of "regulations" on the child: "From infancy many of us are forced to accommodate to the rhythms of others. We are told when to eat, sleep, speak or move and admonished never to experience the extremes."[3] With increased socialization the unconditional spontaneous love that ideally the child experiences, the kind of love that illuminates its spirit, seems harder to come by. The love it now receives has a conditional component—given for performance: walking, talking, eating, reciting songs, conforming to parents' expectations and demands, and so on, and doing them well.

Conditional love is not true love. It is approval proffered by the halfmind for behaving according to specific rules and regulations or meeting prescribed expectations. Unconditional love—pure love—is spiritual, given because a person *is*.

A child raised with conditional love might think, "If I don't do what Mommy and Daddy want me to do they might not love me at all. They will get *angry* with me and not love me any more . . . ever."

As pressure for social conformity continues, a child might say, "At one time when Mommy and Daddy looked at me I could see only love and adoration in their eyes. Now I see anger. I don't please them as much. Sometimes I am unable to do what they want me to do and I can't help it . . . maybe I'm a *bad* person because I don't please them. I make them unhappy."

But the spirited two- to three-year-old child doesn't buckle under to social imperatives without a fight. The "terrible twos" are a protest of the spirit against socialization—most of which just doesn't make sense to kids. The oracle within battles with external authority. "After all," a child might say, "why shouldn't my happy and playful 'free' spirit be allowed to sleep when I want to, eat when I want to, toilet when and where I want to, and play when I want to with the people that I love?" "No way," say its parents. "You have to be put on a schedule and trained. You must comply to the order of things, just like us."

The essence of "training," as any horseman knows, is the tempering, even the subjugation of spirit. But this must not be overdone because, as one horse trainer said, "Spirit is fire in the animal. The wrong kind of training and the spirit isn't subdued, it's broken." This can easily happen to children. Look around.

Of course I am *not* advocating that children be left untrained. They have to learn how to live in the world. The half-mind is necessary to civilization. What I am trying to show is that a spiritual price is paid for this training and that we must recognize and consider this in the way we raise our children. I'll get to this in a later chapter. For now it's enough to know that insensitivity to the spiritual effect of training on children can damage their wholemindedness.

Spirit is reflected in children's eyes. It radiates magnetically from them and touches the spirits of all who gaze within. Eyes, after all, have been described as the window of the soul.

Children's eyes always reflect their misery. One teacher is aware of this. "When the school year starts," she told me, "I look deeply into each child's eyes, and I know them already. I can see if they are happy, sad, hurt, whatever." Subjective as it may seem, the condition of the eyes—their luminosity, the intensity of gaze, activity level, and the length of time a person can maintain eye contact—is helpful in clinical assessment. The brightness in children's eyes supplies me with a litmus test of how well their therapy is proceeding. When children are suffering, their eyes get dim. When they get better, their eyes get brighter and livelier. When they sparkle, they are okay.

There is scientific support for the contention that the eyes reflect the person's emotional and spiritual health. The eyes are unique in that as a part of the central nervous system, they are the only anatomical part of the brain that is on the surface of the body; they are, in computer terminology, a "sensor" of the brain. That's why direct eye contact is such a powerful experience and so uncomfortable for many. A specialist in the field has said about eye contact that ". . . in revelatory moments of mutual gazing a type of union occurs in which one feels no barrier between oneself and the other."[4]

Anything that affects the brain affects the eyes. But look for yourself. Gaze into the eyes of people around you. Do you notice differences in the luminosity, the energy, the "life" in their eyes? Have you seen people with lifeless, "dead" eyes? Gaze into a mirror for a while. What do you see in your own eyes?

As the child grows, the state of its spirit becomes more and more dependent on its interaction with the spirits of its loved ones.

Now here is an obvious but most important point: Love is necessary for the well-being of a baby's spirit. The infant spirit must be gardened.

In the latter half of the eighteenth century, Anton Mesmer, the founder of the ill-fated school of animal magnetism, recognized the effect of spiritual interactions between people. "Everyone knows," he wrote, "of the characteristic found in healthy young people of being able to rejuvenate old men and strengthen them by their emanations; the Holy Scriptures speaks of it." He compared it to a "weak magnet being revived by a stronger magnet."[5] I have often witnessed what Mesmer has described as "rejuvenation" taking place between the young and the old (the Annie phenomenon) and suspect that a spiritual resonance takes place between mothers and their babies (or how older people who marry younger ones get "young" again).

In early life, spirit depends on kindred spirits for love, nurturing, and happiness. The child draws people to the self with its abundant and natural endowment of personal magnetism. The infant spirit cannot nourish itself, it needs communion with others. An infant can't indulge in spirit-illuminating activities. It can't paint, take long walks, play in nature, look at the stars, or find a private way to recharge its spirit. If there aren't enough people to enthusiastically love the baby and spend time with it, its spirit may wither.

Is it possible that when the child absorbs the spirit of another both are enhanced—that a reverberating spiritual circuit exists between babies and some people?

Scientific evidence supports the idea of "spiritual resonance." Physicists have described the "ERP effect," after Einstein, Rosen, and Podolsky. Briefly, it contends, with experimental support, that "two particles, once in contact, separated even to the ends of the universe, change instantaneously when a change in one of them occurs."[6] If this is true, then we are all interconnected by a force that travels faster than the speed of light. This demonstrates, as physicist Nick Herbert has stated, a simple consequence of the oneness of apparently separate objects . . . a quantum loophole through which physics admits not merely the possibility but the necessity of the mystic's unitary vision: "We are all one."[7]

Furthermore, it may explain so much of the mysterious communication that takes place between mother and child, as well as others—mysterious phenomena, like telepathy, that defy logical explanation. It gives credence to the view that we are all part of one another, whether we like it or not!

If loved children prosper, the opposite is certainly true—unloved children suffer. Studies have shown that children who are abandoned early in life by their mothers, left alone and unstimulated, even though their physical needs are cared for, can get severely depressed and even die unless they are loved by someone. This is called marasmus. Rene Spitz, a noted psychiatrist, observed in his classic study that "infants apparently receiving adequate physical care but little stimulation frequently become apathetic, developed severe symptoms of wasting and died."[8] In another study, he found that infants with close relationships to their mothers for the first six months and who were separated from them for three months thereafter also developed marasmus and often pined away in spite of heroic medical measures.[9] Why did these children die even though they were physically cared for? Is it possible that they died because of a malady related to spirit? Was their will to live impaired? Certainly the mechanism of marasmus may be explained immunologically, in terms of a breakdown in certain lymphocytes that help the immune system fight infection, but that's not the cause. That's *how* it happens, not *why*.

Pining away one's life is a malady of spirit.

It is within reason to speculate that if . . .

love resonates between spirits, and
the vulnerable spirit of an infant needs love to flourish,
it is possible that children who are deprived of loving
parents' spirits could die from spiritual deprivation.

This doesn't seem at all farfetched to me. What is the ingredient that makes or breaks relationships? Love, of course. And where is love rooted? Certainly not in the halfmind or the body, although it is experienced there. It is within the spirit. Is the attention, care, and love from another spirit essential in some ways to the healthy growth of a baby?

I think so.

If misery is a communicable disease and children respond to the spirits of people around them, what damage is being done to our children's spirits by well-meaning parents who are unhappy with their own lives?

As a toddler, the child can begin to move its spirit about, in a manner of speaking. Spirit supplies the vital fuel for the engine of intelligence. With mobility, the senses are highly stimulated. This accelerates the development of intellect and the construction of the psyche that Freud so brilliantly explained. The older the child is, the more "training" it receives. A vulnerable spirit is worn on the child's sleeve. Young spirits bruise easily. This is especially recognized in Africa. In certain tribes, for example, the penalty for slapping a child in the face is death. Ancient wisdom states that hitting a child in the face breaks the child's spirit. On the other hand, those children regarded as "tough" are prized. But what has happened to their spirit?

What often appears insignificant to an adult can deeply

hurt a child. Children often suffer in the process of growing and of meeting parents' and society's demand for "performance."

Polly, five years old, eagerly anticipated the first day of kindergarten. Her mother dressed her in her nicest dress. Her father stayed home from work so he could drive to school with Polly and her mother. They took her to her classroom and left. After school Mom met Polly at the bus stop. When Polly got off the bus she looked at her mother and started to sob. "Everyone laughed at me because I couldn't skip and hop," she said, crying. "I hate school and I don't want to go back."

When I asked her why she was so upset, she told me that she was mad at herself because she couldn't make her legs skip like the other children. I asked her to try again and showed her the movements. It was apparent after she made two attempts that her neuromuscular coordination had not matured enough to allow her to skip. She became more and more agitated. I asked her if she was "thinking" she was mad. "No," she screamed, jumping high in the air and throwing herself on the floor, "all of me is mad."

In young children, what is commonly called a "temper tantrum" often could also be described as a protest of spirit.

AFTER CHILDHOOD

As growth proceeds, the pressure increases to separate spirit from halfmind-body.

At the time of the alleged "age of reason,"* (about seven years old) the halfmind, having been "educated" and having absorbed "life experience" and "social programming," begins to make its influence felt on the self as the child becomes more and more separate from its parents.

This is when trouble starts.

---

*Dr. Ian Stevenson, in his remarkable investigations of children who have experienced previous lives, has noted that their recollections begin to wane at this age.

How much trouble depends on where the self lives. If the self lives in a society where spirit is respected—where social imperatives mesh with spiritual imperatives, all will go well. If not, a battle will take place between the socially programmed halfmind and spirit to determine how the self will live its life.

An inner-city ghetto, for instance, is not a good place for spirit. "Joker" Polk, twenty years old, lived in Harlem until he was eighteen. On his eighteenth birthday he was arrested for trafficking in heroin and sentenced to a farm prison for one year. After his release he entered therapy to "find out why I am so screwed up." Two weeks after he started therapy he got lucky. A kindly parole officer found him a well-paying job, in an affluent suburb, as bodyguard/driver for a wealthy businessman. Joker liked his job a great deal. "I am living like a rich man. Good money, good clothes. No hassles. My boss and his family are straight. Feelin' good, Doc. A lot better—a lot better."

"What's better?" I asked.

"I'm lighthearted. I see the trees and the flowers. I have come to life."

He paused. "When I was in the city I was a dead man. I died when I was six, after my grandmother died. She was my light. She called me 'Sunshine.' I did good in school when she was checking up on me. I was a clown, for sure, but I did my homework. I went to church with her twice a week. Then she got sick and died. There was no one else. My mother wasn't around much, so I got into the street and that was it. I was the walking wounded. There was nothing that I couldn't do that would bother me. I did it all. Hurt people, hurt myself. Shot up a lot. Beat up on people—and worse."

"What died in you when you were six?"

"The good part, the part that had fun, my power, the part that laughed, that liked dogs and cats. I don't know if it really died altogether but after my grandmother died that part went somewhere, because there was no one that understood it. Well, one teacher did, an old lady teacher. She knew my grandmother and she called me 'Sunshine' sometimes, too. She told me that I was smart. 'You're not a joker,' she would say. She tried to straighten me out. 'Providence'—that's my real name, not Joker—'Providence,' she used to say, 'you straighten up now and don't keep bad company.' She used to keep me after school and give me stuff to eat. But then I got promoted out of her class, started cuttin' classes—and that was it."

"And now?"

"The sun is comin' out again. Maybe Sunshine is coming back, too. Maybe the part that I put away wasn't killed, after all. It's funny, I don't want to be no Joker no more."

In the next year Joker enrolled in night school to get his high school equivalency diploma and planned to continue his education. His employer said that he had "become like a member of the family. The kids love him."

What enabled Joker, raised under adverse circumstances, to find his way out of the ghetto to a better life? Did the love of his grandmother, still a vital force within him, serve as a beacon and a reservoir of strength? Was it the resiliency and power within his own spirit that "went underground" until it found the right time to emerge? Although the answers to these questions are elusive, we may safely surmise a strong influence of spirit. After all, Joker's mind and body had little to do with his Renaissance; his body was weak and bedraggled from living in the streets, his mind dulled, poisoned by drugs. The only thing that was possibly functioning within him was spirit, present within his devastated mind and body.

His time at the farm prison helped to rehabilitate his body. Abstinence from toxic drugs helped heal his mind. As a result, the "temple of his soul"—his mind and body—were now able to function harmoniously with his spirit. This accomplished, all he needed was a break, a bit of luck to pry himself loose from the malignant culture in which he lived. And he found it. Harmony in his self was reestablished. Joker took over from there. The last time I heard from him he was taking prelaw courses in night school.

THE FIRST ORDER

A human being is a part of the whole,
called by us the "Universe," a part
limited in time and space. He
experiences himself, his thoughts and
feelings as something separated from
the rest—a kind of optical delusion of
his consciousness. This delusion is a
kind of prison for us, restricting us to
our personal desires and to affection
for a few persons nearest us.

—*Albert Einstein*

As Einstein explains it, although man is part and parcel of a greater universe, his concept of individuality, an "optical delusion of the consciousness," confines his vistas to the everyday world. In other words, although man is naturally whole-minded—part and parcel of the universe—he prefers to delude himself and live separately, like a child who closes his eyes and says to his parents, "You can't see me anymore, I have disappeared." This "delusion" of separateness is accomplished through the halfmind.

The "self" exists in one universe but tends to divide it into an immediate "everyday" world (of going to work or school, paying bills, living, and so on) and a distant universe. The halfmind-body lives in the everyday world. It interacts directly with people, places, and things. I call first-order knowledge what the mind's thoughts and the body's feelings, gleaned from the immediate, knowable everyday world, are. The halfmind is thus limited to a part of the "whole" universe that Einstein mentioned. Rudolph Steiner, the mystic, recognized the pitfalls of living with a halfmind. He wrote:

When a man loses hope of having the hidden revealed to him, all force of life must be introduced from without if such a person is to get possession of any life force at all. He then perceives the things, beings and events that appear before his senses; he analyses them with his intellect. They give him pleasure and pain and drive him to actions of which he is capable. He may carry on in this way for a while, yet at some time he must reach a point when he inwardly dies. For what can be drawn from the world in this way becomes exhausted.[10]

Because it may be uncritically programmed, the halfmind is impressionable, vulnerable to images. Easy to fool. A good example of this is the way in which television can hoodwink young children.

The halfmind is initially gullible. Jacques Brel, the Belgian songwriter, summed it up in one of his songs. A sad young man sees an advertisement showing a smiling individual ecstatically devouring a hot dog. He bites into one of his own and is disappointed and laments to the effect that if he is eating a hot dog he is supposed to be having fun.

The halfmind responds to external images reflexively. For example, a young man watching television is led to believe that by drinking a certain beer, he will join an elite group. "You will become what you see in the images on the screen—young, handsome, sought-after." The halfmind reflexively swallows this line.

After drinking the stuff he finds that none of the promised benefits materialize. No group acceptance, no uproarious fun. Just a hangover. The halfmind then measures the image against what is perceived by the five senses and rejects the message as a lie. Only after comparing the image to the reality does the halfmind learn: It has no built-in instinctual knowledge.

The eminent psychologist Phillip Zimbardo has demonstrated experimentally how easily the halfmind learns antisocial, even sadistic and violent behavior.[11] Children are especially vulnerable to what Zimbardo has demonstrated. If you don't believe this, ask any parent who is bombarded by unrelenting requests from their television-mesmerized offspring for the latest toy or who are upset by their youngsters mimicking the violent behavior they see on television. The child's halfmind is like a sponge, uncritically vulnerable to society's teachings—an easily programmed computer.

The first-order mind is complex, like a bank of small computers. In his book *Multimind*, psychologist Robert Ornstein postulates a system of small "minds" within the brain, each serving a specific function. He writes: "Our mind is really a coalition of competing entities. We do not always, even often, know what we think and believe. Part of us, probably somewhere in the self part of the brain, constantly tries to compare and sort out our own thoughts and beliefs."[12] For Ornstein, the "self" is part of the mind, too: "The self, although possessing a privileged place in the mind, is more isolated than we would have ordinarily imagined. It is just another independent talent of the mind, located in a specific portion of the brain."[13] Ornstein is intuitively aware of the limitations of his construct and alludes to "something more" than the multimind: "Something has to command the wheeling in and out of the small minds," and further: "Where in all this is the 'me' responsible for our actions?"[14]

An emerging discipline known as molecular psychology[15] views the mind as a functional assemblage of molecules and claims that one day technology will be able to alter the mind at will. This is certainly within the bounds of possibility, and can be beneficial to humanity. But let's not fool ourselves. Most of the exciting new concepts and discoveries concerning the mind, as exciting as they are, are limited to the structure and function of the first-order mind. Researchers are working on only a part of the whole, and although what they are doing is impressive, it's still nuts-and-bolts work. The "whole" is largely ignored. This seems to be a common oversight even among the most brilliant researchers and innovative thinkers.

The empirical doctrine of philosopher John Locke claims that all knowledge is derived from experience. As far as it concerns the halfmind, his statement holds true. But Locke leaves out the rest. When Descartes wrote, "I think, therefore I am," he was thinking with his halfmind. A more wholeminded person would retort, "am *what!*" Although intuitive psychologists like Ornstein ask "Where is the *me* in all this?" others boil down the total self to the level of a biological computer. Behaviorists, for example, claim that their limited, although unquestionably valuable, theory of the way the mind works explains the *totality* of mental operations. In spite of its beneficial applications, this shortsighted approach is circuitous—it is only good for that which is helped by the behaviorist approach, a category that unfortunately is limited.

Behaviorism, in a manner of speaking, has lost its spirit.

The first-order "computer" mind is molecularly structured, biochemically driven, easily programmable, and, until it learns better, highly suggestible. It reacts to the everyday world. But humans laugh, smile, love, experience joy, ecstasy, grief, and so on. Does the halfmind have a sense of humor? Does it wonder at nature? Does it laugh? Does it want to save whales, to help the poor and needy, to house the homeless?

No. Of course not. And because the mind does experience these things, we may surmise that there is something more within the mind than the nuts and bolts of the first order.

Do you think the halfmind could make sense of these lines written by Wallace Stevens in "The Snow Man" . . . "the listener . . . Beholds Nothing, that is not there, and the nothing that is."

I have no doubt that this phrase would short-circuit the halfmind. In fact, one of the reasons that poetry can't be speed-read is that it must be savored. Poetry is read with another order of intelligence, beyond the halfmind. That's where the seventh sense comes in.

•THE SEVENTH SENSE•

If the first order is nuts and bolts—deals with perceived reality—the seventh sense deals with the meaning of life. Spirit unites the mind-body with the cosmos. It is the self's connection to the "whole" that Einstein mentioned. The wisdom that spirit imparts to the mind, and the emotions it generates within the body, connects to the halfmind via the seventh sense. The halfmind has a great deal of difficulty perceiving spirit. What it does perceive, in the words of William James, is: "the strange phenomenon, as Kant assures us, of a mind believing with all its strength in the real presence of a set of things of no one of which it can form any notion whatsoever."[16]

The seventh sense is an enigma that mystics like Rudolph Steiner have sought to unravel throughout the ages. (Other mystics make the mistake of ignoring the halfmind altogether.) In Steiner's words, man has constantly sought "to develop another kind of cognition. This then would lead into the supersensible world. Because the 'supersensible' cannot be proven does not rule out its existence." Steiner was emphatic on this point: "We cannot deny anyone the right to ignore the supersensible, but there can never be any good reason for him to declare himself an authority, not only on what he himself can know, but on all that a man can not know."[17]

In his book *Ecstasy, A Way of Knowing*, Andrew M. Greeley, the noted writer, describes a "mystical" form of knowledge:

concerned with the ultimate and . . . [that] does not deal with logical propositions or the laws of discursive reasoning, and is like science in that it comes into contact with the hard data of external reality . . . it takes possession of the whole personality . . . it is immediate . . . it requires neither logical proposition nor symbolic representation . . . it is possible for the Real to "rush in" . . . hence the passivity that characterizes virtually all mystics in the course of their experiences. [18]

The seventh sense supplies us with an "oracular" voice from beyond the halfmind. Our awareness of this information—being "tuned in," so to speak—can be likened to a mental radio attuned to what Greeley describes as "mystical knowledge." Imagine, for a moment, that all people have a mental radio containing a broad spectrum of frequencies. These frequencies receive specific, though diverse, information via sensory "waves." The information may be spiritual, emotional, physical, intellectual, social, financial, familial, and so on, each arriving on a specific frequency. Children, for example, are primarily tuned into an emotional and spiritual wavelength that transmits how things feel. Unfortunately, most adults are tuned out on these particular frequencies. They are listening to those of the everyday halfmind.

When I spoke with people during the interviews, I tried to tune into this "oracular" channel. To do this, it was often necessary to clear away other voices, the static of other wavelengths—the "party line"—the everchanging voice of the halfmind that reflects the daily trends and mores of the day. This was not an easy task. The party line works by pressuring people to conform to what is "trendy" in the society even at the expense of health and happiness. It does this by creating "social imperatives."

There is no better example of an oscillating party line in action than social attitudes toward breast-feeding and how they change over the years. The incontestable biological facts are:

- Women have babies.
- Their breasts fill with milk to feed the baby.
- Mother's milk is beneficial for babies.
- For the most part, mother and child are happy when the baby feeds at the breast.
- Following this natural system is simple, inexpensive, and healthful physically, psychologically, and spiritually.

Enter the party line, society's self-appointed (first-order) "experts" who establish their authority by "studying" the issue.

Their "studies," often impelled by social, religious, political, business, or other forces (in this case immature fringes of the women's liberation movement, the puritanical who deplore breast-feeding in public, nurses and doctors who don't want to take the time to teach insecure young mothers breast-feeding skills, artificial milk companies that stand to gain immeasurably if women stop breast-feeding, and so on) "prove" that breast-feeding is not "necessary"—that formula feeding is as good, thus "liberating" those women who so desire from their babies and lining the pockets of the companies that make artificial milk.

What's a dutiful mother who feels impelled to nurse her baby to do in the face of the "experts"? Don't the "authorities" know best? Soon breast-feeding not only goes out of style, it becomes condemned. Things get so bad that when a nursing mother wants to breast-feed her child in public she is looked upon as "strange" or with "disgust" or even shunned.

Thus, as a result of listening to "experts," a generation of blindly obedient mothers started to feed their babies artificial milk or formula, even though their common sense told them it was not right to abandon breast-feeding.

But the party line, as it always does, changed. Other "experts," for one reason or another, now proclaimed that breast-feeding is "best." Back to Mom's breast go the happy babies. But what about the mothers who were "cheated" (as I have heard many say) out of breast-feeding their children? Whom do they get angry at? Do they rail against the forces that initiated the anti-breast-feeding movement? Do they blame themselves for not trusting their instincts and giving in to social fads?

What about mothers who didn't follow the party line, who continued to nurse their infants when it was unpopular to do so? To those who maintained their balance between cherishing their motherhood and meaningfully participating in the fight for "liberation" from unfair social discrimination? What enabled them to continue nursing their young in the face of social condemnation? How could they do what they did? The answer is simple.

They listened to their seventh sense—the oracle within them—and turned a deaf ear to what was in fashion. They gave credence to a biological imperative, breasts were put there to feed babies. And they acted according to this imperative, as opposed to what social imperatives were espousing—in this case that breast-feeding was "out of fashion." "Fashion" is a first-order concept that often flies in the face of biological and spiritual imperatives.

There are plenty of "fashionable," malignant party lines that are currently being "imputted" into our halfminds; social ways that people swallow hook, line, and sinker. The "thin" ideal woman: How many women are really thin? "Name" college education: Can everyone go to Ivy League schools? Warehousing children in day care, full time: What are we doing to our kids? Isolating elders in old folks' homes unnecessarily: Is this what life is about? The idea of total "retirement": Dropping out of life after fifty-five, leaving one's children and grandchildren to fend for themselves. And so on.

All for which an emotional and spiritual price will be paid in the future. The seventh sense is aware of basic and enduring truths and is directly opposed to the first-order ways of society and the malignant institutions these party lines create.

The difference between social imperatives and the seventh

sense was stated by the philosopher Rudolf Otto, who wrote: "Laws of the spirit are fundamentally different from those of the natural world." He believed that "spirit is the source of concepts, principles, intuitions and valuations. And that although the spirit develops under the influence of external stimuli, it is something unique in its own right which cannot be derived from sense experience." What Otto claims to be the source of "concepts, principles, intuitions and valuations of the spirit"[19] is the seventh sense.

This seventh sense generates emotions within the self that the halfmind cannot tag.

Often it is difficult for the self to differentiate a genuine seventh-sense emotion from a reaction that originates in the halfmind. This can be quite confusing. My friend Scott told me about an overwhelming "patriotic" experience he had.

"Last July 4 I was in Sardinia, on a boat trip with a Greek friend. We were docked between a large Syrian ship on one side and an Arab ship on the other. My host was raising our ship's flags in the morning. He went down into his cabin and brought out a small American flag. We raised it. For fun, I 'bugled' the call to arms by putting my closed fist in front of my mouth. But something amazing happened. What started out as a joke became deadly serious. There I was in this port, the only American. Tears came to my eyes. I began to bugle louder and louder. I got goose pimples. When I saw the flag raised, a sentimental feeling for my country rushed over me. Call it patriotism. I couldn't believe what I felt."

Was the profound emotion that Scott experienced due to patriotic (first-order) "conditioning," or did something beyond his halfmind respond to the event? In answer to this question, the (first-order) behaviorist would say that Scott was conditioned since childhood to respond in an emotional way to his country's flag and that he reacted in this manner because he missed home and his loved ones. This makes sense as far as it goes.

But viewed through the lens of the seventh sense, another

possibility arises. Perhaps the intensity of Scott's "patriotism" arose from something deep within him that was attributable to something more than conditioned nationalism or a feeling of homesickness. Could spirit have been involved?

I think so, and for one important reason—the very intensity of the emotion he experienced. Deep emotions can arise from spirit. The halfmind does not experience profound emotions—computers don't feel. What the halfmind experiences as feelings are immediate, concrete, and body-centered: physical pain, physical relief, gratification of needs.

One other point hints that my friend's reaction arose from beyond his halfmind—the event itself was related to (and this is most important) a spiritual imperative.

Spiritual imperatives are mandates from spirit to the mind that are always positive and contain an agenda for living a happy and meaningful life. I suspect they are transmitted to the mind via the seventh sense. When they are received, they create strong emotions within the self.

Because this idea of spiritual imperatives may seem confusing at this point, I will give a brief example of the concept.

Everyone knows, and common sense tells us, that most people have a considerable attachment to their place of origin— a sense of "home." All would agree on the universality of this concept; "home" is expressed in thoughts, feelings, and behavior, extolled in the arts, and strongly felt in an emotional (and often sentimental) way.

What Scott experienced was a strong emotion. It was about home, the place and the people. *It is my contention that when a particular event has at its core a universal theme and elicits a strong emotion, it is an indication that spirit is involved.*

Experiences generated from spirit are identified by their universality, by the "gut feelings" they engender, the common-sense thoughts they produce, the universal behaviors they invoke, and the inability of the de-spirited halfmind to explain what is happening.

. INSPIRATION .

"Inspiration," experienced by the wholemind as an unusual thought, feeling, or concept that is apparently beyond the knowledge we learn from the everyday world, comes from the seventh sense. Like Kant's idea of "knowledge before experience," it is a way of "knowing" something without having learned it from the everyday world. The body learns first-order information through the five senses that "input" the halfmind: touch, taste, smell, sight, and hearing.

A "sixth" sense—intuition—also exists. Intuition is a mental process that takes place when information is either consciously or unconsciously derived from the world, placed out of consciousness, exposed to intricate neuroanatomic connections in deeper recesses of the mind, and restructured within a new cognitive framework. It ultimately emerges as a new "original" idea or a mental construct. Silvano Arieti, a distinguished psychiatrist, described intuition as "a kind of knowledge that is revealed without preparation, or as an immediate method of obtaining knowledge."[20] Part of this process occurs in the halfmind, part in the wholemind. The borders between the two are quite fuzzy.

Inspiration is easier to explain. It originates in the seventh sense. In the past inspiration has, like much of what is contained within the seventh sense, often been attributed to divine sources—a "God-given gift" or an artistic achievement attributed to "a work inspired by God." Beethoven, who felt that his talent was God-given, is quoted as saying

> But well I know that God is nearer to me than other artists; I associate with Him without fear; I have always recognized and understood Him and have no fear for my music—it can meet no evil fate. Those who understand it must be freed by it from all the

miseries which the others drag about with themselves
. . . music is the one incorporeal entrance into the
higher world of knowledge which comprehends mankind but which mankind cannot comprehend.[21]

It is the nature of inspiration that it creates within a person
a seminal idea or concept. What issues from the seventh sense
is "classic," universal, enduring, like art, music, and literature.
Inspirational figures, who exemplify enduring principles like
freedom, charity, reverence for life, goodness, beauty, have, in
their lifetimes, relinquished the ethos of the first order and lived
their lives according to spiritual principles. Great human beings
stand in testimony to this statement.

The concept of a seventh sense contradicts Locke's narrow
notion of empiricism. Wilhelm von Leibnitz, the German philosopher, apparently without invitation, attempted to expand
Locke's narrow viewpoint. He quoted Locke's first-order statement, "There is nothing in the intellect except what was first in
the senses" by adding "nothing except the intellect itself,"[22]
making a good case for the existence of "something more."

HOW THE SEVENTH SENSE
COMMUNICATES
TO THE MIND

How does this seventh sense get through to the mind? In
my survey, people had interesting answers to this question.

Those who are in touch with this presence feel, as a fifty-
four-year-old woman said of seventh-sense impulses, that they
are, "What a youngster feels in the presence of a strong and
wise old grandparent."

"Can you describe it?" I asked a middle-aged man. He
smiled.

"If I tried to describe it in human terms," he said, "it would be in the following way: If it had a personality, its attitude would be patient and mellow. It wouldn't panic over everyday life events because it lives in another dimension and has a long view of life. It knows that nothing 'daily' really matters in the long run, except what *really matters*, and that is things of the spirit. It views events in terms of outcomes rather than day-to-day fluctuations. It grows more powerful with age. It soothes people around it. It is a source of deep wisdom."

A woman, aged thirty-nine, said that her grandmother was like a seventh sense—"full of wisdom I didn't learn anywhere else. I always went to see my grandmother when things were going wrong because she always knew that things will usually turn out all right in the long run. Recently I was complaining to my daughter about something and she told me the same thing about my own mother. Funny but I never saw my mom like that."

Effective therapists, clergymen, healers, and so on have a strong "ancient" presence within that radiates from them and is calming and healing to those around them.

Carl Jung intuited an "ancient" within. His biographer wrote: "In fact, at the age of twelve [Jung] had already conceived the idea that there was a second personality within him, an old man of great authority."[23] The "guardian angel" in mythology is another representation of the ancient within, often serving as advisor and protector to the youthful spirit. One of the reasons that the young and old get along so well is that the young have the benefit of a real live "ancient" to themselves.

The seventh sense often signals the self physically, creating nonspecific "gut feelings" that are hard to separate from socially conditioned emotions. Gut feelings can be located anywhere in the body. Many of the women I spoke with located these feelings in the chest. Margaret Mead said she "felt all over." Men often locate them in the abdomen. Some people report a tightness in the forehead.

"I know about a person as soon as I meet them," one man told me. "When I don't like someone," a woman said, "my chest tightens, my feet get cold. The funny thing is there is no reason in the world that I should feel like that. I might not even know the person, but I can sense something." The seventh sense acts as a "telephone line" from spirit within and without to the wholemind. It is beyond the sixth sense, which has a root in reality. When we get a gut feeling, something in us "knows better"—has information beyond the first-order information that the mind has been fed. It assimilates this information and eventually urges us to act upon it.

Here is a sample of the internal dialogue that might take place in a person's mind when the seventh sense is operating:

"I did it on a hunch."

"There is no reason for it. I took the risk and had no doubt at all that I would be successful."

"I was looking for a house. I heard about this house that was a terrific deal. It wasn't bad at all and the price was a steal. But it didn't feel good to me. So I didn't buy it. Everyone thought I was crazy. But there was something wrong there that I can't put my finger on."

Some have linked the seventh sense to mystical ideas: having seen it all before in a previous life, *déjà vu*, clairvoyance. Suffice it to say that the seventh sense is a countervailing source of information to the everyday, the first-order conditioning of the mind.

And it must be listened to.

• BATTLE OF THE TITANS •

The halfmind and the seventh sense often have to slug it out within the self. It is like a battle of titans for dominance of the self. The people who just commented on their "gut" feelings were aware that their seventh sense contradicted their halfminded "reason." To make a decision and act upon it, they had to select between contradictory information from their "programming" or from their "gut" input.

All of us experience similar conflicts. It is reflected in every act where there is an internal war between expediency and integrity. It is the ongoing battle between the proverbial devils and angels in all of us.

A young man who was addicted to drugs for three years graphically identified these warring forces. He told me about the conflict between his "mind" and what he spontaneously called "spirit": "My body wanted drugs. It needed drugs. My spirit said to stop taking drugs, that I was killing myself. But my mind wouldn't listen and it would go out of its way to fool the spirit. My mind was tricky. It played games so it could get drugs for my body. I know it sounds crazy but it's true. My spirit would say 'no heroin today.' My mind would agree then . . . it was a battle within my head . . . my mind would say 'I want to walk downtown,' knowing damn well that it had every intention of getting drugs. My spirit would know that my mind was lying but somehow I would end up downtown and get drugs.

"I asked my girlfriend to help me—sort of get her spirit on my side. I told her not to let me bullshit her into letting me smoke or shoot up. Between my own spirit and hers I was able to beat the habit."

ALTERED MIND-BODY PERCEPTION AND THE SEVENTH SENSE

The existence of a seventh sense may shed some light on unexplained phenomena like telepathy, precognition, faith healing, premonition, and other "paranormal" or "parapsychological" occurrences. (See Appendix B.) These phenomena are universally recognized and interwoven into most cultural, religious, or mystical practices. This is especially true of native Americans who, at least in the past, lived in a society where spiritual practices played an important role in daily life. Native Americans honored things of the spirit and expressed them in their customs as well as their rites and rituals. Many of these practices persist today. If someone dies unexpectedly, as in an auto accident, a week-long vigil is held at the victim's home to assure the spirit that all is well. A prayer is offered to assure the spirit of the deceased that things are being cared for. It was not to worry, but to go to the Creator in peace.

The Indian friend who told me this, Chief Raymond, believes in "paranormal" experiences. "The spirit can fly," he said. "When a person is sleeping, the spirit can leave the body and go to other places. But you can't talk about it. To talk about it takes away the power. Some things you talk about, others you don't. You don't talk about the spirit. It is too sacred." And that was all he would say on that matter.

Once when I spoke before the tribal council of the Zuñi people concerning an intergenerational education project, the interpreter warned me not to say certain words, like "warrior" and "ghost." To speak the words would call these spirits into the room. So powerful and alive to native Americans is the sense of cosmic connection between earth and the universe that they believe they can summon their dead ancestors when they wish. Their ancestors are with them. They exist in a world bathed by spirit.

Children are the same. One child I asked to tell me what happened to people after they died answered, "Well, the person hangs around for a while after they are buried . . . sort of floats around the grave to check things out . . . maybe for just a few days. Then, when they see that everything is okay, they leave to go to heaven." And she had never met Chief Raymond.

THE SEVENTH SENSE AND DREAMING

Something is telling us something when we dream.

Dreaming is related to the seventh sense, since the state of dreaming removes the self from everyday life. Like everything else in this area, there is much controversy surrounding the nature and function of dreaming.

One function of dreams is as the sentinel of the self. When we dream the halfmind idles. Since external consciousness and logical thought processes are diminished during sleep, this is the time when spirit may have access to consciousness, examine the state of the self, and communicate it to the mind. Because dream language is often garbled, spirit has trouble getting through to the self. It doesn't make logical sense to the conscious mind. The language of dreams is akin to the illogical, magical, fantasy thought process of the immature mind, before we attained the age of reason, before the halfmind assumed precedence.

While the halfmind sleeps, the seventh sense is active and forages through the halfmind. It gains access to past memories, symbols, scenarios (similar to what Jung called the "collective unconscious"), and assesses what is happening to the self in everyday life. In proper circumstances, it can then communicate its findings to a receptive wholemind when it wakes up. Perhaps the seventh sense can even reprogram the halfmind in the service of spirit.

Of one thing I am sure. Those scientists who say that dreaming is a useless function caused by random electrical activity in the brain are wrong. I have been privy to too many reports of rational people having predictive dreams, achieving insight, or solving problems during their dreams to believe that these phenomena are uniquely caused by nerve cells randomly firing during sleep.

Something is happening, we just don't know exactly what it is.

Consider your own experiences with dreams. Have you ever had a predictive dream or awakened with a solution to a problem that you couldn't figure out in your waking life? Have you ever wakened in the morning a lot happier than when you went to sleep and wondered why, since the world hadn't changed while you were sleeping?

Certain cultures have institutionalized the mystical aspects of dreaming. The Senoi people of Malaya believe that the dream state is as important as waking life. Children are taught to take control of their dreams and to face the fears embodied in their nightmares. It is incumbent upon a person who has an "offensive" dream about another to apologize to him or her as soon as possible. Mesopotamians felt that their soul left the body with sleep and that dreams represented the nightly voyages of the individual's soul. Many cultures believe that sleep releases the spirit from its corporeal form and that dreams result from the spirit's boundless nightly adventures.

Of one thing I am sure. In sleep the spirit is the great detective, uncovering aspects of life hidden from consciousness. Freud was right about dreams being the "royal road to the unconscious." They might well be the royal road to spirit, an idea not dissimilar to what Freud described as the regions of "id."

Turmoil in dreams arises when the self is unable to express its spiritual imperatives in the everyday world. A terrifying dream alerts the mind that something in real life, unrecognized by the halfmind, is threatening the self, and for one reason or another the conscious mind does not acknowledge the problem or is unwilling or unable to deal with it. How many children's nightmares are a statement that their waking lives are emotional nightmares? Are their parents ignoring problems bubbling under the surface of the family? Problems that are beyond the grasp of the child's halfmind but that spirit can detect? Children, with oracular clarity, see right through social cosmetics to the core of reality.

No wonder they have night terrors.

A SEVENTH-SENSE CONSCIENCE

Guilt is an emotion linked to spirit. There are at least two "types" of guilt that I can identify. The first, halfmind guilt, occurs when the self transgresses the party line—socially accepted first-order rules and regulations. It results from a person's actions. The halfmind easily discards this type of guilt. One way is by attacking the rulemaker; the guilty self can turn the tables and get angry at those who inflicted the rules in the first place. For example, a teenager, prohibited from staying out late on a Saturday night, will indeed feel guilty if he or she comes home late . . . but will deal with guilt by getting angry at "strict" and "prudish" parents. If the young person wants to go out the following night, all that is necessary is to serve penance, like bringing his or her parents breakfast in bed. Thus, first-order guilt is easily forgotten. In fact, situations that create it can usually be chuckled about years after the fact. "Remember when Mary put clear plastic over the toilet seats on April Fool's Day . . ."

A second form of guilt arises from an affront to spirit. It results not only from what a person does, but goes beyond the act to determine what a person *is* as a being and as a result of how a specific act affects the person's *being*. This is a pervasive form of guilt, for which restitution is not easily made, and it may last a long time. It is experienced when a wrongful deed is done even though a given society's party line may sanction the deed. Such guilt is an internal, private experience. It is felt whether or not another person knows that a deed was done. It is a transgression against the spiritual integrity and character of the self, and is guilt peppered with a deeper, more pervasive negative emotion called shame. Shame invades spiritual consciousness and is not easily discarded. It is an emotion that represents a negative attitude toward the self for *existing*.

A clinical illustration of how shame operates is evident in the fact that many people who have had extramarital affairs feel not only guilt but shame, and suffer a compulsion to confess their perceived transgression (and potentially hurt an unknowing spouse). Unable to tolerate the level of shame they have piled upon themselves they search to confess to unburden themselves, to clear their conscience and regain self-esteem. A person who can't find a satisfactory way out of such a quandary may punish themselves severely and often be unaware why they are doing so.

Shame is deep, pervasive, and very difficult to live with. It occurs because of an infraction against another set of rules that are, I believe, universal, natural, cosmic, basic, and rooted in spiritual imperatives. One of them is being "whole"—intact, integral—not living different lives with different rules, being harmonious.

A good illustration of how this conscience operates appears in Victor Hugo's novel *Les Misérables*. If you are familiar with the story, you know it concerns the lifelong pursuit of Jean Val-Jean by Inspector Javert of the French police. In the story Val-Jean, who stole a loaf of bread in his youth, was jailed, subsequently escaped, and tried to start a new life. Inspector Javert pursued him relentlessly over many years. As Javert closed in, ValJean has to flee his home, where he had become a kind and generous pillar of the community. Javert pursues him. In the end Javert finally arrests ValJean, but, knowing what a fine man he is and too conscientious not to do his duty and bring ValJean to prison, Javert commits suicide. In the end the policeman was forced to choose between his sworn obligation to bring ValJean to justice, enforcing the first-order conscience of society, or obeying the dictates of his second-order conscience—his spirit—by committing a wrong against a brave and valiant man. Caught between his two consciences, Javert chose not to choose at all by destroying himself.

Spiritual conscience isn't learned from the everyday world, and its "values" are not *rooted* in ephemeral social rules and regulations (ideally a society will reflect its values). It serves as a countervailing force against a socially learned "superego" that can be so easily corrupted. This makes for an ongoing drama that rages in everyman—the good guys versus the bad guys—conflict that theater is made of.

There is a difference between spiritual conscience and the conscience of the "superego" as Freud has postulated it. The superego is constructed with the bricks and mortar of first-order experience. It is a conglomeration of rules and regulations "programmed" into the halfmind by parents and society. Because the oracle within the self is pressured into adhering to these rules, there is a natural conflict between the oracle as "ego" (self) and the superego when the rules don't match. The battle starts early in life, as soon as society's rules impede the child's needs (feeding upon demand versus feeding on an arbitrarily determined "schedule"). In reaction, the child complies and gets angry. The child defies and risks disapproval. Guilt is the punishment for defying the party line. Frequent infractions makes for a "bad" child. Parents who are especially stern often use shame as a disciplinary measure and do great harm to their children. Children may be made to feel guilty for a "naughty" act but should not be shamed for it.

Guilt deals the self a superficial wound, shame a deeper one.

A young secretary told me that she takes anything she can get her hands on from her office: staples, pens, pads. "I take them all home." I asked her if she felt guilty about what she was doing. "No, not at all. The boss can afford it. Besides, maybe I wouldn't do it if they treated me better." It was clear that she had assuaged her superego by rationalizing her act. Since she felt that she was being exploited, she believed she had the right to avenge herself by stealing.

In talking with her, I pursued the issue to a deeper, more personal level. "But what you are doing makes you a criminal in the eyes of the law," I said. "More important is what you are doing to yourself." This comment added another, more personal, dimension to her act.

The remark took her aback. "I never thought about it like that. I would be ashamed of myself if I look at it like that. I don't want to be a criminal. They [the employers] are the criminals for treating their help the way they do. I shouldn't be compared to them."

She reflected for a moment, then her anger waned. "To tell the truth, now that I think about it, I really did feel bad once I took the time to look at the stuff I took. I mean, I knew I did wrong . . . a little voice told me. I guess I tried to justify it."

This comment brings to mind another, more lighthearted issue that I came across during this study. It concerns the subject of the "little voice" and brings up an interesting question.

Can spirit be heard?

A seven-year-old youngster named Kelly thinks so: "When I do something wrong, sometimes I hear my mom saying, 'Kelly, don't do that.' I know that she's going to find out what I did. But when I think about doing something wrong that no one will find out, another voice tells me, 'Kelly, don't do that.' Sometimes there is even another voice that says, 'Yeah, Kelly, do it anyway.' Those voices say things that my mom doesn't know about."

Socrates heard a voice, too: "By favour of the Gods, I have, since my childhood, been attended by a semi-divine being whose voice from time to time dissuades me from some undertaking, but never directs me what I am to do." He went on: "The prophetic voice has been heard by me throughout my life; it is certainly more trustworthy than omens from the flight or entrails of birds. I call it God or daemon. I have told my friends the warnings I have received, and up to now the voice has never been wrong."[24]

Many people reported that they can hear a "voice of their conscience" that comes inside their heads (if they heard it from outside their heads I would wonder about hallucination). Ed, a

Chicago businessman, hears "voices," too. "Of course there is a conscience that straightens me out when I need it. And it lets me know when I am doing wrong. Look, if I do wrong to someone, I do myself harm. If I cheat someone out of a million bucks I should feel bad about it. But I can say, 'Shit, I got a million bucks and that jerk doesn't.' Sure I could make excuses to myself. My mind can do that, but it will only last for a minute. Those types of excuses fade quickly and I am left with the deed. Every time I spend a penny of that money it will remind me of what I did. I just won't like myself. 'Ed, you are a creep,' it would say. If I cheat someone, I am harming my own self, my spirit. If I did that, my spirit wouldn't leave me alone until I made it right. The money wouldn't matter—and religion has nothing to do with it."

For what it is worth, Socrates, Kelly, and Ed are not alone. Since ancient times people have believed in guardian spirits. In ancient Egypt a "guardian genius" called Ka was known to accompany people throughout life. To the native American, a guardian spirit appears in dreams in the form of an animal. Moslems believe that man has four guardian angels, two to watch over him during the day and two at night.

Have you ever heard your conscience?

• THE SEVENTH SENSE AND RELIGION •

Spiritual conscience and religious conscience may be congruent or divergent.

Religious conscience is based on the specific rules and regulations of the religion, which may or may not be synonymous with spiritual imperatives. (Obviously, such religious beliefs that lead to something like the Spanish Inquisition or the Salem witch trials have little to do with spiritual imperatives.) Religious rules serve as guidelines for living life in a specific man-

ner and for a defined purpose. One who adheres to these rules
will, according to the religion, benefit at some time, somehow,
and in some way. When rules are broken, appropriate religious
punishments are administered. Methods of atonement for infraction of most of these rules are also spelled out. Halfminded
individuals can act pseudoreligiously, in the sense that they can
certainly follow religious rules. But they are merely religious
"robots," going through the motions, totally unaware of the
spiritual aspects of what their religion propounds.

Spiritual imperatives—love, charity, caring—are as close
as spirit comes to having "rules." When religious rules are compatible with spirit—with these spiritual imperatives—the self
experiences no conflict. When religious rules and obligations
diverge from spiritual imperatives (killing people because they
belong to another religion) as well as social imperatives (religions that proclaim supremacy), the self can experience conflict. When religion diverges from spiritual imperatives and
becomes its own "government"—a salesman for the hereafter,
in effect—*religious conscience then becomes just someone else's
rules, which may be far removed from the conscience of spirit.*

There is no more poignant illustration of this than what
happened to many native Americans who were "converted" to
the white man's religion. Native Americans are well aware of
the rules and regulations that the white man's religions have
interposed between the "Creator" and themselves. Chief Raymond was bitter that his people surrendered their own ways.
"Our ways are the ways of nature," he told me. "All living
things have a spirit. When we talk to people we try not to hurt
one another's feelings. The Earth is our mother. We respect
her. We have no shame or guilt over physical things, like the
white man does. There is no heaven or hell. There is no sin.
No evil. The Creator is good. There are just bad people who do
bad things because they are not living right. We should be good
to one another and the family and respect the earth. We should
walk right and give thanks to the Creator for the sun every

morning. And we honor the spirits of our ancestors, to join them one day. We need no priests, no middle people who tell us what is good and what is bad and then give us repentance. For what? Something they think is bad. Look at the wars they make for religion. At least, in the old days, when my people made war they would paint themselves black afterward, because they knew they had done wrong. I know what is bad. My parents and grandparents have told me. The spirits of my ancestors tell me. The Creator tells me. It was my grandfather who told me to apologize to the trees before I entered the woods to go hunting and to say a prayer, 'Please forgive me, trees, for bending your branches as I go hunting in the woods.' It was my grandmother who told me, as her grandmother did before her, to thank the spirit of an animal when I killed it. 'Thank you, rabbit, for giving up your life so my family may eat you and be nourished.' The Creator is all around us, within us and between us. No man has a monopoly on this.

"The Creator is the spirit, the true conscience."

For Chief Raymond there is no middle person, no translator, no enforcer, no bureaucracy between spirit within the self and the "Creator." The chief explained that the conscience of his spirit was in harmony with his organic religion, both rooted in the rhythms of observable natural phenomena. He said he did not need a "man-made" conscience when the "Creator" had already supplied him with one.

In our conversation, he alluded to the ongoing battle between spirit and halfmind: "Once we started following the white man's religion and his rules, we started to follow other rules. We allowed our minds to be poisoned because white man's religion says it is of the spirit, but it is really of the mind. With this lie he has taken our lands from us. By following his rules we have allowed him to break our nation's hoop [its continuity]. Many of my people have surrendered their spirit to the white man's rules and regulations. Now these people have been broken."

For the most part, man is a religious animal. People take

naturally to organized religion. An institutionalized religion is at its best when it truly serves its adherents' spiritual needs, as opposed to being primarily devoted to its own perpetuation. It is best as a potentiator of spirit rather than as a proprietor. When it works, it works well.

Bob, a forty-five-year-old automobile salesman, had searched for years for the right church community. "I went from this one to that one. Then one day I walked into this little church in the next town and found people who believe the way I do, who think the way I do, and who feel the way I do. Before that there was always something wrong with every church I went to. What they said was good and evil didn't correspond with how I saw real life. Too much politics. In one church the pastor was a jerk. Ran the thing like a business. Too much talk of money. I don't want money to be a factor in my religious life. I go to church for my soul. Too much gossip. Too much hate. Maybe that's normal when people get together.

"Maybe my new church is abnormal. The life in my church matches the life I want to live. Its rules are my own rules for living. I feel that I am together, sewed up nice and tight—a neat little package, me, my church, and God. It all fits. We are a real community."

When a religion bases its ethos and ways upon a foundation of spiritual imperatives and its institutional body "lives" this philosophy in word and deed, then it offers its adherents the best of both worlds: a spiritual sanctuary on earth; an earthly place to conduct spiritual affairs. Bob has found it within his church. Chief Raymond has found it in nature.

• "EQUIPMENT" •

The expression of spirit into the environment via the self depends on the latent abilities of mind and body. The quality of the self's "equipment"—how gifted, able, or disabled a person may be in diverse areas of functioning—is directly related to the self's ability to fulfill its aspirations within a given environment: high personal self-esteem, a feeling of being fulfilled and happy in everyday life, and, most important, the expression of its spiritual imperatives.

The more a person depends on "feedback" from the everyday world for his or her self-esteem, the more dependent that person is on the performance of his or her equipment for giving the world what it demands. There is no better example of a failure of equipment to meet social expectations than what happens to a child afflicted with hyperactivity.

Jimmy, a little boy so afflicted, is unable to sit still no matter how much he would like to. He is always on the move. His body, through no fault of his own, is "revved up." If he lives in an environment where school performance is valued and where it is necessary to sit unmoving for a long period of time in class, he gets negative feedback and becomes a social "failure," because he constantly disrupts his class with his fidgeting and relentless motion. Parents and teachers are always on Jimmy's back. He is miserable. What is even sadder is that his handicap is "invisible"—to everyone he looks fine, unlike a child with a physical disability, who would elicit sympathy. Jimmy knows that he is a pain in the neck to everyone, but he can't do anything about it. It's not much fun for him to look up into people's faces and see how angrily they look back at him. All this happens because he can't control his activity—his body equipment has failed him. He becomes sad, disillusioned, then angry at a world that doesn't understand him and at not being able to be what he would like to be.

Even a minor mental or physical deviation from the "norm" has an impact on spirit. Dottie, a thirty-nine-year-old secretary, was born "a small person"—under four feet tall. She said that sometimes she felt that her spirit was "trapped" in her body.

"My spirit is bigger than my body." She smiled. "As a kid I didn't think about my size and I did everything. I remember being surprised when I couldn't reach something everyone else could."

I asked how her size limitation affected her. "Say, for instance, I couldn't jump from the ground to the porch as others could. I would try to think of another way to do it and if I couldn't, I'd get angry. This bothered my spirit. It made it sad, because it was such an ordinary thing not to be able to do. If my spirit could talk it would probably say 'Ahhhhh!'" She said this sadly. "I don't think of my spirit as being in my body. I think of it as riding around with me, like on my shoulder . . . or sort of piggyback." She smiled. "Maybe there is not enough room."

Many other conditions affect the balance among mind, body, and spirit. The way these conditions affect the self depends on the individual's other attributes—the love and support of the family and the love, support, and attitudes of society toward the affliction.

A child with Down's syndrome, one symptom of which is mental retardation, has a relatively intact body but a disabled mind. The sweet dispositions of these children is legendary. They are lovable kids. Although mind and first-order consciousness are obviously impaired, spirit is there . . . and in the past they were locked away.

What about persons afflicted with a functional physical deformity like cerebral palsy? Most often these people are gifted with highly intelligent minds and are frustrated because their intellect is imprisoned in a handicapped, anarchic, and uncontrollable body. What heroic effort of spirit is necessary for them to bring forth their brilliance into the world?

An impressive demonstration of how spirit can triumph over faulty equipment is a Special Olympics, which features games for the disabled. On view is true testimony to how triumphant and noble spirits can overcome faulty mental and physical equipment. The onlooker will emerge from this experience humbled and wiser. It can be compared to witnessing a birth, and will increase the "spiritedness" of everyone who sees it.

. QUANTITY OF SPIRIT .

Some people seem to be more "spirited" than others.

"This "spiritedness" is not a result of biochemical metabolism, psychological characteristics like character, temperament, or anxiety, or anything other than the fact that these people have been endowed that way. I wondered if those who have an abundance of spirit could consciously put it to use. I asked this question of Jeff, the champion athlete, during our conversation: "Did spirit have anything to do with your becoming a world champion?"

He didn't think so. He answered that his mind-body and his spirit were separate and that they didn't interact. But he didn't deny the possibility.

I have asked other athletes the same question. Most felt strongly that "heart" and "spirit" were important in a champion. Phil, a popular baseball player, said, "Spirit is the whole ballgame. Give me a kid with some talent, some brains, and a lot of spirit and I'll give you a winner. Look at the athletes that you see on the winning teams. Full of spirit. It pours out of them and infects their teammates. Spirit is contagious. It's not psychology that wins games, it's spirit."

He continued. "I'll tell you something else—you can't buy it or make it. You got it or you haven't—and some people have more than others. God isn't fair. We all didn't get the same amount. Look at some of the faces around you. Dead. Look at others. Alive, bouncy. Sunshine coming from their eyes. No spirit, no champion. It's not their body or their minds. It's how much spirit, energy, they have."

Phil believes in "quantity of spirit" and that spirit is present in abundant amounts in champions. In his words: "Spirit is the essence of a champion. Spirit converts whatever the person has to work with into greatness. If a person is lucky enough to have great talent and great heart, or spirit, then he, or she, will be exceptional. Without spirit the greatest natural talent will never, never be realized. It would be like having the fastest car in the world without fuel."

There is a lot of truth in these words. Visit a newborn nursery at your local hospital and spend some time observing the babies. You will see that some are more active than others, some more peaceful than others. Then there will be a few who are more attractive than the others. Not necessarily in the physical sense, but they will have a "glow" more "charisma." (Make sure that there are no babies whose parents you know in the nursery—otherwise you'll be biased.)

Martha, a nurse I worked with, once mentioned to me that newborns were different from one another.

"In what way?" I asked her.

"You should know," she said. "Some are full of it and some aren't. Some have more pep than others, some just have more life to them, something special. And some are miserable—and will probably be all of their lives."

At the time I discounted a great deal of what she said, because of that last remark. How could she say that some of these cute innocent infants would be "miserable all of their lives"? I wondered. But, in retrospect, as much as I don't like to admit it, I realized there was some truth in what she had said.

A rabbi I spoke with strongly believes that people have differing quantities of spirit. He talked about Holocaust survivors who were "wonderful spirits."

Dorothy, a fifty-three-year-old executive trainer, believes in the idea of quantity of spirit, too: "You can send a horse to water but you can't make it drink," she said with a smile. "You can send someone to school to act like an executive, but you can't make one. You can't make a leader. They are born, not made." I asked her what makes them different. "Spirit," she answered. "It comes out of their pores."

·4·

SPIRITUAL IMPERATIVES

*Methinks in thee some blessed spirit
does speak
His powerful sound within an organ
weak.*

—*Shakespeare,* All's Well That Ends
Well

It is human to wonder what life is all about; what we are doing here on earth; or what is the point of all this life surrounding us.

Not easy questions for most, but some people I have met have personally come to terms with these issues. I mean *personally* because they told me that their answers arose from "inside" as opposed to what anyone or any institution told them. Others have had the answers to these questions supplied for them by an established religion and find them satisfactory enough, in varying degrees. Yet others refute the necessity of such questions in the first place. Nevertheless, these matters remain part of the human experience; everyone, at one time or another, wants to know what the heck is going on!

If I learned one thing from my experience both as a physician and as a psychiatrist, it's this—the most satisfied and fulfilled people I have met, not only during this study but during my entire lifetime, say that they live their lives according to "principles" that, as one elderly man claims (and as Shakespeare, in the quotation above, seemed to know) "comes from inside."

I believe them. I further believe that the "principles" that these people mentioned arise from beyond the halfmind, are rooted in spirit, and supply the self with an agenda for living a good and meaningful life.

I call these principles spiritual imperatives.

Edmund S. Sinnott, a leading American botanist, wrote the following in 1908. His words well describe the nature of spiritual imperatives. "That man loves beauty, seeks righteousness, pursues truth, and reverences the Divine, and does so not primarily from outer compulsion or inner necessity but because these are things that he earnestly *desires*, should put us in good heart about his future."[1]

Spirit is not just a passive presence, manifested as another consciousness within the self. It is a force, as well, one that manifests itself as powerful imperatives pressing for recognition by the halfmind and for eventual expression, via the self, into the surrounding world. When these imperatives are acted upon, the self feels happy, peaceful, and harmonious. When they are frustrated or repressed, the self experiences a broad range of negative emotions, from mild unhappiness to great turmoil, and these may eventually flood over mind and body and lead to the dissolution of the self. Then you have the phenomenon known as a "mental breakdown." This concept of spiritual imperatives, and the ability of the mind-body to fulfill them, adds another dimension to current psychological theory. Until now psychology, the science of mind and behavior, has focused on the development and workings of the mind as it concerns the five senses, plus perhaps the sixth. The time has now come to begin to consider how the seventh sense, via spiritual imperatives, affects mind and behavior.

Freud postulated an ego, id, and superego, but never "proved" them to be "real." Nevertheless, when put into practice, his "unprovable" theories were of inestimable benefit in healing mental suffering. Perhaps spiritual imperatives can never be proven, either, but, in the same way, they can be of inestimable value in helping people to confront and deal with important questions in their lives and can offer a meaning to their existence.

Is it possible for people to become aware of their spiritual imperatives, since they are often unrecognized by the halfmind? Indeed, most often these imperatives are perceived as a confusing tangle of emotions and thoughts that create emotional turmoil and intrapsychic conflicts. Other times they may nudge the self to action, without its knowing why.

The great majority of people with whom I spoke were not consciously aware of such things as spiritual imperatives, even though they may have been using them as a guide for living. When they did have a set of values, it was usually based on a religious belief. They lived their lives according to spiritual imperatives, but weren't able to give them a name. They just *did* it. Numbered among these people are the sung and unsung heroes and heroines who appear throughout history: artists, prophets, religious leaders, healers, mystics—all those whose lives serve as an example of the importance of one single person's life that is dedicated to the expression of spiritual imperatives.

THE SPIRIT OF . . .

One clue to the existence of spiritual imperatives is that they have been imbued by mankind with a life of their own and a collective form. In platonic terms they are "givens, existing independently of human affairs."[2] In this way spiritual imper-

atives become something that all people have in common, acting as a binding force. "Liberty"—an imperative of spirit to be
harmonious within the self and to express itself in the everyday
world—becomes, extended beyond the individual, *the* spirit of
liberty. Translated into a social concept, it becomes a gener-
alized principle, like "human rights." Our Constitution is a
manifesto embodying this principle, and is the most "spiritual"
of such documents.

"Love," the most powerful spiritual imperative of all, becomes, as Shakespeare wrote, the "Spirit of love."

For Plato, a spirit of justice exists whether or not people are
cognizant of it or apply it in their daily lives. Plato's "forms" are
similar to spiritual imperatives. When they are achieved, they
enhance mankind. They serve as an ideal for the individual and
the collective.

But imperatives are often difficult to attain because the majority of mankind is primarily halfminded. Take "justice," for
example. The spiritual imperative of "justice," both for the self
and collectively expressed as "justice for all," is theoretically
woven into a collective American spirit. The framers of the
Constitution recognized the importance of this spiritual imperative a long time ago. But the principle has not yet been fully
achieved. Why? Simply because not enough Americans are
wholeminded enough to recognize, accept, and behave according to it. What they do is remain in the first order and re-create,
with their own children, a culture that perpetuates an unjust
ethic. Justice for all will not be achieved until enough people
have become spirited enough to shape society according to spiritual imperatives. If this doesn't happen and the halfminds dominate, the concept of "justice for all" could be repressed,
especially when it interferes with the interests of halfminded
people who usually control governments. An example of that
having already happened is the status of human rights in the
Soviet Union and the fate of those unfortunate dissidents who
proclaimed the spiritual imperatives of justice and liberty and
now inhabit the gulags in Siberia.

In every society there reside people who alone and collectively speak out and do battle for the cause of spiritual imperatives. What enables them to do so? Knowing what is "right"—being aware of the spiritual imperative—is one thing. Doing something about it is another and requires considerable spiritual force and courage.

Great men and women can do what they do because they are gifted with an inordinate amount of spirit and a strong will. Furthermore, because they are aware, on one level or another, that there is "something more" to human existence than everyday life, they do not fear the first-order world.

Spiritual imperatives appear as major dramatic themes in the mythology and literature of all cultures as the triumph of good over evil, strivings for freedom from bondage, the search for love, and other goals.

When Ralph Waldo Emerson wrote, "Heroism feels and never reasons and is always right,"[3] he was alluding to a spiritual imperative that motivates heroic acts. Writing about the Eroica symphony in his book *Beethoven: His Spiritual Development*, Sullivan stated: "[It] is not because the symphony is 'about' Napoleon or Abercrombie, but because Heroism, as a state of being, was realized by Beethoven . . . It is his conception of the heroic that matters to us, and which is a clue to the greatness of the soul which is expressing itself."[4]

SPIRITUAL IMPERATIVES

Below are some of the spiritual imperatives that I have identified in people I have known, studied, or worked with therapeutically. Each imperative has many corollaries. There are surely many more. Search them out within yourself.

- The need for giving and receiving love and intimacy. Spiritual joining, communion with the spirit in others. Within this communion, there is fairness, justice, compassion, charity, refraining from inflicting pain.

- Harmony. Within the self (between spirit and mind-body) and between the self and the world.
- Communion with creation, whether it is called God, cosmos, Brahmin, nature, or by some other name.
- Communion with beauty—artistic expression in some form.
- Continuity in the material world, rootedness in the past and future, expressed as an imperative for belonging, for procreation, for friends and family, for "immortality," to be remembered.
- Freedom to express spiritual imperatives within the self and surroundings, whether it be family, community, society, or the cosmos. Liberty, social conscience.
- The imperative to know—learning.
- The will to exist in the world and to celebrate life.

These imperatives may be closely intertwined. Love, for example, is all-pervasive. The imperatives of procreation, continuity, love and intimacy, as well as communion with creation can find simultaneous issue at any age within the context of a satisfying and meaningful family relationship.

Specific imperatives dominate at certain ages. Babies are pure love and continuity. At old age the self would ideally have fulfilled all of these imperatives.

THE NATURE OF SPIRITUAL IMPERATIVES

The fruit of the spirit is love, joy, peace, . . .

—*Galatians* 5:22–23

Of the most pervasive spiritual imperative, love, Carl Jung wrote: "Love needs the spirit and the spirit love, for their fulfillment."[5]

Spiritual imperatives transcend cultures. Love is love no matter where a person lives. Babies are loved in the same way whether they are in California, New York, Siberia, or Bali. But, on the other hand, cultures can affect the priority, quantity, and quality of satisfaction of an imperative. For example, although babies are universally loved, the degree to which this love is celebrated and expressed depends on where the baby lives. The more "agrarian" and "primitive" the culture, the longer children stay close to their mothers (because people are close to one another physically and emotionally. Home, school, and work are in the same place). In so-called advanced, time-pressured, people-separating cultures like our own, where home, school, and work are in different places, most babies who are enrolled in caretaking institutions are there because their mothers are (out of need or desire) unavailable. Thus the spiritual imperative of connectedness and love is frustrated in both mother and child.

SPIRITUAL IMPERATIVES
WITHIN THE SELF

The satisfaction or frustration of a spiritual imperative creates powerful feelings within the total self. When an imperative is fulfilled, the wholemind easily recognizes feelings of joy, even of ecstasy. This can happen with "organic" experiences: the birth of a child, a walk in the woods, loving, visiting the land of one's ancestors, an outstanding achievement, fulfillment of a dream. Like any appetite or need, once satisfied, the exigency of the imperative disappears, at least for a while.

When spiritual imperatives are unrecognized by the half-mind, or when their expression into the world is blocked by the realities and situations of everyday life, or both, the self suffers. But unlike other sources of frustration, the self may or may not be fully conscious of what is taking place. Often the discomfort is wrongfully ascribed to other sources: illness, dissatisfaction with family or friends, jobs, and so on. But the real cause can be traced to a frustrated spiritual imperative. Such people often benefit greatly from a form of psychotherapy that can make them aware of the existence, and the importance, of spiritual imperatives and how they affect the person's life. I have seen this happen. What is known as "insight"—an important realization accompanied by a strong emotion—often occurs when a spiritual imperative makes itself known to the conscious mind. A very sensitive man I know who described himself as a "paper pusher" suffered repeated bouts of depression triggered by stress related to his work. "It hit me one day at work," he said. "I had a feeling with great clarity. I realized that since I love to learn and to teach, what the hell was I doing in a job that I hate? I couldn't study and learn there. I couldn't give of myself to any-one there—we were all competing for promotion. I decided then and there to quit my job, go back to school, and get cer-tified as a teacher. Sure, it'll take courage, but you only live once." This man did carry out his plan to become a teacher and, to my knowledge, hasn't been depressed since.

When a spiritual imperative stirs within, the self feels it very strongly. When the person is not able to identify what's going on, the mind-body experiences anxiety. But when an in-dividual does recognize the origins of these feelings, it can lead to positive action. Sometimes the feelings are so strong that they induce people to sacrifice their lives in order to correct per-ceived spiritual wrongs. One person who was ready to do so was Patrick Henry. I would guess that this famous American patriot had valid complaints about the world in which he lived. Under the British regime, he was materially deprived and politically and militarily oppressed. His spiritual imperatives for freedom and justice were thwarted.

What could he do about his sorry state of affairs? Two. options were open to him. The first was to ignore the situation and go about his business. The second was to take action. As history shows, he chose the latter option, fully prepared to suffer physically and intellectually the consequences of his strong desire to express his spiritual imperative for liberty. He wrote this about his decision: "It is natural for a man to indulge in the illusions of hope . . . Are we disposed to be the number of those who, having eyes, see not, and having ears hear not, the things which so nearly concern their temporal salvation? For my part, whatever anguish of spirit it may cost, I am willing to know the whole truth; to know the worst and provide for it."[6]

The nature of the feelings that arise from spiritual imperatives are distinct from the first-order emotions, which arise from the halfmind-body's reactions to the consciously identified stresses of everyday life—what physiologists call the "fight-or-flight syndrome." When something is wrong in everyday life, the reasons involved, at least most of the time, are evident to the self. For example, in Patrick Henry's case, he was (halfmindedly) aware that his everyday life was being compromised by unfair taxes and political and military oppression. But his passionate need to correct these conditions went beyond a narcissistic, self-serving solution, which would have been to remove the oppressors, and substitute himself in their place. This would simply have improved his own condition. Instead he acted wholemindedly, on the basis of at least two spiritual imperatives: liberty and harmony (within his self and between his self and society). His purpose was not only to relieve personal stress but to remove the oppressive system that afflicted his country, and in its place substitute a new politic based on liberty for all people and harmony between people and politic.

This illustrates a most important characteristic of spiritual imperatives. They are universally good when applied. The work of people like Gandi, Mother Teresa, Albert Schweitzer, and the like are examples of spirit in action.

What drives a person to risk life and limb in order to implement a spiritual imperative? What motivated Patrick Henry to do what he did? Where did he obtain the necessary strength of purpose to risk all in order to confront the reigning powers of the day?

These questions can be answered in one simple sentence. Patrick Henry was a spiritual genius (if someone can be an intellectual genius, or a musical genius, why can't someone be a spiritual genius?). He was spirited, aware and intelligent, and he acted according to his spiritual imperatives.

The political situation of the day distressed every part of his self: mind-body and spirit. His halfmind was uncomfortable in everyday life. His spirit desired liberty. To alter this condition, it was necessary to change the oppressive system that was causing this distress. Since his halfmind was no more than a computer (and computers never lay down their lives for a cause), he had to reach beyond his halfmind and call upon his spirit for wisdom and courage.

Thus it was not his halfmind but his spirit that proclaimed "Give me liberty or give me death."

He could do what he did because he was rooted in another, spiritual, dimension of life. He based his life on spiritual priorities—the first order was not enough for him. His courage was easy to come by. This is in contrast to those halfminded people who are rooted in the everyday world and have no courage. Why? Because they place a priority of self-interest upon their existence and find their world impossible to relinquish. For them, the everyday world is all there is.

Thus no risks; nothing ventured, nothing gained.

As in the case of Patrick Henry, making a conscious, informed decision to die for a noble cause (such as laying down one's life for a child, or a principle, or for one's comrades) is a decision, I believe, that originates from spirit.

What I am describing is not to be confused with suicidal behaviors, which have a different genesis. What may often appear to be an expression of a spiritual imperative may be bogus. Like other qualities of the spirit, this ability can be mimicked and perverted by those people like Kamikaze pilots, the "Red Hordes," or Iranian suicide squads, who have been conditioned to destructive belief systems that make their actions appear to be spiritually generated. This bogus spirituality does not originate in the dimension of the second order. It occurs as a result of mental conditioning from the everyday world. *These acts differ from an act originating in spirit in that they are not universally good.*

Let us return now to examine how the self can know when spirit is trying to make itself heard. When was the last time that you listened to spirit, followed your instincts, so to speak, and rebelled against a consensus of opinion from the "outside" world? How do you know what is right or wrong? How do you know when spirit is knocking at the door of your halfmind?

SIGNALS

Spirit, mind, and body send signals to one another.

Emotions are an experiential barometer that help the halfmind to assess the state of spirit—if it pays attention. Emotions that arise from the satisfaction or frustration of spiritual imperatives offer a clear personal signal, if one is attuned, to the state of the spirit's well-being and are a call to action to correct problems.

Pleasurable emotions, generated by spirit, are beyond halfminded explanation. Humor, for example—belly-laugh humor, not the kind that is sexual, aggressive, or clever and intellectualized—is spirit-linked. Spirit-generated feelings are often described by people as loving, warm, content, happy, or sentimental. Smiles illuminate spirit. No behavioral or psychological explanation suffices to explain the complex emotions and behaviors that are engendered in humans by a simple smile. These emotions are different from those that arise in the halfmind (although they can exist simultaneously). Feelings within the halfmind arise as a response to an external event of no enduring consequence. These are feelings related to gratification from first-order conditioning: winning a tennis match, an increase in material wealth, attaining status, and so on. People who "have everything" but still don't feel good usually have confined themselves to the superficial realm of the halfmind and the everyday world have along their way lost the ability to plumb the deep reservoir of feelings that comes from spirit.

When a spiritual imperative is fulfilled, the mind perceives its fulfillment with satisfaction. A ninety-two-year-old farmer whose final illness I attended when I was practicing family medicine told me on the day before he died that he was "ready to go." He was, in his words, complete, full, happy and fulfilled in life. "Whatever I did, I hope was right," he whispered to me. "I did what I had to do. I followed my heart, which was a better judge than my head. My spirit is at peace." At that time I really was unaware of what he meant when he said, "My spirit is at peace." Now I know that he summed up his happy life in those five words.

Despair is a negative emotion that has its origin in spirit. It signals the presence of an aching mind searching for integration with spirit. I don't mean to say that the halfmind doesn't suffer, too, but it is a superficial pain that results from minor everyday-life disappointments, such as being angry about being late for a train, and so on—the "normal" miseries of life, which sometimes can coexist with spiritual joy. Childbirth is an example of physical pain and spiritual joy taking place at the same time.

Spiritual pain is deeper, infinitely more painful. It spreads to all aspects of the self, affecting thoughts and impairing the functions of the body, often leading to clinical depression. Untreated, spiritually related pain, experienced by mind and body, can become so great that the self may consider putting itself out of its misery—an aching mind has limits to what it can bear.

SPIRITUAL IMPERATIVES AND THE BODY

At times feelings generated beyond the halfmind are accompanied by physical phenomena that feel good or bad, and which cannot be totally explained in neurophysiological terms—physiology, like any science, can explain the "how," but not the "why."

A grandmother told me, "I love my granddaughter so much I get goose pimples when I look at her. I am crazy about her. I just want to eat her up." A high school girl told me that she loved her boyfriend so much "it makes me vomit when I think of him." Sometimes a person feels something but can't explain it. A teenage girl asked me to explain why she got "red and embarrassed" around a young and attractive teacher who was acting seductively toward her. At that time she was unaware that she felt the same way about him. An especially sensitive lady told me: "I can tell about people without knowing them. I am sensitive. I just look inward to see how I feel around them— what kind of vibes they are sending. If I feel good, then I like them. If not, then I avoid them. I'll tell you, some people really give off bad vibes and I stay far away."

Sexual lovemaking, as distinguished from "screwing" or performance sex originating in the halfmind, when carried out in a tender, loving, and intimate way, can generate a tidal wave of profound and ecstatic emotion that carries the body in its wake. Grief, especially after the loss of a "kindred spirit," can incapacitate the body.

SPIRITUAL
IMPERATIVES AND
EMOTIONS

It's important to note that spiritual imperatives generate a diversity of emotions within the self. Love, as the primary spiritual imperative, can create a broad spectrum of feelings that range from the exquisite tenderness expressed by lovers to the kind of voracity expressed by the grandmother who wanted to "eat" her grandchild. Sentimentality is a tender and wistful emotion with its origins in spirit, and is especially evident in a fulfilled grandparent-grandchild relationship. Even Jean-Paul Sartre, not the greatest sentimentalist, warmly recalled in *the word*, that he "could drive my grandmother into raptures of joy just by being hungry." "Nostalgia" is another spirit-linked emotion—a memory tinged with feeling—a bittersweet longing of the spirit, traveling through time to relive pleasure it once experienced.

When a spiritual imperative is thwarted, the mind expresses its displeasure with emotional words like "longing," "emptiness within," or "incompleteness."

These emotions are rarely perceived in a pure and simple way, because first-order emotions, resulting from our interactions with the everyday world, constantly mingle with emotions generated by spirit. This is confusing to the halfmind.

The imperative of "belonging" is an example of how confusing this can be. The imperative of "belonging" may be fulfilled as an attachment to a corner candy store for a city person, a house for a suburbanite, the land itself—the "earth mother"—for a nomadic native American, or a hole in the ground for an Eskimo. "Belonging" is closely linked to other imperatives, such as continuity and rootedness in nature.

Satisfying the imperative for "belonging" can generate complex and often contradictory feelings within the self because spiritual imperatives are often opposed by social imperatives that have been programmed into and stored in the halfmind. Fred, a young man whose family lives in Ohio, got an offer for the "perfect" job in Hawaii. Accepting the job meant that he would have to leave his family and relinquish the security and good times he shared with them. Fred both liked and loved his family. But to refuse the job meant to narrow his vistas by staying at home and to act contrary to a current social imperative proclaiming, for his generation, upward mobility and independence at all costs. This was a difficult, emotionally anguishing decision for Fred, who was torn between spiritual intimacy and belonging on the one hand and social independence and mobility on the other.

"My friends will think that I'm crazy if I don't go to Hawaii," he moaned. "And if I stay home I'll never see the big world out there." Finally Fred decided to take the job, visit home as often as he could while he was away, and eventually return home.

Social imperatives are not the only forces that conflict with spiritual imperatives; there are natural, psychobiological developmental forces that do the same. This is especially common in adolescents. When this conflict inevitably occurs, it creates a great deal of emotional turmoil, not only within the youngster but between the adolescent and his or her family. The conflict between "belonging" (viewed by the youngster as a regressive developmental force encouraging dependency on parents) and "liberty" (in terms of personal independence and autonomy) as it concerns "leaving home" is an especially difficult developmental issue for the adolescent. At the same time an unsettled youth wants to attain "independence" from parents and to put an end to living a life subject to adult authority, but to leave home and parents shakes the foundation of the adolescent's need for "belonging," "love," and "intimacy," as well as his or her basic, first-order needs for food, shelter, and clothing.

The degree of anguish engendered within a given youngster at this point in life depends on many factors, among them the resources of intelligence, talent, and other strengths within the self, the type of family, the character of the society, and so on.

Youngsters who admire their parents and negotiate their career goals with the intention to live near the family would be less torn between their spiritual and social imperatives than a youngster who has lost respect for his parents and can't wait to leave them. For the former, who remain near the family, imperatives of love, intimacy, continuity, and belonging are fulfilled in one neat package. Since nothing is free, there may be an intellectual price to pay because the youngster (if it matters) could be narrowing his or her exposure to a broader world. "Liberty" might be somewhat stifled, but that's not inevitably true.

In the latter case, although the young person may gain intellectually—life experience will be expanded—this is only done by frustrating the imperatives of intimacy, continuity, and belonging, with the result that inescapable problems will be created within the self. These might be slightly assuaged by establishing a "secondary" family, as so many do in our "detached" and highly mobile society.

The latter situation is especially commonplace in contemporary America not only because great geographical distances separate family members but because the social imperative of attaining both emotional and financial independence is a national obsession. It is riveted into our culture, its mythology symbolized by the roving gunslinger of the old West. This social imperative is in direct opposition to the "belonging" imperative of the spirit. Thus a young adult in the United States often feels inferior or guilty for not going out in the world, and is reluctant to remain at home even if it's appropriate because he or she is not following the herd, who obey cultural dicta.

Not all people follow the herd. Ernest, a young man in Appalachia, told me, "Hell, sure, I left the farm and went to Los Angeles. I did like my friends did. Go West, young man. Stayed there for three years, in that craphole. Got it all out of my system. Sowed my oats. Now I am home to stay. This is where I want to raise my family. With my dad, mother, and Gramps next door. That's what it's all about. I am home where I belong.

As Ernest indicated, the self feels good in a good home. At home spirit has communion with the people and the place, and shares in the continuity of events, past, present, and future.

"In love of home the love of country has its rise," wrote Dickens.[7]

Is not home "where the heart is"? Most people report positive nostalgic, sentimental feelings when they talk about home. For children, no matter where or how they live, home is the center of the universe. This is evident in the unbridled enthusiasm of their responses when they are asked to describe their homes and families. "My home is the best place in the world and my parents are the greatest people," said Gretchen, seven years old. Evan, a forty-five-year-old baker, thinks the idea of "home" "is in the bones." The movement toward finding one's roots led many Americans to return to the places where their ancestors were born. Others sought their roots in cultural events. Evan was, in his words, "dragged by my mother" to a performance of Scottish Highland Pipers one Sunday afternoon. "I was born in this country and have never been to Scotland," he said in an interview. "But my grandmother told me a lot about the land and the people. Well, one day my mother took me to Madison Square Garden to hear the Pipers. I never would've believed it could happen, but I tell you I got shivers up and down my spine and I got teary. The music got to my bones. It was like I had heard it a thousand years ago. I never cared before, but all at once I knew I was Scottish. I know I belong in two places. I love it here, but a part of me is there, too."

•THE INEFFABLE LANGUAGE•

Spirit's communications to the halfmind are perceived as vague and ineffable. When spirit, via the seventh sense, tries to get through to the halfmind, it signals the mind in its ineffable language. The halfmind registers the emotion by *thinking* it. It attempts to attach the emotion to an event, thus converting the spirit's signal into a language it can understand. When it is unable to do so, it fumbles around with a jumbled and confused message while the body becomes more and more uncomfortable.

When this happens people often converse internally. When a person feels uncomfortable, something like the following internal dialogue may take place. "I can't put my finger on this but I feel . . ." or "I've got a nagging feeling" or "Something's not right, but I don't know what it is." In a pleasurable situation, the phrases might be "This is so beautiful that I can't express it" or "Don't say anything, because it will spoil the moment" or "I know that I'm right, no matter what anyone says or what the facts are."

This internal dialogue is an area that needs a great deal of investigation. There are those who claim that there are ways to gather information that is beyond the five senses.

Dr. Lawrence LeShan, who has extensively studied "sensitives" (people with clairvoyant ability), asked them, "How does the world look to you at the moment you are receiving this paranormally acquired information?" He found that when his subjects were communicating with their sources, they reported: "Individuality and uniqueness were secondary to oneness and relatedness, secondary and almost illusory. All things, events, entities, objects flowed into one another and couldn't be meaningfully separated from each other. Space connected objects rather than separated them. Time flowed as a seamless garment, and past, present and future were arbitrary illusions. From this view all actions and events were part of a harmony."[8]

The quest for access to this dimension of experience has throughout time been one of the main preoccupations, even obsessions of mystics and other students of the unknown. Many credible individuals believe that the mind can be taught, through spiritual practices and techniques like meditation, to be able to translate, perhaps just minimally, the language of spirit. Clairvoyants claim to have the ability to do so.

I do believe spirit can reveal itself to consciousness in the form of a brief and often intense emotion accompanied by a flash of a thought. This is the closest thing to a "voice of spirit" that I know. Unlike Socrates, I don't mean this is a literal voice, saying words. Others do, however.

During a television interview a young bassist was asked, "Why play the bass since it's bigger than you?" The child smiled. "A little voice told me to play it," he answered.[9] Thoughts issuing from the seventh sense are unique, extraordinary, and profound. Conceptually, they soar beyond first-order boundaries and course past things concerned with the everyday world into ideas, philosophy, principles, values, religion, and the cosmos. Some exceptional people are born with extraordinary access to the seventh sense—a form of spiritual genius. The noted clairvoyant Edgar Cayce has clearly demonstrated these unusual abilities.[10] One sensitive, claiming that everyone has the ability to tune into the seventh sense, said that "People who have a severe foreboding about an act before they do it are receiving information from a spiritual source . . . they should change their plans."

But for most the ineffable language is often hard to hear.

Simone, a twenty-seven-year-old mother, left her three-month-old baby with a nanny and returned to work as a high-salaried investment banker. "Things aren't right," she told me. "I am doing what my friends are doing, working and being a mother. I am tired. I feel out of sorts. I am questioning the meaning of life. All day long my baby's picture is in my mind. I see what she is doing. I don't have room for anything else in my head. Something is wrong. I can't express it."

Two months later I saw her again. "I figured things out," she said with a smile. "I don't want to leave my baby. I don't care what my friends are doing. I care about my baby more than my career. I know that's not a popular point of view today, but I don't want my baby raised by a stranger." She smiled. "This is not for everyone, but it's right for me. As soon as I decided to leave my job for as long as it takes, everything clicked into its right place. All my doubts lifted."

Explaining her situation in the light of spiritual imperatives, it could be postulated that Simone was unable to concentrate on her work because thoughts generated from her spirit were overwhelming her halfminded consciousness, which itself was filled with thoughts pertaining to her work. This conflict occurred as a result of a social bind: the fact that her society forces women to choose between work or their babies. In a more responsive society, one offering flexible options like part-time work, available husbands and grandparents, and excellent child care at the workplace, her conflict would be minimized.

Once Simone listened to her seventh sense, she chose her child. And once she prioritized her life, she felt happier. But she paid a price for her decision—because her company didn't allow part-time work and made no allowances for her to return in the future, she (unfairly) lost her job.

Usually a person pays a price for expressing spiritual imperatives and living a life that gives them primacy. This is because spiritual imperatives are often in opposition to social or biological imperatives. Every spiritual genius, throughout time, has known this to be true and suffered accordingly.

Simone acted according to her seventh sense. If not, she would have continued as only a part-time mother.

There are some other aspects of the ineffable language that, although clearly perceived by the halfmind, don't make sense to it.

Memories are part of the ineffable language because they transcend time and place and can be related to spiritual imperatives. Memories are, at the same time, both real and illusory and subject to expansion or romantic distortion. They are mental reflections that allow the mind to recall, make sense of, savor, and even edit previous experience. Memories, custommade to the specifications of the self, are pictured in the mind by thoughts, reexperienced by the senses, and colored by feelings. Like Evan, who often reminisces about the day he heard the bagpipes play, "Every time I think of that day I feel great. I hear the music in my head and feel it in my soul . . . and my body gets goose pimples."

Fantasy occurs on two levels. First-order fantasy is a process of wish fulfillment that serves as an emotional safety valve to relieve frustration of the halfmind. Fantasies originating in the first order are transitory, usually nonrecurrent in theme, simple in content, goal oriented, situationally focused. You succeed in burning off emotional energy by imagining you are telling off the boss, eating a good meal, having sex with a movie star.

Fantasy is the springboard of creativity. In an internalized ineffable language, fantasy, consciousness, and spirit merge into mental themes that are related to spiritual imperatives. This level of fantasizing is a conscious activity that uses spiritual "input" in the service of the self and deals with the kind of long-term, enduring, creative material that is the serious stuff of existence. It is akin to wonder, an emotion about which the halfmind knows nothing.

These higher fantasies are rich in content and color, full of wonder and creativity. Under adverse circumstances, they help keep the self in touch with spirit. This is what the ghetto child does when dreaming about a bright future one day. Recurrent fantasy serves the self by make-believe, satisfying a frustrated imperative and causing a pleasant emotion to take place in the body—fooling it, in a way.

Fantasy may also serve to keep an imperative in the forefront of the mind so it isn't forgotten. The ability to do this is cited as an important reason that some individuals were able to survive the horror of Hitler's concentration camps. Their will to live, their search for meaning in the experience, and their ability to fantasize, as Viktor Frankl so well described, kept them alive while others perished. Fantasy may also serve as mental rehearsal for when the time arrives to express an imperative in life. Fantasy is linked to the hope, as Pope wrote, that "springs eternal in the human breast."

What is the purpose of hope if not the expectation that, in the future, an opportunity will arrive to express a presently frustrated spiritual imperative? As Shakespeare so aptly put it, "The tender leaves of hopes, tomorrow's blossoms."

HOW THE MIND NEGOTIATES
SPIRITUAL IMPERATIVES

The halfmind responds when a spiritual imperative is frustrated and psychologically maneuvers to limit the extent of damage to the self. It does this via certain mental mechanisms so brilliantly described by child psychoanalyst Anna Freud.[11] The mind maneuvers by denying the importance of the need or by accepting the fact that the imperative will never be fulfilled.

For example, let's suppose a child called Liza yearns after her favorite dessert. (While this is far from a spiritual imperative, we can use it as a model.) She is not permitted to eat it before she finishes her dinner. What can she do?

She can wail for hours to protest her disappointment and frustration, but her parents won't give in and she still won't get her dessert.

She can invoke her halfmind to intervene and end her frustration. The mind has many ways to do this. It can rationalize the situation; she will say that she never wanted the dessert in the first place. Denial will have her saying that she doesn't like the dessert at all and wouldn't eat it if she was offered it anyway, so there!

If Liza can never hope to have her dessert because, for one reason or another, she never finishes her dinner, she remains frustrated. Then her mind has two alternatives: either accept the situation (which kids rarely do) or create a reaction formation. This is an oppositional attitude that will lead her to say that the dessert is awful, that she will never, ever eat it again, and, taking it one step further, that all people who like that dessert have something wrong with them.

When the halfmind becomes aware of a spiritual imperative, new attitudes and values are created that are subsequently acted out in behavior.

A POSITIVE RESOLUTION— ACCEPTANCE

When a spiritual imperative is satisfied, it recedes from the forefront of the self. The force behind it is spent, the self achieves inner harmony, and there is a release of tension. It is like a baby who is well nursed. The wholemind rests.

When a spiritual imperative is unsatisfied, however, turmoil is created. The self can deal with this turmoil in different ways.

After ten years of seeking medical help for infertility, Celia, a thirty-five-year-old librarian, finally accepted the fact that she was unable to become pregnant. Her husband, Gary, was sensitive and understanding about the problem. He assured her that, although he was disappointed because, he said, sharing the responsibility, "they couldn't become pregnant," he was happy with their relationship and loved her no less because of "their" problem. "It could've been me with the problem," he said to Celia, "and you wouldn't have dumped me."

But Celia, sadly grieving the loss of her dreams of motherhood and in spite of Gary's supportive attitude, was angry at herself, as if her spirit were railing. "My body has failed me. Why has God done this to me? What have I done to deserve this? All my friends have kids. Gary wants one. I feel I am a failure. I have a hole in my heart for a child and nothing to fill it." Her anger, turned against herself, turned into depression. She became angry at Gary, as if she wanted to drive him away. "He should marry someone who could have a baby with him," she cried. "I am no good."

Usually gregarious, she became reclusive. "I don't want to see my friends with their babies. I hate them because they have children."

It took several months of therapy, together with Gary, before Celia came to terms with the reality of being childless. Her mind worked to soothe the wounds of her spirit by repressing her need to become a mother and searched for other ways to "mother" that were available and appropriate for her. This is a mental mechanism called "sublimation." "There are other things in life," she said. "I can be a wonderful aunt to my nieces and nephews. I can help the kids who come to the library. If that doesn't fill the gap, then I could adopt, but I am not ready for that yet."

In order to enable Celia to function in the world, and to relieve her from the pain and disappointment arising from her body's inability to fulfill a most powerful spiritual imperative, her mind redirected the imperative toward being fulfilled by being a "wonderful aunt" to her lucky nieces and nephews.

"I know I am getting better," she told me. "I am no longer upset when I see someone with a new baby. I have a lot to be thankful for. I have a lot to do." Reflecting for a moment, she continued, "I don't know if I could ever manage if I did have a baby." (This was a rationalization.) "Maybe it's better that I don't." (A reaction formation.) "It would take so much time from Gary and me. If this is meant to be, I won't question the will of God." (Finally, Celia reaches acceptance.) "I am at peace with this issue now."

This mental process works well as far as an *internalized* frustration, the frustration of the imperative for procreation by a physical deficiency, is concerned. It doesn't work as smoothly when interpersonal conflicts, like a marriage without love, or social conflicts occur. Often compromises aren't possible.

A NEGATIVE RESOLUTION— SELLING OUT

There are those individuals whose minds cannot negotiate a positive deal between an unreceptive reality and their spiritual imperatives. Unlike Patrick Henry, they relinquish their imperatives and sell out. When people do this, they join the ranks of the miserable. Martin, a twenty-one-year-old carpenter, is one of these people. He compromised his values in order to keep his job.

At one time Martin, who lives in Georgia, enjoyed his work very much and especially enjoyed the contacts with his customers, many of whom he had known since childhood. This all changed when Pete Wilson, an aggressive and arrogant man "from the north," bought the construction firm for which Martin worked. After two months of building houses for his boisterous boss, Martin noticed that Mr. Wilson was dishonest. He overbilled his customers, ignored the building codes, and skimped on the quality of construction materials.

This bothered Martin. When he hesitatingly confronted Wilson with these complaints, he was bombarded by the man's rationalizations. Martin recalled being told that this was normal procedure, "everyone did it," and that the customers didn't care about it—they could afford it. Wilson's attitude was "what the customers didn't know wouldn't hurt them," and that if Martin "didn't like it, he wasn't cut out for the business and he could leave."

Martin slept on Wilson's words for a night and made a decision to stay at the job. Work was hard to come by. His mind began to work to quiet the outrage in his spirit. Martin had to repress his need for joy, honesty, fairness, justice, and intimacy with the people whose homes he was building. To do this his mind had to diminish them.

The fun went out of his work and he began to avoid talking to customers. They were no longer just "people" to him, they had become "them." Soon he even began to dislike "them" and started criticizing and derogating "them" in conversations with fellow workers and Wilson. He stopped going to church. As time passed he became Wilson's favorite employee and was promoted to foreman.

The changes in Martin's attitudes and values made life difficult at home. His wife claimed that Martin had changed for the worse since he had been working for Wilson. "He used to be so kind and considerate, now he's macho and has such a negative attitude. We have no church life anymore. He is not the same person . . . and if I try to tell him something, to reach him somehow, he yells at me. Martin is not Martin anymore. He has lost his niceness."

Martin made a trade-off—financial security and occupational success for relinquishing his spiritual imperatives. In the process he had become de-spirited.

HELGA'S DILEMMA

Spirit drives the mind-body complex into action to fulfill spiritual imperatives. Patrick Henry, for example, after identifying the oppression he experienced, communicated the situation to others, formulated a plan for change, and did something about the state of affairs under which he lived. If action is not taken when an imperative is frustrated the self suffers. Martin's inaction, for example, led to his eventual de-spiritment.

Helga, thirty years old, had not taken any action about her dilemma when I spoke with her. Her problem started when she succeeded in having a child after trying for seven years. After her child was born she hesitantly told me that she had "secret misgivings," ambivalent feelings, about being a mother. "Well, first the thought of not being able to have a baby panicked me. Now that I have a child the mature woman in me is happy to be a mother. I love my child dearly. But there is another part of me, a part that I am ashamed of, that resents the dependency of Bucky [her child] and the fact that I no longer have a life of my own. I think that when I was out in the world I was a person— now all I do is take care of someone else. But when I look at Bucky I feel happy and 'right.' There is a deep part of me that is content to be a mother. There is another part that resents the inconvenience. It's a battle. If I can stay in touch with my love for Bucky it's okay. But it's not okay all of the time."

Helga's mind and spirit battled within her. Her spirit wanted to stay with her child and be happy. Her socially conditioned halfmind wanted the stimulation of going out in the world. Why?

Helga lives far from any of her relatives, in a small northeastern town. Her husband, Klaus, works as an auto mechanic. They have no family in close proximity. So she received no "applause" for bringing Bucky to the family and little personal "fame" or sense of accomplishment from her environment for being a mother. No one was there to celebrate the child's birth. Helga was, however, locally well known as a businesswoman before her baby came. She owned and worked in her own cleaning and pressing business in a local shopping center. She knew everyone there.

Helga's roots were in a "traditional" immigrant family where, in her words, "women worked very hard at home, not in the outside world, and children were important. They raised their children by themselves or with the help of their family. Housekeeping was important." Helga was trained to raise her child at home—her family (although far away) disapproved of putting her son in a day-care center. Helga's spirit wants to be with Bucky and so does the part of her mind that was conditioned by her family. Being a mother makes that part of her feel good. But there is another part of her that resents being a housewife and living a life that she feels derives from her husband. Some of this arises from her spirit, her need for liberty, the right to a nonderivative life. This is a battle that contemporary women are currently waging, and something that Helga will have to work out with her "male chauvinist" husband.

There is also "anti-mother" social pressure on Helga. Her culture tells her that she should be in the workplace and that motherhood is an inferior way to spend her time. Some baby "experts" even tell her that Bucky will be a more "independent" child if she puts him in a day-care center, as if that can be considered an advantage.

It is evident that these complex forces torment her half-mind as well as her spirit, eroding her mental and physical health. Helga's dilemma is an example of the conflicts that we all face, every day. And what is perhaps the predominant spirituo-biopsychosocial ailment of our time.

COLLECTIVE SPIRITUAL IMPERATIVES

Spiritual imperatives are the threads that form the fabric of cultures. Every culture contains similar imperatives but expresses them in its own unique way. This diversity is reflected in the writer Houston Smith's humorous comment: "Although He is unity, God finds, it seems, His recreation in diversity."[12]

In response to an imperative like "belonging," people, acting in concert, put their territorial imprimatur on the place where they were born. They act to name the site as "my property" or "my home." They then lay claim to land collectively by creating national boundaries, and designate customs, culture, architecture, food, clothing as "theirs." They place a mantle of sentimentality and symbolic meaning on "their" places ("Fatherland," "Mother Russia," and so on). This love is expressed spiritually in art, literature, poetry, music, and symbols that extol the object of their "belonging."

Unfortunately, the imperative of "belonging" can be distorted by a disturbed halfmind. When George Hegel, the philosopher, wrote: "The German spirit is the spirit of the new world. Its aim is the realization of absolute truth as the unlimited self-determination of freedom—that freedom which has its own absolute self as its purport,"[13] he had no idea what Adolf Hitler would do with these words.

When people decide to institutionalize their common spiritual imperatives by creating a structured bureaucratic system with authority to confirm, control, and channel them, it can make for serious problems. Institutions have the propensity to run amok and no longer serve the individual. Indeed, the individual often ends up serving the institution.

Institutions that reflect spiritual imperatives may be tangible or intangible entities. Educational institutions, for example, are tangible entities designed to enhance the individual's imperative to know and to learn. But some educational institutions have taken on an elitist, self-serving life of their own, barring entry to the "outsiders" they are supposed to serve. They create rules and regulations for learning—rules that cater to the society's needs rather than the individual's. They are staffed by teachers who have a vested interest in perpetuating their own positions.

An intangible institution like marriage comes into being in response to imperatives like love, procreation, intimacy, happiness, continuity, and harmony. Civil and religious authority have carved out a terrain for overseeing marriage, making rules for the making and breaking of marriages: filing fees, blood tests, divorce courts. These institutions in turn affect social attitudes— unmarried people, for example, are viewed with different eyes than married ones, whether favorably or unfavorably, depending on what's "à la mode."

Institutions can be dangerous. They too easily evolve into fixed entities with lives of their own, thus creating a purpose for existence that is often far removed from their original reason for being. They continue to assure their own perpetuity even after they have outlived their usefulness. Institutions can become despirited, too.

In sum, spiritual imperatives, when identified and acted upon offer the self a meaningful agenda for living. But another thing is necessary to live the fullest life possible. One needs kindred spirits.

· 5 ·

KINDRED SPIRITS

. . . it is a fire that kindling to its
first embers in the narrow nook of a
private bosom, caught from a
wandering spark out of another
private heart, glows and enlarges
until it warms and beams upon
multitudes of men and women, upon
the universal heart of all, and so
lights up the whole world and all
nature with its generous flames.

—R. W. Emerson, *"Essay on Love"*

Have you ever met someone and not only just "liked" that person immediately but felt an overwhelming attraction that impelled you to want to know them better? Have you ever wondered why you reacted like this? And about what part of your self was reacting? Do you think that what you felt was emotional, sexual, empathetic, intellectual, physical, spiritual, or . . . ?

And what did you do as a result of this attraction?

Did you pursue the relationship, build on the initial reaction, and end up with a lifelong friend?

Or did you pursue the relationship only to be disappointed and left with the thought that you shouldn't trust your own feelings?

Have you ever been exploited by an individual who first kindled this kind of reaction in you?

If we have even a modicum of agreement on the possibility that spirit exists and that the way we deal with spiritual imperatives has an important influence on our lives, it should then follow that spirits can take to one another. They can sometimes skirt around the halfmind and touch one another directly. When they do, something extraordinary happens, something similar to the encounter between Annie and Mrs. Boyce. An emotional switch is thrown. A person may be deeply touched, inspired forever by even a brief contact with another's spirit. A politician I know told me he spent ten minutes with Franklin Delano Roosevelt when he was a youngster and his life was changed forever.

A significant contact with another's spirit can lead to different outcomes: While it could lead to an important kindred relationship, the initial spark could, on the other hand, simply fizzle out. The emotional switch can only turn the relationship on. Reality determines its outcome.

A kindred phenomenon may be experienced not only between two people but among members of a group. Will Olsen, fifty-one years old, mentioned the words "kindred spirits" when he told me about his high school reunion: "There they were, my old friends, all worlds apart in experience, in social status, education, the things of this world. But when we got together, none of that mattered. Everything was so easy among us all. It was like we were kindred spirits. It was a beautiful moment, when everyone there knew what had happened, knew that it was a magic time, knew that time and space didn't matter, that 'who' and 'what' we were didn't matter—that there was a palpable something else between us that seemed always had been and always would be, even if never we saw one another again."

The idea that spirits take to one another and become deeply attached in an evolving relationship sheds new light on the interpersonal process that heretofore has been limited to terms like "ego psychology," "field theory," and so on. The concept of kindred spirits explains what keeps people together. In addition, it points the way to a therapy for wounded relationships.

· KINDRED SPIRITS ·

I define "kindred spirits" here as people with a very unique and close relationship that endures over time. Spirit takes precedence over the halfmind in an intellectual relationship and over the body in a physical one. It is the mortar that bonds the relationship. Thus kindred people are connected by more than their common interests, needs, or physical attraction. It is something in their spirits that binds them.

Kindred spirits share a basic unity with one another that transcends the boundaries of time and substance. It is more than a simple sum of the physical, emotional, and intellectual components of a relationship. It is the "oneness" of the two people within the relationship. *I can state with certainty that the amount of spirit vested within a given relationship between two or more people determines the quality, importance, and the meaning of that relationship.* This applies to all types of human connections.

Kindred relationships are not to be mistaken for half-minded, pseudokindred ones that are intellectual, physical, or social in nature. People are easily attracted to another's mind, sexually seduced by physical beauty, or grouped together for mutual interest. But these are instrumental commonalities in which people expect one another to share ideas or "fulfill each other's needs"—to perform in one way or another. They even may exploit, or "use," one another for selfish purposes. These people are not, as happens in kindred relationships, strongly drawn to one another simply because they exist.

• HOW RELATIONSHIPS UNFOLD •

Earlier in my life I became quite interested in the way people made friendships and how these relationships evolved. One of the things that I found especially fascinating was the way that old friends, after being separated for years, could so easily pick up where they had left off after only a few minutes of being together. I was also curious about why some relationships went through a period of being so very intense for a while and then fizzled out. To satisfy my curiosity, I started a modest research project on "friendship." After interviewing fifty people, I began to detect a pattern of how friendships evolved but, more important, I became aware of the major role that spirit plays in long, enduring relationships.

That was when it dawned on me that spirit is the cement that binds enduring, loving, and committed relationships.

What I learned from this research on friendship was:

* Relationships seemed to unfold, dynamically, passing through several phases.
* The intensity of feelings involved in the entire process was often affected by the biological nature of the relationship— whether it was parent-child, friends, lovers, aunts, uncles, and so on. Although a genetic linkage doesn't automatically ensure a kindred bond, people who are related to one another get a head start on closeness because of their shared time and experience.

Relationships seem to evolve through different stages. In the following description, I use "lovers" to refer in a larger sense to any two people in a kindred relationship.

ATTRACTION

Attraction is the first stage. Two people feel an attraction to one another happening all at once or coming about more slowly. In romantic relationships people have been known to "fall in love at first sight." Some family members have a similar reaction to a new baby. Friends "take to each other" or "hit it off immediately."

"Attraction" is experienced emotionally and physically and is accompanied cognitively by happy thoughts. It is essentially a total body feeling. People spend a lot of time savoring a new love. Even the thoughts feel good. This process is different from halfminded "thinking about" someone, which is an intellectual process unaccompanied by any significant emotions. Being in love illuminates the lover. Reflect on your own experience or ask any mooning teenager with a "crush" to describe what he or she is experiencing.

INFATUATION

Attraction can, with varying tempo, easily heat up into infatuation that floods over the halfmind. It is an obsessive preoccupation with the beloved, usually accompanied intellectually by an exaltation of the positive aspects of the beloved and obliviousness to the negative.

"Love is blind" aptly describes this state of affairs. Love also truly enhances the beloved, bringing the best qualities to the surface for all the world to see. To be able to say "I am loved" makes a person feel good. Being loved makes a person feel a lot better about him- or herself. Love is good for people.

This stage is abundantly spiritual—unbridled joy in the company of the beloved; unconditional love and acceptance of the beloved's shortcomings; delight in the beloved's mind, emotions, body, and spirit.

Romantically put, lovers glow in the light of their kindred spirits. Their S-Connection opens fully within their selves. Love pours in. Lovers hunger for each other's presence. Nothing material, like money or status, matters. All that matters to them is that they touch the spiritual essence of one another. Together they stroll in a spiritual garden (as I write this I am struck how closely this romantic description resembles the state of Adam and Eve in the Garden of Eden—before the "first-order" fruit was eaten). Their spirits merge—become joined—they attain a "kindred" state, just as can happen, in varying intensities, between anyone, from a grandparent and a grandchild, to new next-door neighbors.

In lovers there is an urge to union. "I am aware," a young man told me, "that a part of me that I can call spirit wants to merge with another spirit, a woman's. Mine is not complete alone. Maybe it's complete in itself, but it's unfulfilled. It has to be so I can grow—be better. I can't explain this any better but I am very conscious of it."

DISCOVERY

Although love may well be blind, the mind isn't. This leads to a third stage, discovery, which operates intellectually. At first lovers enjoy one another's spirits, and the fact that they exist. But as they begin to discover one another, they inexorably start *thinking*. With thinking comes critical assessment. They begin to measure and judge one another. As they accumulate knowledge of one another, a door to the first order opens. The honeymoon is over.

So begins a process of "making sense" of the relationship— fitting one another into their own socially programmed mental cubbyholes of race, religion, education, physical appearance, status, profession, manners, dress, peer attitudes, personality . . . *ad infinitum*.

"Does the person measure up?" asks the halfmind.

Their personal differences in style, character, values, interests, and so on lead to confrontation. The fight between their halfminds begins.

They try to change what they perceive as one another's faults. Sometimes, when lovers agree about the fault and work on it, things get better. Sue, a sensitive young woman, helped her husband change or, in his words, kick my drug habit by tuning in to his spirit.

"I know my spirit has feelings," she said. "It learns, it grows by learning and listening about Hal . . . and I feel *his* spirit. My spirit helped his."

"Spirits meet each other," Hal added. "To help each other. My spirit was torn down. I met your spirit," he said to Sue, "for a reason. Your stronger spirit helped my weaker one. Your positiveness helped me to overcome the negative in me. It lifted my spirit up. I changed."

Sue smiled. "Yours did the same for me," she told him. "It was like our spirits met and then we got to know each other afterward."

Love is constantly subjected to pressures of the first order. Lovers must, after all, adjust to one another's ways, parents must socialize their children. During this discovery phase, personality quirks inexorably surface.

From this point on, the well-being of the relationship depends on how the self balances itself on the tightrope between romance and reality. If spirit predominates over the halfminded intellect and its instrumental philosophy, the relationship becomes permanently "kindred." If not, the relationship dissolves.

RESOLUTION

•DISILLUSION AND ABANDONMENT•

The resolution of the relationship can be either disillusion and abandonment or, on the other hand, permanence.

When a relationship doesn't pass the varied instrumental halfmind tests of the first order, disillusion occurs. The minds of the lovers do not "take one another in," even though initially their spirits touched. Conflict ensues. The light of spirit becomes dimmed, then extinguished, and the first order predominates. Competitive power struggles for the upper hand in the relationship take place, romance gives way to instrumentality. Unfortunately, some people don't know when this is happening and for one reason or another stay together in a disillusioned state for reasons of money or from habit. Sometimes relationships dissolve because one party is psychologically unable to tolerate long-term relationships, or too much "judging" occurs and the loved person fails to measure up to one standard or another. Social forces may exert negative pressures on relationships—the extreme example is that of Romeo and Juliet. These can strain the bonds of love until they break . . . and love lost becomes a part of life lost.

But most often relationships crumble when the parties involved relinquish the spiritual nature and priority of their attachment and thus surrender the stuff of romance: joy, spontaneity, passion, wonder, imagination, or love itself.

This is what often happens when marriages fall apart.

When the halfmind and its instrumental philosophy runs the show, a de-spiriting ethic results that insidiously erodes a relationship. This can happen between friends, marriage partners, parents and children, family members, at home, at work . . . anywhere to anyone.

When disillusion reaches a critical point, disengagement occurs. The relationship loses its vital substance. The light goes out. Eventually the relationship is abandoned.

• PERMANENCE •

When lovers pass the first-order "test" of "acceptability," the relationship proceeds from spirit, past the mind, and arrives at a loving, nonjudgmental station. Friends and lovers open up their minds to one another and "take one another in" (the psychological term is "incorporation"). As spirit and mind join together, their selves achieve a commonality of philosophy, purpose, and trust that transcends all diversity. The relationship achieves a sense of "oneness" and permanence. It becomes a "given"—stable, durable, and capable of absorbing many of the miseries of everyday life. William Merry, seventy-two years old and married for forty-five years, said that when he married, "My spirit had to learn to work with another spirit. You don't plan for one person anymore. It's two. If you ask me, spirits have a need to share things. You know. They need a soulmate. If you marry a good person, you get happy. Living and planning your life with another person—together—influences my spirit in a good way. A problem that would make a person depressed if he was alone doesn't have the same effect if he is with another—two spirits are better than one, I guess. But it's gotta be the right fit to bring out the best on one another. Like a lock and a key."

It is important for parents to achieve a state of spiritual permanence in order to raise secure children. When people reach this state and have problems, they are able to deal with them and maintain the relationship. With permanence, spirit becomes forever imbedded within the relationship, and the half-mind becomes immune to negative first-order input. Children thrive in this kind of emotional and spiritual soil. It makes them feel safe.

Kindred spirits are secure. There is no price that would lead them to betray one another. Only the halfmind has a price.

This is why Will Olsen's friends felt the way that they did at their high school reunion. Their timeless relationship, tinged with nostalgia and romance, was untainted by the first order just because they lived in different everyday worlds. There was no power, no competition, no authority, and no "conditionality" to their attachment. Although they might have had little to "say" to one another because their lives were so different, they were communicating on a much more profound nonverbal level.

Spirits communicate without words. Have you not noticed how a beautiful experience can leave you speechless?

A great many enduring bonds are formed early in life, perhaps because they are established before the halfmind takes over. Lifelong idealized and adoring relationships between peers or youngsters and their elders remain long after the elder dies. Lois, twenty-two years old, talked about Mrs. Walker, her neighbor and "old friend who saved me when I was fighting with my parents.

"When I was a teenager, my mind was not programmed to love, but my spirit was loving. My mind was screwed up with drugs and boy problems. My parents had their own problems, and too many kids, to pay attention to me. Mamie Walker saved me with her kindness and understanding. She died last year but her spirit lives in me, because she taught me so much. If I close my eyes, I can see her. I talk to her at night and I can feel that she is there in the room with me. When she died I know that part of her spirit went into me. I learned grit from her. Her goodness can never die. It's all around me, like radio waves— we don't see them but they are there. To me her soul or spirit is permanent."

The idea of permanence also may explain why old friends

are so comfortable with one another, why they feel so good together although they may have grown very different from or have not seen one another for a long time. What is it they see in each other's eyes and in their smiles?

AS SPIRIT GOES, SO GOES
THE RELATIONSHIP

Spirit is love. When spirit is present, relationships endure. When spirit leaves, the relationship perishes. To be happily married, it is critically important that the partners be acutely aware of the spiritual state of the relationship. This is not an easy task.

Phyllis and Ted met in college and married after graduation. Phyllis worked while Ted attended medical school. They were happy; Ted enjoyed his studies, Phyllis enjoyed her job, while eagerly looking forward to the day when Ted would replace her as breadwinner so they could have a baby. They shared a "spirited" relationship; they were loving toward one another, had the same dreams, and anticipated the future with eagerness. Power and authority in their family was distributed equally between them. Phyllis never abused the financial power she had because she was the one in the family earning their living. Ted did feel "a bit threatened" by being supported by his wife, but he joked about it. They were true partners, united in mind and purpose. Their spirits were kindred and shared a oneness. Their lives were fashioned of a common substance.

Before I go any further I would like to explain a bit more thoroughly what I mean by "oneness." As I use the term, both parties to oneness share a mutual "ego" (in addition to their own) that is a joined part of their selves. It is something like a "team spirit." The whole is greater than the sum of its parts. This is in no way a symbiotic, malignant mutual dependency that is pathological and leeches psychic energy from each of the participants. No, this state of oneness is synergistic, enhancing both parties. Oneness takes account of all the quirks and differences of each person and accepts it. A couple that has achieved such unison will find that energy resonates back and forth between them. Thus, both are enhanced. A man who married a woman thirty years his junior said that his wife "made him young" and that he was "bootlegging her energy." A seventy-year-old woman I know, energetic, involved, and married for forty years, said of her husband, "Sixty-eight years old and he is still an enthusiastic, crazy kid. God knows he's kept me going. His energy gives me life. He's got enough for two people."

A symbiotic system tends to homogenize differences and blend two separate personalities into one disturbed and tortured ego. In such a state, like the siblings in the classic tale of the Corsican brothers, people merge to a point where they lose their individuality and no longer know where one begins and the other ends. In oneness the two people remain independent entities, although they do adjust and accommodate to one another. Although partners in oneness can't feel one another's feelings firsthand, they can empathize with them. Most of all, they do not want to hurt one another. There is little meanness in kindred relationships. Oneness is a responsive system. If I were to continue this line of reasoning, it would return, full circle, to the ERP effect (see page 52) and to the idea of elemental oneness of the universe, what the poet Charles Williams so aptly described as "separation without separateness, reality without rift."[1]

But to return to Ted and Phyllis: As time passed, they slowly began to lose that state of oneness.

Ted graduated from medical school and started a practice. He unabashedly relished the mantle of authority that his newly won medical degree conferred upon him, especially when his proud parents began to act deferentially toward him. To put it bluntly, he got a swelled head. He began to spend longer and longer hours at work because he liked the way people treated him there. At home he became more judgmental and critical— "bossy," Phyllis described it. Her little quirks, which he had found "cute" in the past, now irritated him. He began to measure and judge her. "He comments on everything I do," Phyllis lamented. She became increasingly unhappy and started to withdraw from the relationship. This infuriated Ted, especially because Phyllis was uninterested in making love. "I don't like the way you are acting," she told him, "and I don't feel romantic."

As Ted became more authoritative, controlling, and despotic, Phyllis withdrew all the more. She began to take what was for her an inordinate interest in "things" like clothes and decorating their home. The more money Ted made, the more she spent. They no longer talked about their dreams and hopes. Ted was evasive when she brought up the subject of children. When they did speak, their conversation was superficial, about daily events and finances. Their spirits, once kindred, were drifting apart. Where once was substance was fast becoming an empty shell of a relationship.

Ted's unhappiness began to show outside of his home. He began to speak of his patients disparagingly. He was losing interest in his practice. He became obsessed instead with the stock market, often buying and selling stocks between patients' appointments. Usually a rigidly honest person, he sought out an accountant who was known for walking the fine line between cheating and being straight to do his income tax. He worked long hours, leaving little time for Phyllis.

Finally, because Phyllis threatened to leave him unless they sought help, Ted agreed to go to a marriage counselor with her. Once in therapy, Ted learned that something he hadn't previously recognized had been eating at him: He was unhappy and disappointed with the reality of practicing clinical medicine. He was, in effect, in love with the image of medicine, but the reality of it was unpalatable to him. "People get in the way of the beauty of medicine," he said. They don't pay their bills and there is so much paperwork. Bills, paperwork, malpractice insurance, difficult patients, they're all a pain in the ass. It's not the way I imagined it would be. It's not satisfying."

Once aware of the problem, but not wanting to quit his profession, Ted found a way to have an interesting and rewarding life as a physician. He entered the field of medical research and was much happier for it. In fact, he has since made several major contributions in the field of biotechnology. As soon as he made the decision to change medical specialties, he felt better and was more relaxed at home. He spent more time with Phyllis and they started enjoying one another again. A vacation helped. Phyllis relaxed. Their sex life improved. Spirit returned to the relationship. They became partners once more.

"We have less money, but who cares? Just the fact that he is happy with what he is doing and we spend time together seemed to make most of our problems disappear," said Phyllis. Which brings up a very important point.

For kindred spirits to stay that way they must spend a considerable amount of time with one another. Furthermore, whether it is at home, work, or play, this time must have a spiritual quality.

This is a most important admonition. In my clinical experience, one of the most common reasons for divorce is that married people don't spend *enough* relaxed, pleasurable time with one another. Because they are in a rut, they usually are oblivious to the fact that they need time together in the first place. On the contrary, when married people are angry with one another, they avoid one another. The last thing they want is to spend time or go off on vacation with the person they are mad at.

What they do is complain incessantly and harp at one another about false issues: their sex life, interpersonal issues like control or domination, money, or some other substitute for the real problem. The truth is that when people first get married, these things don't matter. What happens to married people who have fallen out of love is that, over the years, they have allowed spirit to bleed out of their relationship. And the most common reason for this is that the former lovers have gotten too involved in a halfminded existence. This is the bottom line.

Kindred relationships, especially in marriage, must be constantly nurtured. When they are not, the halfmind takes over and trouble is guaranteed. Then people withdraw, or even go looking for spiritual contact (romance, attraction, infatuation) elsewhere. The sad thing is that most of the time it's to be found at home. Frequently both partners feel exactly the same way but have lost the ability to communicate with one another.

KINDRED SPIRITS WITHIN THE FAMILY

Although family members, for the most part, all share a kindred feeling, they sometimes pick favorites. This isn't simply due to one person identifying with another, because these preferences cross gender boundaries. One grandmother told me that she couldn't help that her granddaughter Celia made her "crazy with joy," and much as she loved her other grandchildren, it was not true of them. Of course, she didn't want the others to know it. "It's not their fault," she told me. "It's something between Celia and me."

Family members share a commonality of spirit that binds them (for better or worse) and helps them overlook expected differences in personality or values because they share something more profound, something beyond their common genetic origins. That something is derived from spiritual imperatives like "love," "belonging," "continuity" . . .

This is why family and family gatherings have a meaning for people that transcends the nature of the personalities involved. A twenty-one-year-old student told me that she "swells with happiness when I am with my family—because—" She paused for a moment and then smiled. "They are like me."

Someone asked me how my belief that family members were "kindred" in one way or another affected adopted children. Do adopted children fit into the family "spirit pool"? And does this really matter?

It surely does. An understanding of this matter may help in limiting some of the confusion and turmoil that both adopted children and their loving and devoted parents often experience. I have worked closely with a considerable number of adoptive families and have come to enjoy, respect, and admire them. Most adoptive families are alert to the normal problems that arise concerning their children but rarely think about conflicts related to spirit. I never did, either, until I talked with a Caucasian grandmother-to-be who was having a great deal of trouble accepting the idea that her daughter was going to adopt a one-year-old Vietnamese child. She was concerned that she wouldn't "take to" the child. Since she was a compassionate, liberal, church-going social activist, her negative feelings about grandparenting were repugnant to her and she felt guilty about them. I assured her that her feelings were not "weird" and certainly understandable but that she should wait and see if they might not disappear when she became acquainted with the child. Fortunately, this was exactly what happened.

Once she saw the child, she quickly became a devoted grandmother "but," as she said two years later, "although I love Kim very much, and she loves me, she doesn't know the difference, I do . . . She's not my flesh and blood. There is something missing." Three years later her feelings changed even more for the better. "Kim is still not *of* me, but I am totally in love with her. We are of like minds and spirits and every day I get joy from her."

Their spirits were becoming kindred. Kim, of course, didn't know how her grandmother used to feel, which is so much the better, and was a happy, healthy youngster. It is true that adopted children don't have the built-in "kindred" head start that blood kin do. I must emphasize that this certainly does not have to interfere with their sense of closeness or their happiness. Being adopted understandably affects their sense of completeness—an additional issue to be handled by the adopted child, along with those of identity confusion, questions about ethnicity, curiosity about the biological parents and other relatives.

How much does this spirit-removed-one-step-from-their-family affect parents and youngsters, especially as the latter reach adolescence? Does this partially explain the children's hunger to know their spiritual and biological parents (which I believe is spirit-centered) no matter how much they love or are "kindred" with their adopted ones?

Myra, a twenty-eight-year-old woman, was adopted when she was one month old. She told me, "My spirit was different from those of my adoptive parents. They are dear people and I love them, but they are not like me. When I was young I hid my real self, because they didn't like it. There was no one in the family who was like me except for my wild Uncle Joe, who is my 'soulmate.' My parents gave me everything I wanted, but I don't feel complete with them. I would never tell them how I feel because it would break their hearts, but there's a little place within me that is empty. It's not in my mind, either. I know it will be filled when I have a child because then I will be complete. It's like I can fill the hole with something that came before or will come after but I can't do it in this world right now. It's something that is not of this world."

The spiritual head start that nature accords blood relatives must be nurtured in real life. With time and undivided attention to one another, family members can form a spiritual connection.

AVERSIVE SPIRITS?

If the idea of kindred spirits is acceptable, is it possible that the opposite can be true? That spirits can have *aversive* reactions to one another? Certainly the halfmind does; all forms of prejudice are lodged there. Can an individual's spirit feel out its counterpart in another person, and then choose to ignore it, to become infatuated, or to repel it?

Lily, thirty-two years old, who claims to have "psychic" powers, told me that she can "sense" people's auras, the energy fields that allegedly surround them. "Some have beautiful golden auras—they are good. Others are bad, black surrounds them, and these people frighten me."

When a person says that someone is a "bad influence" or when people claim that someone affects them "the wrong way," is an "aversive" phenomenon taking place? What is someone responding to by saying "There is something about that person that I don't like. Don't ask me why . . ."

Of course these reactions may all be explained away by psychology, but not entirely satisfactorily so. There is mythological and cultural support for the possibility that aversiveness exists, embodied in such concepts as good and evil, devils and angels, good or bad spirits. Mystics who believe in reincarnation agree with the idea that spirits may repel one another. "Of course," one explained, "people have that reaction all the time. That's because they met the person in another life and the person was bad to them."

When you dislike someone, is it your spirit or halfmind that is reacting?

FOOL'S GOLD—CHARM, SEDUCTIVENESS, AND THE PSEUDO-KINDRED RELATIONSHIP

On a lighter note, I would like to comment about "charm," or personal magnetism, which can be abused as a pseudospiritual imitation of genuine charisma. Let's call this seductiveness. Seductiveness can fool people into thinking that a relationship is more than it is. Most people that I interviewed had encountered seductive individuals in their lives. They were people like the man one woman met at a party: "He was terrific the first time I met him. Full of the old charm. I couldn't help but like him, everyone did. I was crazy about him at first but he turned out to be a shallow, self-centered louse."

True charm is the stuff that superb salespeople are made of. The infectious enthusiasm of charm, both personal and verbal, is a potent one-two that would assure any salesman great success. Like charming people, seductive ones are able to form instantaneous connections with other people that appear to be kindred in nature, but in reality they offer only a pseudokindred relationship—emotional fool's gold. There is no substance behind it. They have the ability to flip a bogus switch on and off at will. Charming people possess an unbridled ability to be entertaining and to infectiously make others feel good. Charmers make for great entertainers. When people meet such a person they are charmed. When they take their leave they are eager to see the person again. But with seductive people, they are inevitably disappointed because the seducers' talents are meteoric, short-lived, and do not endure past several brief encounters. Unlike true charm, seduction has little staying power.

Charm is like "charisma" in the sense that one has it or not. Like any talent, it can be used for good or bad purposes. If it is present in a spirited person and used nobly—to earn a decent living in show business, as a part of a physician's bedside manner to cheer the sick, as a teacher, to raise funds for a worthy cause, or to inspire for worthwhile purposes—that's fine. In its purest form charm is an outward expression of spirit.

The ability to charm, in a de-spirited person, becomes seduction. It is worst of all, for without the constraints of the second order a disturbed, halfminded person may use this trait to exploit others for malignant purposes: to form cults, sell trash, "con" people, lie, cheat, and destroy.

Look around to see what I mean. There are a great many people like this who have the public eye and ear. They are among the ranks of de-spirited people that abound in our society.

·6·

THE DE-SPIRITED SELF

A wounded spirit, who can bear?

—Proverbs 18:14

How much are you in touch with your own spirit? Are you balanced, whole? Or are you isolated from the spiritual aspects of your self?

If you feel that you have lost at least some of your spirit or that you have to fight furiously to maintain contact with it, you are not alone. Most of the people I interviewed felt like this.

As sad as it is to say, spirit is, in one way or another, always in danger of becoming a casualty of human existence. People fight the world every day in order to remain wholeminded. This is tiring. Few among us are able to keep our halfmind in its place and function with a wholemind. Few among us are lucky enough to choose the way we spend our days, and can sidestep the everyday world.

For the fortunate few, the rewards are great. Indeed, when the halfmind and body and spirit are merged, the self feels happy and whole. The self is at ease both with spirit and the world outside. Such a person can be said to be spirited.

But unfortunately, most of us are not this lucky. We are either ignorant of things beyond the halfmind or too trapped in the first order of things to pay attention to spirit in the first place.

When we ignore spirit, we pay a price. For without spirit, the halfmind dominates the self and the self becomes de-spirited. The condition of de-spiritedness is a major cause of misery in our culture. It is a pervasive and, until now, unrecognized malaise that few escape.

DE-SPIRITING THE SELF

The seventh sense is a dissident—an oracle that must be silenced for the first-order halfmind to dominate and eventually de-spirit the self. This conflict is ongoing, from cradle to grave.

Hans Christian Andersen's story, "The Emperor's New Clothes," humorously illustrates this conflict. If you remember the story, the emperor's unscrupulous tailor runs out of new ideas for the royal clothes. When the emperor arrives at the shop for his annual fitting, the tailor places him naked in front of a mirror and enthusiastically goes through the actions of draping him in what he says are magic garments that can be seen only by those who are pure in heart. In reality, he has clothed the emperor in nothing at all. The puzzled monarch can't see any clothes on his body, but, not wanting to admit that he is something less than pure in heart, agrees that, indeed, his nonexistent clothes are beautiful and rare.

His entourage, also afraid to admit to bad characters, enthusiastically congratulate the tailor, agreeing that these are indeed fine garments, worthy of their emperor. As the emperor, "wearing his new clothes," parades naked through his kingdom, the people, with the same disinclination to confess their "black-heartedness," applaud the beauty of the emperor's garment. Only when a small boy pipes up and cries, "But, Mama! The emperor has no clothes on!" do the people realize that this child, who is certainly pure in heart, cannot see the clothes, either, and this means that there are no clothes there.

Like the small boy in the story, spirit can't be fooled. And since all of us are born with spirit, it is necessary, for the self to be de-spirited, that the process begin at birth. And that's what often happens.

THE DE-SPIRITED CHILD

Children easily become de-spirited. How much and for how long this happens depends on several factors: the child's age, the degree of spiritual giftedness of the child, the circumstances causing de-spiritment, and others.

De-spiritedness is communicable, too. Circumstances that de-spirit a child's caretaker affects the child, as well.

De-spiritedness may last a lifetime. Robert Johnson, an intelligent, successful businessman, remembers that he "jailed his spirit" as a result of his family falling upon "hard times."

"I was a happy kid but at five my life changed. We fell upon hard times. My mother had to go to work and Dad wasn't making it. We had to move into a relative's house. I was unhappy. I got headaches. No longer was I happy, carefree, spontaneous. When my parents got depressed I lost my audience. But I adapted, at what cost I do not know. I subdued my feelings. I came away from the experience with an ability to encapsulate what was tender, open, and gentle in my spirit . . . at will. I walled off my spirit but there was a door that I could open or close. I had found a place to hide my spirit. Then when I started to work I locked it away for keeps. Sometimes I would take it out on a Sunday afternoon and I would say 'Hello, here we are in this absurdity we call life.' My spirit has been in this jail most of my life. In my work, competitive and hard, I felt as if I was in a war and my spirit had no place in that until I'd won my battles. In business I did what was expedient. I view my employees as chessmen. I do not get involved with them emotionally although I am not unfair at all . . . at work people are business."

Did Mr. Johnson lose anything by "jailing" his spirit? "I used to write poetry before I was six and I never did that again. I locked myself away from people. I was—I am safe. I made myself insensitive. I feel no fear or emotional pain even though it's happening. I've cut myself off. I have trouble being loving with women. My wife tells me that I am inexpressive, unromantic, too dutiful. My kids . . . tell me that I am a cold fish. I have a hard time reaching my spirit now. Maybe it's in jail for life."

Loss of a beloved person (especially a kindred spirit) is spiritually painful and can be quite de-spiriting for children. Ellie Lloyd, an emergency room physician, who recalls being "blithe, funny, and whimsical as a child," fled into the first-order world as a result of losing her beloved father, her "soulmate." "Before my father died, people smiled at me all of the time because I was so cute. I used to make people happy and I knew it. They called me 'love child.' Then my father died. He was my soulmate.

"My mother remarried when I was seven. I missed my dad, part of me had died with him. All his love had suddenly disappeared. I hated the man my mom married—he was so mean to me. He wanted my mother all to himself. She withdrew from me, too. She was in the middle, between me and my stepfather. I began to lose her love, too. I wasn't happy any more, I had lost some happy ingredient to my life.

"I was smarter than my stepfather, and he couldn't stand that, so he criticized me and told me I was too big for my britches. In school I was the smartest in the class; I used to stay after school every day, for as long as I could, so I wouldn't have to go home. Naturally, I excelled scholastically, although the other kids called me a 'nerd.' After a while I became immune to what anyone said about me. But I also lost warmth and fun in my life. I know I gave up my emotions and my spirit. I became grim. I became angry at men. I had walled off the fun part of me. "I was even scared of having children because I thought the love had been drained out of me. Now I am amazed to feel how much I love my new niece. Maybe I still can love.

"I must say that there is one advantage to having numbed out my spirit. As you know, a lot of my work in the emergency room deals with really bad accidents. But I have no trouble handling almost any kind of catastrophe. I never get upset or disgusted, even with badly wounded victims of an auto accident. I just switch to 'computer mode' and I function as a very effective doctor. If it was my spirit that saw the gore in some of those auto accidents, it would make me throw up."

Patrick Waddell, a fifty-four-year-old engineer, contracted a bad case of polio when he was four years old. He remembered how this crippling disease affected him: "[It] broke my spirit—sure. I remember being able to run around and play before I got sick. After that—well—as I got older, I closed off my mind. I never got picked in the games, and I love sports. I became iron-fisted—hard—angry. I got fed up being picked last in ballgames—you know, being used for third base and the like. I put away my spirit early because I hated my body. My spirit became like a turtle, peeking out when I was alone, or learning. I liked learning. My spirit learned the tools of public nonexistence. But when I did math it was happy. I have a private spirit, but as far as the world was concerned I kept my spirit in jail." He paused and smiled. "My spirit—the lifer."

In children it is pure, and uncomplicated. Spiritual imperatives within the child (and the resulting way that a child views itself and life in general, before the first order takes control) are continually being assaulted every moment of the child's life by de-spiriting factors. These factors impair the child's access to the abundant love that resides within his or her own spirit and the spirits of those who love him or her. Below are some factors that assault the spiritedness of children and may ultimately de-spirit them:

- Removal of love by a beloved person. This may happen unwillingly, by the death or illness of a parent, or be done willingly, by a parent who abandons the child. This absence of a beloved person happens with varying degrees of acuity and permanence, as in divorce or when both parents leave a young child every day to go to work.
- Cruelty to the child by a trusted authority figure in the family or at school.
- An environment during the growing years that diminishes the importance and special state of childhood and doesn't allow the child to feel worthwhile, and to make others happy just because it is alive.
- Lack of attention to the importance of a loving attachment.
- An instrumental relationship in which the child is constantly criticized, rated, and judged by its primary caretaker and given love and approval conditional upon performance rather than for existing. Thus the child perceives itself as a product rather than as a lovable human being.
- Frequent disappointments from an important, idealized person.
- Inadequacy of equipment of the mind or body—mental or physical disabilities—as a vehicle for spiritual expression and the possible social avoidance that such conditions engender in others.

In sum, what de-spirits children is the loss of contact with a beloved spirit or, on the other hand, exposure to a person who derides, diminishes, or assaults the child's own spirit.

The de-spiriting person may be a parent, caretaker, relative, teacher.

De-spiritedness is transmitted from generation to generation. Only an extraordinary gift of spirit will enable a child
whose caretaker is destructive to escape such a legacy. To be
wholeminded and happy, children need abundant love, nurturing and respectful relationships with important authority figures, and close contact and joyful interaction with other spirits
who love and treasure them.

It's that simple.

THE DE-SPIRITED SELF

As children grow, the influence of the first order on them
becomes more and more powerful. As the halfmind dominates,
spirit is pushed aside. If this continues, spirit becomes effectively separated from the mind-body and the self becomes unidimensional, cut off from spirit.

De-spiritedness has far-reaching effects: mental, physical,
and emotional. Usually the self is not consciously aware of its
de-spirited state, because it is left in a halfminded condition.
Therefore, it loses spiritual insight—the ability to examine itself
through an "outside" spiritual porthole. The self becomes like a
broken computer that has reached the limits of its program for
repairing itself and needs a human to do so. This is why mildly
de-spirited people seek help. Whether or not it is ever stated in
the therapy, their "cure" will depend on their becoming re-spir-
ited.

Seriously de-spirited people never seek help and usually deride those who do.

•TEMPORARY DE-SPIRITEDNESS•

A de-spirited self is like an eye trying to see itself. It can't
do it. As a result, it becomes more and more immersed in the
first order of things. Thus a person who, for one reason or an-

other, has their S-Connection shut down, may "go down the tubes" relatively fast. Sarah, a twenty-year-old college student who became temporarily de-spirited in her freshman year of college, told me, "In college there were so many confused and unconnected people in one place—it was so different from home. I felt like I was let out of a cage. I went crazy with no parental supervision—drinking, sex—there were no brakes. I got rid of my spirit. I was like a mindless body for a while. I was responding to the environment; the bars, the boys. I tried to go along, to please everyone—at least for a while. When I was alone I felt awful, so I would go back out again. But one day my spirit came through, like a dam bursting. It said, 'no more.' Then I straightened out."

De-spiritment can occur at any time in life. The well-known "midlife crisis" is certainly a reflection of a state of de-spiritment that may be temporary or permanent.

Peter, forty-three, a criminal lawyer, had (at my request) reluctantly consulted with me because I was treating one of his children who told me (remember the oracle?) that he was worried about his dad. His father revealed during our conversation that his boss was worried about him too and had recently told him to "get rid of his problems" or he would be fired. Peter was angry at his boss, his wife, and his children. He said that he wanted to be "free."

He told me angrily, "I have come to see you because I have to, otherwise my kid won't come to visit me. I don't want to talk to a psychiatrist." He talked about his job. "I hate what I am doing—defending the dregs, people who I know are guilty. Getting them off and then they are back on the street. At first I thought that I was doing good. Justice and all that. Now I am burned out."

"When did you start 'burning out'?" I asked. He sat up straight and a blank look came over his face, as if he had realized something. Tears came to his eyes. (I thought then that his tears signaled an important internal event—a "breakthrough" of sorts, but I was unable to pinpoint its meaning. Today I understand that his emotional reaction was a signal of the "breaking through" of his seventh sense into awareness.)

As tears welled up in his eyes, he started talking more seriously and appropriately about relevant issues. After the session he agreed, again reluctantly, to return "for the sake of my kid."

During our work together, I learned that Peter's life was in total chaos. He was an alcoholic, was involved in multiple affairs, and occasionally used cocaine. Separated from his wife, he rarely visited his five children, and was guiltridden about this. The spectrum of his life was limited to his job, the corner pub near work, and his escapades. He complained about his attitudes. "I am so negative, so grouchy, so cynical. I used to be outgoing and cheerful. I was a choir boy, and I kind of liked it. But now, life has lost its meaning. Every day is the same. I try to feel—with sex, drugs, booze—but it's all the same.

"Life is like a Mexican restaurant that I used to go to. The food looked great but everything tasted the same."

Peter's "midlife crisis" was a sign that he had become despirited. Several months after he had joined Alcoholics Anonymous, stopped his destructive behavior, and was trying to reassemble his life, he said, "I think that I got a swelled head and gave up the best part of me. I let myself get in a rut and stopped listening to the part of me that said 'watch out,' my conscience. I lost contact with my family and the loving part of me. There was a turning point. I lost my values and I didn't know it. As I said, I always was a family man but . . ." He stopped for a moment. "Maybe this started it. One time I went out of town for a week and I met this woman. I was so horny, but my conscience was saying 'no'—and then I did it. I started an affair. Hell, my friends did it, why couldn't I? It was after that that I started doing worse and worse things. I went over some kind of line. It didn't matter any more what I did, I had lost a certain state—of grace maybe—now the Catholic in me is coming out. It was like I went through a door but it was a door to a hell for me . . . It was then I pulled away from my wife and kids. I guess what I learned was that I was too guilty to continue my relationship with my wife and that I didn't want my kids to find out what a hypocritical father they had. How could I criticize them and guide them when I couldn't control myself? Especially since I was pretty bossy before that. I realized that I was a fraud. I got so bad I didn't know what I was doing any more. If my boss didn't tell me that I would be fired if I didn't get help, I would never have been able to pull myself out of it."

Summing up his experience, he told me with great emotion, "What I thought was wrong wasn't what was wrong at all. What I did to cope with what was wrong made it worse and made me lose the ability to correct my situation. It wasn't that I was bored or mad at my job or hated my family. It was that I had become too wrapped up in my job and work. I was a drone and lost my perspective as to what life, for me, is all about. I know what mentally unbalanced means now. That was me."

In cases of "temporary de-spiritedness," like Peter's, with a psychotherapy that responds to the spiritual aspects of the condition and can help to identify and cope with the de-spiriting agent successfully (whether it be an event, an attitude, or whatever), harmony can be reestablished and the self healed.

Temporary de-spiritedness can occur in wartime, as a side effect of combat. The military is aware of this. In fact, the training that new recruits receive includes more than the obvious intensive physical and intellectual conditioning designed to strengthen the soldier physically, teach the skills of war, and enable the recruit to bond with fellows. Something more takes place. The soldier's seventh sense is dulled so that he can commit acts in battle that would normally be intolerable to his spirit. When the war is over, it is expected that a soldier is able to repress his experience, shed what he has learned, reintegrate himself, and reestablish his spiritual integrity—often a tall order.

PERMANENT
DE-SPIRITEDNESS

I see this hath a little dash'd your spirits.

—*William Shakespeare*, Othello

Temporary de-spiritedness can become permanent. Some war veterans never snap back; those who find it necessary to cut themselves off from spirit in order to survive may lose contact with it forever. One veteran put it well: "I had to turn off my conscience or blow my own brains out."

Don, a Vietnam veteran, described what happened to a buddy who "lost his spirit."

"Jack was a nice clean-cut Baptist kid from Florida. He was very outgoing and funny at first. We saw a lot of action together. After three months in the bush, he was shooting at anything that moved. He used to weird-out and vomit after a firefight. He started drinking and using drugs. He stopped talking to people and became more into himself—a totally different person. One night he was especially upset after we raided a village. 'I lost my soul, I lost my soul,' he kept telling me. The next day we were caught crossing an open field and were taking mortar rounds. They were firing at us from the edge of the clearing. Jack was next to me in a ditch. He stared at me. 'Don, I am a dead man. I have no soul.' Then he jumped up and ran toward the enemy and was cut to pieces.

"I think that Jack really died when he told me he had lost his soul. Then his mind went. He was walking around like a zombie and there was no light in his eyes any more. I remember that blank stare. A lot of the guys looked like that before they bought it. It was like they gave up the ghost. Jack was like a machine."

What Don calls "giving up the ghost" and becoming a "machine" well describes what happens to people who sever the S-Connection. It is not surprising that sensitive people who suffer abrupt severance of spirit may lose their will to live. In a sensitive person spirit comprises a large part of the self. Those, like Jack, who placed a spiritual priority on life would rather not live than face a life without spirit, an existence without love. It is like the best part of them had already died while their mind-body lived on.

Broken spirits no longer savor life.

But total de-spiritment rarely happens. Most often it varies in quantity and quality. It can even be turned on and off. Some people who may act extraordinarily well under certain circumstances, with certain people, at certain times and places, can be tyrannical under other circumstances. One teenager I know said, "I can't stand my father at home but he's great at his office." The mind, to suit its needs, is capable of ignoring the seventh sense for a short time for a particular, and expedient, purpose. For example, bomber pilots understandably disconnect while they are at "work," dropping bombs. After a bombing run, it is perfectly possible that they reconnect—go to church, make love to their wives, play with their kids, and attend community functions. And some have done it all on the same day.

A person can become so spiritually exhausted that if nothing is done, he or she becomes de-spirited. This might explain the grouchy and disgruntled attitudes of some of those who work in the service, or helping professions like civil servants, hospital workers, and social workers. Although these people started out in altruistic professions, to *help* people, they end up being rude and uncooperative. Dealing with poverty, chronic illness, and crime often brings on "burn-out." The altruistic reservoir, rooted in the spirit of these people, ran dry. When their limited supply of compassion and altruism is "used up" by the overwhelming demands of the first-order world, they give out. In a sense, they are spiritually exhausted. Having no chance for respite because they must continue to earn a living, "burned-out" people disconnect from spirit. It's the only way they can go on. The ones who don't "burn-out" are undoubtedly gifted with an abundance of spirit.

ROBOTS: THE HALFMINDED
PERSONALITY
●————————————————————————————————●

When stress is chronic, spirit becomes increasingly disassociated from the mind-body until, in essence, it becomes *functionally disconnected and the self becomes de-spirited.*

Certain de-spirited people act like robots.

People like this can be dangerous, because in relinquishing spirit their remaining halfmind is easily exploited and programmed by others. Robotlike individuals can commit, or be easily coerced into committing, a broad range of horrible acts, from designing gas chambers, to polluting the environment, to beating up their grandmother to obtain money for a heroin fix.

Some people are born robots. Some criminals (even those with relatively high intelligence) who sadistically murder without compunction are like this. Obviously, not all robotic people are criminals. They may even function well in society, but they are devoid of "spiritual intelligence." They seem to be ignorant of the emotional and spiritual aspects of life. They may be classified as spiritual morons, just as a person with an intellectual deficit could be classified as an intellectual moron.

Polly, a thirty-five-year-old personal secretary to the president of a large corporation, is an example of a person who spent a good deal of her life robotically. She was a spiritually ignorant person. Polly was first deprecatingly described to me by fellow workers as a "robot." "She dresses in a sterile way and she has no body odor," said one of her colleagues. A male associate said that Polly had no sex.

When I first met Polly, her manner was terse. Her communications were brief and her conversation monotonous. She couldn't talk about ideas, but was concerned with day-to-day (first-order) things. She talked about her impending move to New York City. Her body was lean and stiff. Her lips were closed tight around her tiny mouth. Her thinking was unimaginative. Her grooming was impeccable.

Before her "nervous breakdown," she served her boss well. He called her an "automaton." In psychiatric terms Polly would be described as an obsessive compulsive personality with depressive tendencies. To her sister she was an "old maid" and "always a nonfeeling tight-ass." To her mother she was "born a Miss Priss." Before her depression occurred she told me that she was satisfied with herself, liked living alone, and didn't "need other people like others do. I like to go to work, come home and neaten up my house. I don't like messiness and too many men are messy. Sex is messy, so I'll be an old maid and like it."

At this point I wondered if her robotlike personality resulted from a damaged mind that allowed no issue for her spirit, or was it because of a congenital absence of any spiritual connection? Was she simply short-changed by nature? As hard as I tried, I was unable to find even a little trace of spiritedness: whimsy, warmth, joy, or any similar traits in her personality. In its place was responsibility, punctuality, repetitious behavior that appeared to be dutiful. The term "robot" well described this unfortunate, de-spirited woman at that time in her life.

The next time I heard about Polly, I learned she had suffered a "nervous breakdown" and had been hospitalized in New York City for the past three months. I went to visit her and found that she was a different person. Emotion poured out of her. She was animated and active. She didn't care about her appearance. She seemed more alive than ever before. She had lost her robotlike characteristics. Her spirit had emerged.

How did this happen? Simple. It was love.

Love had hauled out her spirit. After she went to work in

S P I R I T • **152**

New York City, she had, all of a sudden, fallen for a married
fellow worker. At first she couldn't identify the turmoil and the
longings within her. Instead she experienced restless nights, fatigue, and assorted physical ailments. The quality of her work
deteriorated. She became pensive. When she was near the object of her repressed affections, she became uncomfortable and
agitated because of the new confusing sensations she experienced. Finally she experienced panic attacks and phobias,
stopped going to work, and became more and more withdrawn,
until she was hospitalized.

With hospital treatment she gradually loosened up and lost
some of her robotlike qualities. It was not a complete transformation, of course, but her spirit had been liberated. Today she
no longer acts like a robot. Her "nervous breakdown" was, for
her, a blessing in disguise. What really broke down was her
limited halfmind. When that happened, spirit flooded in. For
her to relinquish a robotic state and be able to love, it was necessary that she disassemble her previous narrow, limited, and
rickety personality structure to rebuild a self better suited for a
happy life. One that had plenty of room for spirit. She eventually met and fell in love with another man and today is happily
married with two children. "That crack-up was the best thing
that ever happened to her," her sister told me.

Halfminded, robotic people are not always born that way—
they can be created. Robotic parents, through fear and intim-
idation, can create robotic clones who emulate their elders' behavior. Fortunately the average child doesn't capitulate easily. If
the child is emotionally or spiritually intelligent, he or she will
usually put up one hell of a fight, and the fur will fly. Especially in the teenage years.

Cultures roboticize people. I will deal with this more extensively in the next chapter. For now it is important to understand that factors like the climate in which people work (and
this includes any endeavor that is creative and artistic, like art,
religion, or medicine)—the social attitudes toward work, i.e.

work as a basis of self-esteem, how much time one spends at it, what kind is available—directly affects the "roboticization" of people. In some societies people work to live. In others, like contemporary America, people more and more are living to work.

How does this affect spirit?

Badly. This is because the modern work ethic emphasizes a first-order ethos whose philosophic cornerstones are the pursuit of material products, technological progress, and economic growth. For its people, it proclaims an ethos of power and control, competition, a "pecking order" for authority, and "personal productivity."

This system is de-spiriting to people because it is the product of a halfmind-driven, materially acquisitive culture and its competitive ethic is anti-emotion and anti-spirit. In its purest form the code of this culture states:

Feelings are to be hidden.

Emotional expression is weakness.

There is no room for humanity. The job is more important than the person.

Those who adhere to these rules are rewarded. Maureen, a thirty-six-year-old office manager, follows them faithfully. "Of course I have to act like Adolf Hitler. I mean hard, with no feelings. In my office it is the work that counts, not the person. I can always find another person. At first I had a hard time acting like a rat and it took me a long time to get like this, but this is the attitude that helps me get ahead." She reflected for a moment. "And people who think this way get promoted."

"What do your employees think about you?" I asked.

"They probably hate my guts. I've gotta keep them in line." She laughed. "As long as they do the work, we get along."

THE DE-SPIRITING PERSON

Do certain people make you feel bad? Do they give you a nagging oppressive feeling when you are with them and yet you can't explain it, because things seem okay on the surface?

If you have had this feeling, you have been in the presence of a de-spiriting person.

Some people have the ability to illuminate others spiritually.

Others have the ability to extinguish spirit. I call people like this "de-spiriters," individuals who, knowingly (by abusive behavior) or unknowingly (by subtle manipulation) have an adverse effect on the spirits and spiritual well-being of others.

De-spiriters are to be found everywhere—at home and, especially, at work, where they may be imbued with realistic authority, playing the role of the boss, controlling the lives of the people who work for them.

De-spiriters assume authority within a relationship, choosing victims from inside a family, work or social constellation. In the community, de-spiriters may even appear to be altruistic. On the surface—they may be doctors, clergymen, teachers, others whose ostensible role is to serve. These are the worst kind and the most demoralizing, because they exploit in the name of humanity.

CONDITIONS OF DE-SPIRITMENT

Certain conditions are necessary for de-spiritment to take place:

- The de-spiriter must be in authority (realistically, as a boss or parent, or because the victim neurotically offers him- or herself to the power and control of the de-spiriter).

- There must be a competitive aspect to the relationship.
- The relationship must be lived in the first order of things—the everyday world is given primacy.
- The victim may be in any relation to the de-spiriter: a child, an employee, a student, or a spouse.
- The victim wants something from the de-spiriter and is willing to engage in the relationship for some presumed reward.

The de-spiriter calls the shots and sets halfminded rules for the relationship.

- "If you project spirit, I will not acknowledge it or receive it."
- "I will judge you because I know that you need me or want something from me." (Imagine if someone's mother said this.)
- "You will put your self-esteem in my hands and allow what I say and do about you to be an important element of how you feel about yourself—and I will make you feel bad, inferior, and doubtful of your own perceptions."
- "I will not show any emotion toward you, nor will I love you or allow you to make me illuminate your spirit. In fact, we will function only in a first-order universe limited to well-defined areas in which I dominate. If you know more about something than I do I will not discuss it with you."
- "Therefore, no spiritual stuff. No hopes or eagerness. No dreams or sharing expectations. No fun or joy. You will have no part of my spirit—only part of my mind."
- "We will not venture into any territory beyond the half-mind."
- "You play the game the way that I want to, or I will not play."

The victim must relinquish his or her seventh sense in order to accede to these rules, for spirit would not tolerate such an arrangement. De-spiriters know that adult victims aren't always guiltless or helpless. That, in a way, they collude with their "enemy." They willingly submit to the de-spiriter's authority for their own motives, conscious or unconscious.

And the de-spiriter uses this conferred power to advantage. This concept of "de-spiriter and victim" explains why some people stay locked into destructive sadomasochistic relationships.

A young mother of three tolerated daily insults and weekly beatings by an alcoholic husband (who refused to seek help) for many years before she finally left him. Why did she stay? "Because," she told me, "a drunk for a husband is better than no husband at all." She was a frightened, insecure woman, afraid to meet the world alone, so she settled for an unhappy life.

A housekeeper I know told me that she served her mistress for thirty years and hated every minute of it. Her mistress's insults and her disagreeable personality were "unbearable." She said, "I was patiently waiting for her to die so I could collect the money she left me in her will."

A college student said, "Sure, I hate my chemistry teacher's guts. He insults me and puts me down all the time. I won't tell him, but he is a pompous ass, but I am happy to kiss it so I can get a good grade and go to medical school."

"I am waiting for my father to die," a young lawyer told me, "so that I can spit on his grave and take over the business." Why did the young man work at his father's firm in the first place? "Because I probably couldn't make it anywhere else."

Children don't naturally collude with de-spiriters. That's why de-spiriters don't like kids. If the children are unlucky enough to have a de-spiriting parent, they are helpless to do anything about it. As a youngster cried to me, "Why does my father have to drink and call me names and beat me? Why me? The other kids don't have fathers like that. I don't want the one God gave me."

TECHNIQUES OF
DE-SPIRITMENT

How do de-spiriters do what they do? In the hope of learning more about this, I asked people how they would "destroy" or "break" another's spirit if that's what they desired. Here's what they said:

"Don't respond to the other person's spirit," a young student said, grinning mischieviously. "When you feel a person getting personal, sense their spirit reaching out, snub them. Be businesslike. Above all, don't play."

"Simple," said a ten-year-old girl. "Don't love them."

"Judge them," said a law student.

"*Gaslight* 'em," said a psychology student. "Make them doubt themselves. When they say something, ask them if they are sure, or to prove it. Don't believe anything they say. Be serious all the time. Don't fool around. If it isn't bad, don't say it."

"It's easy to break a kid's spirit," a teacher said. "Just tell 'em something and don't do it. Disappointment really hurts kids. It blows their dreams. Then humiliate them in front of their friends."

"Very easy," a well-known attorney told me. "Don't be a spirit receiver. All of us start out in life being a spirit projector, like babies. We find out quickly that this is not acceptable behavior, because the receivers are being made to feel uncomfortable. So one is asked to turn it off. So, to kill someone's spirit, don't be a receiver. Be indifferent to that part of them. They'll dry up soon enough . . ."

THE SCROOGE SYNDROME

Why do de-spiriters do what they do?

Without a seventh sense, the infinite spiritual vistas of life are closed off from the self. The range of functioning becomes narrowed and finite. The self's views and attitudes become bound to the material everyday world.

Not only does disconnection from the spirit limit the quantitative scope of the self's life view, it affects it qualitatively, too. Divorced from spirit, the de-spirited self begins a campaign to diminish the importance of what it has lost by de-spiriting the environment.

The unidimensional self therefore is not only deprived of spirit, it becomes anti-spirit. It doesn't want to be reminded of what it has surrendered.

Therefore the de-spiriter undertakes an effort to remove traces of the spirit from the surrounding world and to minimize, even eradicate spiritual things. The more material power and authority a de-spiriter attains, the more potential he or she has to affect others adversely. The de-spiriter has a plethora of potential victims within the family and at the workplace. De-spiriters are especially at home in a work environment that has a competitive and adversarial ethic, congruent with their worst qualities. In fact, in some workplaces de-spiriting qualities may even be considered desirable.

In a compassionate and humanistic environment, a de-spiriter wouldn't last five minutes.

A classic example of a de-spiriting character is "Scrooge" in Dickens's classic story, A *Christmas Carol*. Remember how cruelly he treated Bob Cratchit? Scrooge showed no trace of empathy, compassion, or consideration for Cratchit's family or his financial problems. For Scrooge, Cratchit was an instrument— a chess piece in the game of work. What concerned him was how much work he could extract from the man, and at the least expense possible. Scrooge personified a unidimensional, despirited view of life.

The first half of A *Christmas Carol* is devoted to setting the scene for Scrooge's cruel, insensitive, greedy, and downright miserable behavior. He is a de-spiriter par excellence. Dickens portrayed Scrooge's characteristics well in the following passage. "A merry Christmas, Uncle. God save you," cried a cheerful voice. It was the voice of Scrooge's nephew, who came upon him so quickly that this was the first intimation of his approach. "Bah," said Scrooge. "Humbug."[1]

As the story proceeds, Scrooge is visited by "Spirits" ("ghosts") of Christmases past, present, and future who, by frightening the blazes out of him, allow him to relive the past, to preview the fate he is destined to encounter, and, in general, to show him the error of his ways. Scrooge heeds the message and reforms. His spiritual switch is thrown, and he accepts the spirit of Christmas. He comes to his seventh sense. Scrooge then becomes a happy, generous, and compassionate man, especially toward Bob Cratchit and Tiny Tim.

There are a lot of Scrooges around. Joe P. claimed that his boss was a lot like Scrooge. Joe, a successful investment banker, remembered having "paid his dues" when he worked for a tyrannical mentor at the beginning of his career. "I always sought out bright and more experienced people and tried to learn from them, and tried to have fun at the same time. But not with Mahoney.

"Before I went to work for him, my routine was to do all of my work in two hours and socialize the rest of the day. Not with Mahoney. He was all business. I couldn't sit down when he was around. He never smiled. When he was frustrated he screamed at everyone. He never looked anyone in the eye—he treated everyone like furniture. Never asked about their families. A real Scrooge. He told me he didn't want to be nice because he might have to fire people some day. If I went into his office with a smile he would never respond. He was all business. I tried every trick I knew to get personal, but it wouldn't work.

"He never paid me a compliment. He only told me what I did wrong. Every time I left his office I felt bad, as though I had caught his foul mood. I felt deflated, too, like he had diminished me. He was very powerful—charismatic. He could walk into a room where everyone was having a good time and in two seconds set a somber and serious tone. Men were afraid of him. Women thought he was a jerk. But they were afraid, too. He was a lonely guy.

"I left after a while because I knew that if I bought the way Mahoney was acting I would turn out to be just like him, and that's just not worth the price. In fact, I started to be that way, but my wife straightened me out. When I left Mahoney insulted me. He was angry because he knew that when I quit he lost his hold over me. He was a power maniac. And cheap? What a miser! He thought working for him was reward enough. Mahoney almost annihilated my spirit. If I stayed there I would have turned into a work zombie and a curmudgeon just like him."

The Scrooge syndrome affects a great variety of people; not age, gender, social status, or occupation confers immunity. The syndrome can occur within the family as easily as in the business world. Luella, seventy-two years old, the mother of six and grandmother of sixteen, who I thought was cold, austere, and reserved when I met her, was described as a female Scrooge by her oldest daughter, Sheila. "I hate to say this, but there is nothing to that woman, not an ounce of compassion or sympathy. She never even hugged one of her children after they learned to walk and talk because then she couldn't control them," Sheila continued. "Ask her sisters about her. They say that she hasn't changed since the day she was born. She was always a bitch. And she's such a hypocrite. Would you believe it, she goes to church every day, but what does she use religion for? To invoke the Lord's backing as a mother so she can boss us around. She is about as Christian as Attila the Hun. It's a sham. When we need her, all we get is a lecture. If it weren't for my father we would all be neurotic wrecks. For as cheap, stingy, cold, joyless, and unspontaneous as my mother is, he was just the opposite. The funny part of it was that in public she was the epitome of the devoted mother. Her friends never knew what a phony she was." Sheila reflected for a moment. "And with the grandchildren. She never touches them; she just worries about them messing up her damn house. The kids don't like her. They complain that she's boring and strict and no fun. If she was a failure as a mother, she is a disaster as a grandmother. Totally self-centered, that's what she is."

People afflicted with the Scrooge syndrome are either born with it or acquire it during their lifetime.

It may be due to a congenital condition—for whatever reason, *some people* are born with an impaired capacity to use their spirit. They are, as I have stated earlier, spiritual morons, ignorant of the emotional and spiritual dimensions of existence. Furthermore, they lack the ability to put themselves in another person's shoes, to see things from another viewpoint. They are usually without kindred spirits, and often friendless entirely, unless they have enough money or power to buy "friends." This has nothing to do with intelligence or other mental or physical faculties. Scrooges may be quite gifted in many areas.

Sheila's mother is a case in point.

Some Scrooges who have acquired these characteristics did so to survive a difficult childhood. One successful lawyer I know told me that he knew that he "stowed away" the best part of himself when he "couldn't keep up with the other kids because I was too fat." He decided early in his life that "if I couldn't beat them at sports, I would beat them at life." He became an excellent student and grew to be a "hard-driving, no-holds-barred son-of-a-bitch attorney." He found himself "respected but friendless." Fortunately he was aware of what he had become because he had not completely silenced his spiritual voice. "I hated what I had become."

The Scrooge syndrome can strike individuals who place a great priority on and spend a great deal of time in a de-spirited environment (where Scrooge-like behavior is rewarded). Slowly but surely they become de-spirited. This occurs most frequently in people of average intelligence who are basically spiritually ignorant. Paula, for example, did what her family and society expected of her as a child, an adolescent, and a young woman. She married soon after high school, had two children, and decided to go to work. She started as a bank teller and, because she was obedient, industrious, and meticulous, did very well at her job. She found that at work she was "special," but at home she was "a slave to my husband and kids." As she progressed in her career, she became less involved at home and, with her newfound authority, became harsh, demanding, unfeeling, and less and less empathic to her colleagues. She started acting the same way at home. This finally led to her divorce and estrangement from her two children (she freely gave custody to her husband). The children resented their mother. "She's a big shot at work," her daughter said, "but she doesn't care about me very much." Paula had several affairs with male colleagues at work, and invited her children to spend a weekend with her and a lover. The children wouldn't go. "That's their choice," Paula said dispassionately. "I don't know what happened to her," her father told me. "It's like she has become an unfeeling bitch."

At that point in her life Paula was still unaware of the emotional and spiritual price she was paying for her newfound "freedom."

Fortunately, except in congenital cases, the Scrooge syndrome is not irreversible. Even Scrooge himself was cured. In the examples I just quoted the lawyer found it necessary to change his behavior when he fell in love and Paula found a more reasonable middle path among work, motherhood, and her social life after she suffered a severe depressive episode that necessitated hospitalization.

THE FAUST SYNDROME

Simply put, the Faust syndrome is an affliction of those who "sell out" the spiritual aspects of their lives for the material/physical benefits they glean from what Goethe, writing in *Faust*, calls the "Earth Spirit." "Contemplating the magic symbols drawn by the renowed master's hand, [Faust] turns from the figure suggesting the workings of the universal spirit as too vast for his comprehension. He hails the Earth Spirit, the lesser deity that dwells in the earth like the soul of man in his body . . ."[2]

"Selling out" is a common occurrence in a materialistic, industrialized society where de-spiriting people abound and some people will do anything to get ahead. Patty, a twenty-seven-year-old advertising executive, was hospitalized after a suicide attempt. "I hit bottom," she told me, "and had nothing to live for. I stripped myself of everything to get ahead in the agency . . . even my clothes. I screwed every boss in the building, stepped on people's toes. I was driven by ambition. I wanted to show the world something. All I did was give up the best part of me. I am a reamed-out person. If I was religious I would say that I sold out to an evil force and lost my soul and my self-respect. For what? A lousy promotion. What the hell is the difference between me and a whore?"

Jim, a teacher, told me that he "screwed his best friend in order to get the principal's job. I knew that it was up for grabs and didn't tell him about it because I knew that he was better qualified. The trouble is, I know that if our situation were reversed he would have told me about it. I think I broke his heart."

A researcher who carries out clinical trials of new drugs told me: "Well, I bend the results on my drug studies a little bit, sure. If I didn't the drug companies wouldn't give me any more studies . . . and I am out of a job. Do you think they spend tons of money to find out that their drug is a lot of crap? So if I want to stay on the team I've got to play the game."

Muriel, a twenty-four-year-old medical student, said, "Sure I cheated in college. How else could I have gotten a grade-point average that could get me into medical school? When I become a doctor I will have the luxury to become an honest person."

Unfortunately, once the Earth Spirit is bought, it is a hard thing to relinquish. Those afflicted with the Faust syndrome must, by necessity, silence the spiritual voice within them.

Could people who are in touch with their spirits create hydrogen bombs, pollute the environment, lie, steal, connive, behave cruelly, and so on? Probably not, and even if they were seduced into such a situation they would soon realize it and extricate themselves. Only halfminded people who have renounced the spiritual aspect of their existence can do these things. Like Faust, they have sold out in the here and now for a materialistic currency: possessions, money, status.

The halfmind fabricates intricate rationalizations to justify the behavior of those who worship the Earth Spirit. The unethical becomes easily accepted. "Cheat a little on your income tax," an accountant once told me. "The government expects it."

Business and the government may sanction this type of behavior and stretch their rules and regulations to embrace it, especially if everyone is doing it. In a Faustian society, who dares to cast the first stone?

Like Faust, every human being faces his or her private Mephistopheles daily. Sure, to err is human and no one is perfect. But, in contemporary society, the Faust syndrome has assumed epidemic proportions. Individuals thus afflicted become de-spirited. Institutions lose their credibility, and their heart.

The Faust syndrome corrupts our children, destroys our institutions, and perverts our lives. It is one of the most malignant de-spiriting forces that afflicts our society today.

Children are especially hurt and confused in the face of the Faust syndrome. They are its natural enemy. Remember the honesty of the oracle:

"Daddy, why are you going sixty-five miles an hour in a fifty-five-mile-per-hour zone?"

"Mommy, why should I tell the man at the movie theater that I am twelve when I am really fourteen?"

"Quiet, kid." Bop!

Spiritually intelligent adults also detect the presence of the Faust syndrome. Mrs. Pelk, a forty-five-year-old homemaker, was aware that her husband had changed since he received a promotion. Mr. Pelk was formerly a "nice guy," a "people person" who enjoyed nothing more than to spend the weekends with his children, in spite of not really being comfortable with their active play and high noise level. But since his promotion he spent more and more time at work. What bothered Mrs. Pelk was that she was losing respect for her husband at the same time that he was gaining more public acclaim. For instance, they agreed that his boss was a "jerk," yet (in her words) Mr. Pelk "kiss-assed" him in public.

"How can he do that and expect me to admire him? How can I make love to him when he is acting like such a wimp, drooling all over that obnoxious asshole just so he can be next in line for his job?"

Mr. Pelk was angry at her. Understandably so, because the Faust syndrome victim ignores the comments of any spiritually intelligent and perceptive person. Mr. Pelk tried drastic measures to stifle his wife's objections. "If you don't like what I am doing, I'll leave. There is something wrong with you. You're jealous, you're ungrateful . . ."

"You know what I told him when he said that?" Mrs. Pelk

said, laughing. "I said, 'And you are a schmuck.' I told him that he was becoming a spineless wimp and if he didn't think things over and straighten up I didn't want him anymore. I wanted my old husband back—the man I was proud of and respected. Well, he sulked away, then he returned and we had a long talk and he came to his senses. In fact, a year later he even bought me a beautiful necklace and thanked me. And he got his promotion anyway and is doing better than ever at his job. Quality tells, I always say. People don't have to sell out."

Like Faust, some who "sold out" can get off the hook, if they try. I wonder if philanthropy has some of its origins here. One businessman, acknowledging his "sellout," told me, "Sure I don't act like the nicest person, but this is temporary. I am doing what is necessary, playing the game until I get enough power, authority, and dough—lots of dough. When that day comes, I will be as nice to people as I would like to be and help them as much as I wish."

What he has unfortunately forgotten is that he will most likely be a different person when that time comes. His halfmind will have taken over.

Only a fortunate few can recover their spirit after they have sold out.

· 7 ·

THE DE-SPIRITED SOCIETY

Like any institution, when a society takes form it first reflects the nature and ways of its people. Soon after it becomes a force in its own right and then proceeds to mold the attitudes and ways of the people who are born into it. When people change, their society changes. Human nature is more cast in stone than the cultures humans create.

Our current society is a de-spiriting one. We have created a culture that is antithetical to spirit, and we all suffer for it.

SOCIETY AND SPIRIT

An ideal society recognizes the importance of maintaining a balance between both the first order and the spirit—of balancing the material and necessary with the meaning and purpose of life. An agrarian or currently existing "primitive" culture, for example, is structured so that the attainment of such a balance is at least possible; demands on the self are congruent, because people have a vested interest in assuring their mutual survival. Thus they spend a great deal of time together to assure and achieve that purpose. In such a culture, the work ethic propounds production through mutual cooperation and interdependence; family and community ties become very important; all generations become closely attached to one another and have their specific functions and roles. The self's physical, emotional, spiritual, and intellectual needs have the potential to be satisfied concurrently, since life is spent in a natural environment. Things beyond the halfmind are respected. Whatever its drawbacks when measured by the yardstick of our modern industrial society, this type of social system creates a minimum of tension within the self and between the self and the culture.

Cultures like these distribute power horizontally rather than vertically. Because there are no real "bosses," in peaceful times the conditions for de-spiritment do not exist in the workplace. Any de-spiriting that took place would be restricted to an individual—someone with an aberration of character who is questing for power, authority, or dominance over others.

This is different from what takes place in our own culture, where demands on the self can be divergent and create a perfect set-up for de-spiritment. In an industrial society spirit must be "broken" so the masses of people can be made to tolerate the unnatural conditions of industrial life. Modern industrial society is a culture of the halfmind.

To illustrate, in a "worst case" scenario of a de-spirited worker, let's take a brief glimpse at the daily life of an average white-collar male commuter who resides in a typical "bedroom community" and works at some distance from his home. If he wants to be successful, Mr. Jones most probably wakes up before sunrise to catch an early train to work. During the day he spends his time in a first-order work world; most often performing halfminded work, at a fast pace, in a high stimulus, multipressured, nonorganic (office) environment. Although on the surface he is friendly and affable, he is wary of his colleagues. They are his adversaries, for he is on a career path, aspiring to be the leader of the organization some day. To get to the top he has to surpass his competition.

The primary ethic of his world is "winning"; the prize is status and material gain. Even though the members of his company may work "together" on a project, the rewards for individual promotion are so great that there is a strong, but unspoken, adversarial and competitive component between team members. When one falters, his mistakes are often viewed by his competitive team members with hidden pleasure, like the understudy who has mixed feelings if the star is too ill to go on.

Jones is isolated from his family (who are involved in their own diverse universes—home, school, work) not only physically but mentally. His attention is focused on processing "outside" information. Not much time is allotted to internal reflection. He doesn't daydream about his wife and kids very much during work hours. He is just too busy and sensorily overloaded. During business hours he spends little time with things of the spirit, nor does he engage in much strenuous physical activity. The physical and spiritual aspects of his self are deprived; he is out of contact with his natural environment.

He is out of touch with anything beyond his halfmind.

Money, and some occasional excitement on the job, are his compensation for these "inconveniences" and his rationale for tolerating them.

When the weekend comes he has an opportunity to shift gears—to leave the ethos of the first-order world. The weekend offers him an opportunity to go beyond his halfmind: to enjoy the people he loves, enjoy nature, exercise his body, and nourish his spirit in any way that pleases him. But does this happen? No. He stays where he is, locked within his halfmind. More quick tempo, more time urgency. He can't switch gears. He may change his activities but changing his mind-set is more difficult. Even if he gets involved in physical activities, he carries them out in a first-order manner—urgently, frantically, and competitively. Even if he does spend time participating in sports, he will be involved in "winning." If he jogs, it will be against the clock.

He views the normal demands of his family as overwhelming. He is so depleted that there isn't much of him left for them. So if he can't give of himself he gives them money, and risks being viewed as a "meal ticket" by his family. If he has a tendency to feel sorry for himself, he may come to resent his family because he is working so hard and they are having all the fun.

Everyone has choices, and Jones has chosen to become a victim of a halfminded culture. There is no spiritual time for him. Even recreation, as it is practiced, becomes an extension of the first order; the competitive work ethic becomes the competitive play ethic.

One of the safe ways out for Mr. Jones and others who are trapped in this culture and are aware that they aren't happy is daydreaming.

As Martin, an "exhausted" forty-three-year-old commuting stockbroker, told me, "I am damned if I do and damned if I don't. I get no rest. It's work all week and another form of work and responsibility on the weekend . . . everyone's pulling at me." How could he resolve the conflict caused by the two opposing forces that were "pulling" at him? He thought about staying in the first order.

"Sometimes I want to just work and work, and forget about my family. That would make life easier. If I needed sex I could have an affair, no aggravation, no responsibility. All my friends do it. On the other hand I fantasize about gathering up my wife and kids and living on a farm."

His quandary illustrates how contemporary life draws and quarters the self between the two orders of existence. Many people, like Mr. Jones, resolve this conflict by settling within in the first order. Life is simple there. Rules and regulations are clear. Relationships with others are uninvolved, intellectualized, and devoid of emotion—formal, without "aggravation," as someone said. It is a world of the halfmind reacting to a limited everyday world.

But these people soon become de-spirited. De-spirited people make for a de-spirited society. In its turn a de-spirited society creates more de-spirited people. One of the results of this vicious cycle is reflected in the presence of a malignant force that has accompanied the ascendancy of the halfmind. This new force is the "businessification" of society. It is an increasingly powerful influence that is affecting every aspect of the way we live our lives.

THE "BUSINESSIFICATION" OF SOCIETY

The philosophy of "businessification" promulgates aggressiveness, competitiveness, narcissism, performance, and "success"—all measured materialistically. At the same time it ignores spiritual imperatives, the importance of emotional attachments and family bonds, and the artistic and nonmaterial aspects of human life. Businessification in the pursuit of wealth creates a de-spiriting society.

At this point I want to make it clear that by "businessification" I do not refer to doing necessary and normal business. Nor do I object to decent people working to make an honest living or to capitalism as a philosophy. "Businessification" is the abuse of business. It is the indiscriminate and anarchic extension of the business ethic to the society at large where it becomes a social philosophy.

The ethics and practices of "business"—competition, success, authority and so on—which are appropriate in the proper arena, have been insinuated into relationships and social institutions, where they have no place. Emotional and spiritual priorities have been pushed aside in the process. Nowhere is the noxious effect of this businessification more pronounced than in the work world, where it has taken hold and affected an entire generation.

• LIVING TO WORK •

The majority of Americans now live to work. The family is being increasingly deprived of its members, who are rushing helter skelter into the work force.

Parents are leaving their children in the care of paid strangers. Grandparents are ignoring their important supportive role for their children and grandchildren.

For what? Money, success, self-esteem? The truth is that many people are increasingly looking to occupational status and material rewards for their sense of well-being and self-worth. But when they get what they want, the majority feel disappointed, empty. They say, "Is this all there is?"

In the United States, working has taken on obsessive overtones. A well-balanced life, it is said, results from spending equal time at loving, playing, and working. In this country all three criteria have become "technologized" and "businessified." Take love, for example. How is love, or even mere affection, viewed in business? There is little place for "unconditional" affection. If any love is given, it is of the conditional type, given for "performance." Even the act of love becomes a competitive performance.

In contrast to true love, which is unconditionally given (as I have previously noted, in true love people are happy not for what the beloved does, but only because he or she exists. The person's faults are easily forgiven), when the businessification ethic is applied at work or at home, love is based on performance: how "good" one is in bed, how much money the husband makes, what colleges the kids go to, what a housewife "does" all day. In the last instance, the husband denigrates his wife's emotional, spiritual, and physical work because her "production" is not evident. How many housewives who are asked at a party "What do you do?" are hard put to find an answer, even though they may work much harder than someone with a nine-to-five job? Then they are made to feel of little worth because they do not have an (allegedly) exciting job or because they place priorities on relationships with their family and their friends. As one recent immigrant said: "Work, work. What's the big deal about work? I'd rather stay at home with my family. What's all this fuss about work in this country?"

In a businessified society, "emotional" work (teaching and other helping professions) are given low status. Emotional and spiritual currency aren't recognized. Good deeds don't make one rich.

Businessification has permeated the professions, replacing, in many instances, its spiritual aspects; the ideas of "calling," "mission" (in the personal sense), or "dedication" become outmoded. The spiritual aspects of the professions are diminished and their financial aspects are emphasized. Comments like "teachers have a good deal because they get long vacations" and "doctors are money mad" are samples of derogatory remarks about the professions. Education, medicine, law, religion—all have traditionally had spiritual roots, for youngsters the fruition of a dream of childhood expressed as a "calling," a "mission," a "dedication."

But with businessification, the professions find it hard to maintain their spiritual qualities.

The "spirit" of learning loses out.

Education becomes a performance-oriented business. Children become educational workers, and are cultivated as fodder for the business system. In fact, an entire "learning remediation" industry has grown up as a result of the obsessive preoccupation with getting kids into the "right" schools. Spiritual education (liberal arts) is de-emphasized; the importance of values, art, music, and literature is diminished. Kids become "educational products" to their parents. Education becomes an "investment," not a romantic quest for knowledge. For de-spirited teachers who would rather be somewhere else, their job is a bore—and the kids know it.

The "spirit" of justice loses out.

Law becomes a business. Lawyers lose sight of principles of justice. Anarchic litigation becomes rampant. The law becomes just a way of making money. The noble principle of equal justice under the law becomes distorted by the businessification ethic; winning is what matters—the guilty are freed on technicalities or because they can pay for good defenses.

The "spirit" of medicine loses out.

Medicine becomes a business. Medical care is given a "price"—in current lingo, "cost-effective care." The business of hospitals becomes more important than the patients they care for. Professionals fight over "turf." Money intrudes into the doctor-patient relationship. Some doctors pay more attention to their financial matters than to their patients. They read more financial journals than medical ones. They become jaded. It's hard to get up at three in the morning to see a sick patient if you're jaded. Patients, unloved, sensing the lack of dedication, become adversarial toward their physicians and quick to sue them. Disillusioned doctors retreat emotionally from patients and defend themselves against them. They start practicing "defensive" medicine. Patients and doctors become enemies.

The "spirit" of religion loses.

Religion becomes a business. Clergymen, exposed to a highly materialistic and de-spirited congregation, are hard put not be caught up in this ethic. There is pressure to become clerical businessmen. Dedicated clergy have a difficult time dealing with religious politics. If they desire to enjoy the pleasures of everyday life, they are diminished in the eyes of those they serve. Like doctors, they lose the special nature of the position that they had when spiritual and emotional priorities were predominant. There are, as well, the TV evangelists, religious businesspeople to a greater or lesser degree, from the sincere to the unscrupulous.

With businessification academics and scientists lose sight of the moral significance and meaning of their work. Breakthroughs formerly sought after to benefit humanity are now pursued in order to enhance the scientists' own reputations and to win a scientific race—to be the first to publish a specific discovery. The scientific literature is flooded with meaningless and useless information produced as a result of a publish-or-perish ethic that pervades the "business" of academia.

Ethical business loses out. Those who "would do anything for a buck" predominate over those honest and decent people whom their business colleagues see as simple or naïve. A businessman told me that he protested at a meeting of his company about some underhanded deal that the board of directors was considering. "The chairman turned to me," he said, "and sneered, 'Harry, *you* are the enemy.'"

Ad infinitum.

Businessification has affected the way people relate to one another. Romantic relationships, mimicking their ways, have become "contractual." Instead of long-term commitments, people live together or stay together for convenience, bound by a "contract" that makes it easy to discard the relationship at the least inconvenience.

WARRIORS AND AMAZONS—THE HALFMINDED PEOPLE

The effect of businessification on the emotions is pervasive. It leaves no room for spirit. Instead of lovers, the business ethic raises de-spirited and halfminded warriors and Amazons. Their training starts early in childhood; they are raised in the ways of war, not the ways of love. The qualities of love, caring, and altruism are discouraged. "Winning" is emphasized. "Competition" is emphasized. "Performance" is emphasized. Education emphasizes competitive sports disproportionately. A premium is put on "entrepreneurial aggressiveness." Emotional displays are labeled as "weakness." The expression of affection is discouraged.

These attitudes pervade the child's mind. At an early age warriors and Amazons learn to regard others as adversaries or as instruments providing some advantage to the individual.

What is valued is not the good heart but good performance. In fact, warmhearted, emotionally and spiritually gifted people are looked upon, one businessman said, as "wimpy."

As children grow they become more concerned with their peers' view of them than with those of their family. They allow their worth to be defined in terms of social success—"popularity"—rather than in terms of their status in the family. Soon society replaces the family as the source of the youngsters' self-esteem. They view themselves not in terms of what kind of person they are but by what they have accomplished as judged by the businessified system. The love of Mom or Dad or relatives is enough to enable young children to withstand cultural forces but they play havoc with older ones. Some crack under the strain of "performance." Youngsters have been known to commit suicide because they didn't get into the "right" college.

Children with a gift for nurturing have an especially hard time adjusting in a businessified society. Nice guys don't win ball games. Emotional and spiritual qualities are not rewarded by peer recognition, social status, or money.

John Lowell is a young man who did something unheard-of in his culture. He gave up a career in professional basketball to become a teacher in a New York public school:

"I wanted to become a teacher ever since I was a kid. I feel good with kids and I am happy in the classroom. I got this love from my grandfather. He taught me so much. I remember how good I felt with him—alone—just the two of us. When I am teaching I remember those times.

"My friends think I am weird because I want to teach. I only played pro basketball so that my father could brag about me. If I didn't it would've broken his heart. I did it for three years. Yes. The money was good. But I wasn't happy. I didn't feel like knocking guys around and all that. All that traveling. I am more of a home-type guy. I don't like to bounce around too much.

"So I quit and went back to teaching. Well, the guys called me faggot and all that. The coach was pissed because when I left the team I was averaging good [points] every game. My father would hardly talk to me.

"A lot of people are disappointed in me. But that's because they are being selfish. Whoever heard of a kid from the inner city not playing ball if he could? Well, I am not sorry I did it. I'm a lot happier."

Young women who are being pushed to go out in the work world have a hard time when they protest. Cathy, twenty-one, reflected about how pressured she felt by her peers to start a "career" as soon as she finished college: "I couldn't tell them how I really felt," she said sadly. "All I wanted to do was get married and have a bunch of kids and be a mom. But I couldn't tell my friends who were all hepped up about going out in the world and starting their careers and making lots of bucks. That didn't interest me in the least. I can't help it, I always liked kids. I adored playing with dolls. I am a homebody. I love to cook— and eat." She smiled. "That's me."

Both Cathy and John would feel a lot more in harmony in a society where one can be a "homebody" without feeling guilty about it, where in order to live as they wish they are not forced to feel, in Cathy's words, "out of synch" with the times.

"Maybe I should have been born thirty years ago," she said, sighing.

Businessification creates in a de-spirited society that, in its turn, fosters social degeneration and abuse of the profit motive.

Businessification creates a society where politicians are corrupted, where treasonous defense contractors supply inferior parts for weapons that their own soldier sons depend on, and where cheating, dishonesty, and skepticism reign and human beings don't matter for beans.

There is no realistic reason that we have to suffer such a society. With attention to spirit it can changed.

·8·

TO BE OR NOT TO BE: THE WILL TO EXISTENCE

A light heart lives long.

—William Shakespeare,
Love's Labour Lost

Every day the self asks itself the question: "To be or not to be?"

When was the last time you felt great about being alive? On the other hand, when was the last time you felt down in the dumps and that life just wasn't worth living? Do you remember feeling terribly sorry for yourself in your teens and having dramatic thoughts of doing away with yourself? (Many youngsters that age do.) Have you ever wondered why some people risk their lives in a foolhardy way? Why some people bounce through life and others drag?

THE WILL TO EXISTENCE

This has to do with a spiritual imperative that determines how much spirit desires to be present in the self—to cling to life, so to speak. I call this "the will to existence."

The will to existence gets feedback from the world. If everyday life is good, the will to existence is reinforced. The person is happy and enthusiastic about being alive. If life is difficult, this imperative can either work toward making things better, or it can just give out entirely. Viktor Frankl showed how, by finding a "will to meaning" in the experience, he was able to survive years in a concentration camp. This "will to meaning," in my view, is just one way that the will to existence operates. Frankl used his intellectual powers to give "reason" to a bad experience. By doing so, he reduced the impact of the experience as a representation of the "whole" of his existence to a "part of the whole," a "lesson," thus diminishing its influence. For example: Louie, a passionate, emotional youngster by nature, was rejected by his first love, Alice, and was inconsolable. "Life is not worth living without Alice!" the distraught youngster lamented. "Alice is all that matters, she's my life." At that point Louie saw his relationship with Alice as a "whole"— the *total* meaning of his existence; and because of this view his life was "all bad."

"But there are lots of fish in the sea," said his father, trying to make his son feel better while at the same time introducing to Louie the concept that Alice is not the "whole" at all, but only "part of the whole" and that life isn't "all bad." It was just his love life that was bad right now. As soon as Louie's intellect grabbed on to this notion, he minimized the incident, and his will to existence strengthened. In Louie's case it took all of five days, and was hastened as soon as he got a look at the "fantastic" new girl who moved into his apartment house.

The will to existence is weakened in a de-spirited person and can be so depleted that the person may die.

By its effect on the mind and body, this will to existence determines the mental and physical state of the self. This proposition is in agreement with the ideas of those who believe that consciousness can directly affect mind and body (and this belief has been supported by scientifically clinical experiments). People have the ability to "will" a good life and to use this "will" to overcome adversity, as well as to destroy themselves. One interesting finding by Dr. Sandra M. Levy, who studied the outcome of a group of thirty-six women who were diagnosed as having advanced breast cancer, was that the only psychological factor that mattered for survival within seven years seemed to be a sense of joy with life.

A light heart does live long . . . or longer.

Are you aware of a "will to existence"? How light is your heart?

Although shamans and religious healers throughout the centuries have recognized a connection between the nonmaterial and mental and physical health, traditional medicine, for the most part, continues to ignore this idea. It's not that people haven't brought attention to the matter. In his excellent book *Persuasion and Healing*, Dr. Jerome Frank wrote: "This review of nonmedical healing of bodily illness highlights the profound influence of emotions on health and suggests that anxiety and despair can be lethal; confidence and hope, life-giving."[1]

Though they were written in 1961, his words still have not been given their due.

Fortunately, today there does exist a cadre of pioneering and perceptive medical and psychological scientists who are braving the "establishment" and seeking ways to explore the regions beyond the halfmind. These men and women, clinicians and researchers, are the pathfinders that will show the way to the medicine of the future. Among them, Dr. Herbert Benson. The far-seeing physician and researcher in the exploration of mind-body phenomena at Harvard Medical school has, in a sicentifically acceptable fashion, been able to use the Relaxation Response[2] to benefit his patients, and to open doors to new areas of research. Dr. Lawrence LeShan, has taught meditation[3] techniques to his patients for many years, not only to help them alleviate their suffering, but to promote health. The study mind-body interaction are interesting more and more investigators including Dr. Steven Locke[4] and Dr. Joan Borysenko[5] of Harvard and Dr. R. Naomi Remen of Commonweal College. Dr. Gerald G. Jampolsky has developed a system of what he calls "attitudinal healing." He propounds seven principles as a prescription for creating a mental mind-set that he feels is conducive to health and healing. They are: "Health is inner peace; the essence of our being is love; giving is receiving; all minds are joined; now is the only time there is; decisions are made by learning to listen for the preference for peace within us; forgiveness is the way to true health and happiness."[6]

THE SUFFERING SPIRIT

Most of the people I spoke with agreed that more than the mind and body was involved in illness. I asked a grandmother called Kirsty if she thought that spirit had anything to do with illness.

"Sure," she replied. "That's just common sense. When people are down in the dumps they get sick. Anyone knows that. And when they are in good spirits they stay healthy. And if a person is miserable they can make themselves sick. And if something happy happens, and they are sick, well then, they get out of bed pretty quick. If doctors don't believe this, well, they aren't much good, are they?"

Spirit fuels the will to existence. Spirit can energize or deenergize the body, according to its own "health," which, in its turn, is dependent on the fulfillment of spiritual imperatives. When imperatives are fulfilled, spirit and the body are in harmony—this is wellness. When spiritual imperatives are frustrated, spirit and body are in disharmony—this is "sickness." When sickness prevails for a long time, the will to existence decreases.

Although it is clear that the mind and body suffer, and that this suffering can be objectively seen and subjectively experienced, is it possible that spirit suffers?

I think so, but not in the way that we usually think of "suffering." Spiritual suffering affects the mind and body and dims the will to existence.

Thus spirit is a factor to be considered as affecting a broad spectrum of illness: from the vulnerability of the self to illness on the lesser side of the spectrum to spiritual suicide on the other. I believe the following examples of spiritual suffering are involved in the process of illness, and there is some clinical evidence to support this belief.

Loss of love.

Disharmony within: when spirit has no issue within the self.

Disharmony without: when spirit has no issue in the world.

The two latter conditions lead to de-spiritment. All three conditions affect the will to existence in a detrimental way.

When these conditions exist, at the least the self becomes more vulnerable to pathogens that are always present in the environment. At the most the individual may self-destruct.

LOSS OF LOVE. A
BROKEN HEART

A broken heart lies here.

—Lord Macauley

The loss of love may cause what is commonly termed a "broken heart." Although broken hearts are not described in medical books, people with broken hearts spend a great deal of time in doctors' offices.

A loss of love affects the person's spirit. With a loss of love, the self loses not only the bounty it received from the beloved but also the personal delights of being in a state of love. A loss of love affects the self in differing intensity, according to the type of relationship lost—whether parent-child, friends, lovers, and so on.

• A LIGHT BEHIND THE EYES? •

The following clinical example concerns a case of spiritual suffering that occurred as a result of the loss of love. I am presenting this case not in a traditional psychiatric way but in a way that considers, and talks about, the effect of events and the patient's reaction to these events as it affects spirit. Remember that up until now spirit is not a word that is often found in the psychiatric literature.*

Mrs. Alton, forty-two years old, and mother of a former young patient of mine, requested a consultation "for herself." She complained of "feeling blue."

Her father had died unexpectedly several weeks previously. She appeared tired and sad, in marked contrast to her former

---

* I use the term "psychiatric" as a comprehensive term that includes medicine, psychology, biology, pharmacology, social science, and so on.

effusive self. Her face lacked expression. She complained that her "body was slowed up" and said she had a "lack of energy, constipation, fatigue." She wasn't sleeping and couldn't "make it to work." Her mind was slowed up, too—her thoughts came more slowly, her attention wandered, she couldn't concentrate. She cried often and felt sad all of the time.

Her psychiatric diagnosis was evident: depression, reactive type, secondary to father's death. If I were to rewrite her diagnoses again, after her treatment was completed, I would include the spiritual ramifications of her condition. It would go something like this:

> depression, reactive type, resulting from "broken heart" due to loss of a kindred spirit. Her spirit was wounded, her body suffered, her will to existence diminished.

Obviously such a diagnosis is not to be found in the *Diagnostic and Statistical Manual of Mental Disorders*; only, perhaps, in literature.

How did I come to this "diagnosis"?

Well, early in her therapy Mrs. Alton complained of feeling "sad all over." I decided to see if she could localize her feelings within her body (she was having diverse aches and pains as a result of her depression). Sometimes this technique is helpful in eliciting deep feelings and memories.

"Where in your body do you feel sad?" I asked.

"I feel sad," she answered.

"But what exactly feels sad? Is it your mind, your body, or something else?"

"My mind, I guess."

"Can your mind feel?"

"Well—I don't know. Something is feeling bad. If it's not my mind, it's my body."

"Does your body feel bad?" I persisted, but gently.

"Well, physically, sore. It's tired and it aches."

"So the sadness is in your body?"

"Not just my body, there's more. It's all over. I feel awful. It's more than my body."

"Can you tell me what exactly is feeling awful?"

"Something more."

"Something more," I reflected the comment back to her.

"Yes, something else, something else is broken. I feel like a part of me is dead. I hope that you know what it is if you are going to fix it."

She started to sob. "I miss my dad so . . ."

During the next three weeks she cried a great deal, grieving the loss of her father. The more she cried the more her other symptoms decreased in intensity (this was partly due to a brief course of antidepressant medication that I prescribed to help ease her symptoms and to ensure that she could function adequately during this difficult period).

"I am feeling better," she told me during the fourth week of her treatment. "At least my mind is clearer and I have more energy . . ."

"Great." That was good to hear. Her body and mind were healing.

"But there is still something in me that's broken. Something very deep that is very sad. Something that hasn't yet been talked about."

Then I knew she was dealing with something beyond her halfmind.

"What's that?" I was puzzled.

"It's not something I can say."

"You are certainly better."

"Wait, don't think I am crazy but I think that my spirit is sad . . . broken, or bent or something. It's deep. I feel it in my mind and body. I feel—that my heart has a burning knife through it. I'm okay but I've got a broken heart. Like I don't want to go on. My mind thinks that life is a pain.

"I don't know what else it could be. I feel that a light within me has dimmed. A light that shines from in back of my eyes. You know how you can see the light in some people's eyes? Their vitality. I was looking in the mirror last night, and—that's it—the light in my eyes has dimmed. They used to sparkle when my dad was alive."

She is right, I thought. Although her mind and body were "clinically" better, her eyes didn't sparkle as they used to do. How would one prove that observation? I wondered. I surely didn't know. If I tried to explain that one at a medical meeting I'd be laughed off the podium. What I didn't know then was all that she was talking about was her will to existence.

Mrs. Alton had groped toward the realization that more than her halfmind and body were affected by her father's death. I wondered whether, although her emotional, physical, and intellectual reactions to the death of her father could be explained both psychodynamically and by a change in the chemical constitution of her brain, this explained it all. The chemical change in her brain was not the cause of her illness, it was an effect. The real cause of her illness lay somewhere else, beyond what seemed to be too evident.

"Was it possible," I asked myself, "that this loss of love so affected her spirit that she was losing her own will to existence? That this event led to a withdrawal of vitality, reflected by physical symptoms she perceived, and mediated through the biochemical changes in her body? Was the 'knife' in her heart a representation of spiritual loss manifested as psychic and bodily pain? Does she perceive that she has sustained a mortal wound?"

Then some doubts set in. "Is this a psychiatric issue after all, or should I suggest that she talk this over with her pastor?"

Finally I did suggest that she seek her pastor's counsel. We agreed that I would continue to work with her until her depression lifted. As long as she was depressed, my involvement was medically valid. Traditional psychiatric theory holds that the loss of a loved one triggers a psychodynamic process within the bereaved that initiates a state of mourning. The process of mourning goes through defined stages of denial, depression, anger, and ultimately is resolved by "acceptance"—coming to terms with the beloved's death. This formulation was fine for treating Mrs. Alton's depression. But what about her "broken heart," which I had come to regard as much more than a metaphor?

I must consider, I thought at the time, and as wild as it may seem, that although medication could reverse the noxious chemical reaction of her mind-body complex to her loss, and psychotherapy could relieve her halfmind psychologically, "something more" was taking place and "something more" had to be done. I felt that she would be fully recovered only when the "light" returned to her eyes.

I knew that the "something more" was beyond biochemistry and psychodynamics and had to do with spirit. I remembered something Shakespeare had written in *Othello*: "Your heart is burst, you have lost half your soul."

Was it possible that people who didn't improve very much with psychotherapy and pharmacotherapy in fact needed a type of therapy that dealt with things beyond the halfmind and body? More recognition of spirit? If this were so, it would explain the fact that sometimes patients get better although their therapists are totally ignorant of how it happens.

From that point in Mrs. Alton's therapy I decided to explore the deeper aspects of her relationship with her father, and in a different way than before. Not in halfminded terms of routine psychological fare like her "Electra complex," nor rivalry with her mother and sisters for his affection, nor her ambivalent feelings toward him, nor her anger with him because he got angry with her when she broke curfew. And not in a religious sense, either, because that was better left to her pastor. I decided to approach the subject with a preconceived idea that her spirit was "kindred" with that of her father and she had lost the immediacy of that spiritual pleasure.

I brought up the word "spirit." What did this mean to her? How did it develop over the years? What part of her bathed in the glow of her father's spirit? What did it illuminate in her? How did this nourish her? Transform her? Help her in her daily life? How much of his spirit was already "built in" her, and how much was "outside"? What did it do for her to love her father so much? These are, at the least, not traditional psychiatric queries.

And she responded to these questions easily. At first I was much more uncomfortable with the subject of spirit than she was. After all, I was the one who was trained in a discipline that ignored spirit. The more Mrs. Alton talked about things in terms of spirit, the better she felt. "Now we are on target," she said. I began to feel better about talking about spirit. If it's helping her, I thought, then it's right.

Both her mind and spirit were affected by her father's death, and both needed help.

What Mrs. Alton was experiencing was more than could be explained by traditional mental constructs like "feedback" or "object constancy." It slowly dawned on me how narrow (in spite of their obvious benefits) were the perceptives of traditional medicine and psychology. I realized that although the methodology involved in therapeutic practice was helpful to the halfmind, it left aside what was most important—spirit. This realization explained for me why some people, although they were A plus students in theory, were poor therapists in practice. It's because they are intellectually halfminded. Effective therapists do a lot more than their halfmind thinks they are doing. They are using their seventh sense, and this is something that can't be taught. Children are very responsive to a talented seventh-sense therapist—many of them improve rapidly with brief therapy. No one has as yet adequately explained this phenomenon. But there is no doubt in my mind that it has to do with spirit, something I never before saw as clearly as I did with Mrs. Alton.

I learned by our work together that there is really such a thing as a "broken heart." If this sounds outrageous to the scientific-minded, let me explain.

If love is spirit and love "illuminates" the self, weaves people together, and represents the good things of existence, it follows then that the loss of love, the material representation of that love, and the constant "kindred" input and illumination of the self it offers deals a devastating blow to the self, because love lost is something of spirit lost. This affects the mind and body.

But all we do is to treat the halfmind. It's like giving an aspirin for a bleeding wound, rather than sewing it up. How much is this approach a reason for therapeutic failures? Or failures in relationships?

No wonder the light went out of Mrs. Alton's eyes when her father died. Her spirit had taken a telling blow and her will to existence decreased.

It was necessary for her to come to terms with the fact that although the immediacy of the pain incurred by the loss of her kindred spirit will fade and that she will maintain him in her mind with tender memories, the wound to her spirit is something she will carry with her to the end of her days.

Spiritual wounds run deep. The mind may heal but a broken heart never heals. Parents who have lost a child, perhaps the worst blow of all, know this. Their lives are forever changed, but they are certainly not over. The will to existence returns when certain mental "arrangements," such as changes in attitude, are made as the mind heals.

A broken heart can be fatal. The loss of love may be so devastating, so dispiriting, that the self can lose its will to existence. This occurs in "hospitalism"—when babies abandoned by their mothers die—and when people "pine away" after loss of a loved one.

• A BIOCHEMISTRY OF SPIRIT? •

Can the idea of a broken heart be reconciled with the teachings of modern medicine? Possibly, *if* we accept the following premises:

- Via the "will to existence"that spirit affects the vitality of the mind-body
- That the capacity for vitality, physiologically and biochemically, is related, at least in part, to the self's immunological system. This medical reality, called psychoneuroimmunology, is gaining more and more attention.

Haven't you ever gotten a cold when you were upset about something?

The will to existence may work through the body's immunological system. The stronger that will is, the healthier the person. The weaker it is, the more vulnerable.

If this hypothesis is valid, it explains the mechanism of action of what can be called spiritual suicide—mysterious "nonspecific" supernatural phenomena like death due to voodoo, to being cursed some other way; death from a "broken heart"—like "pining away" after the death of a spouse; the infant dying after losing its mother; or "intentional death"—when one simply gives up on life, lies down, and dies. Of lesser gravity, psychosomatic and chronic illnesses have been linked to a negative state of mind. Studies have shown that "attitudes typical of pessimists are associated with weakening of the immune system's resistance to tumors and infections." These conditions create measurable physiological phenomena related to hormones and metabolites and immunological changes such as a reduction in the resistance to disease.[7] It's not only a case of mind over matter. More than that. It's a case of spirit over mind over matter. De-spiritment can trigger the mind-body to destroy itself.

Even Freud recognized this: "Expectation colored by hope and faith is an effective force with which we have to reckon . . . in all our attempts at treatment and cure."[8]

There is no better example of mind over matter than the "placebo" response (inducing a positive change in mental or physical symptoms with an inert substance portrayed as an effective drug). It's a medical reality. As Frank puts it: "Physicians have always known that their ability to inspire expectant trust in a patient partially determines the success of treatment. With placebos doctors have demonstrated remarkable cures."[9] This "nonspecific" factor is present in animals, too. Experiments show that when a mouse is put into a cage adjacent to a cat, its ability to withstand infection is reduced. Why? Nothing physical has happened to it. Could it be that, in the face of inevitable death, it has lost its will to exist?

There is plenty of evidence to show that mind affects the matter of the body. Procedures like hypnosis, biofeedback, visual imagery, and relaxation train the mind to influence the body. Some individuals can do amazing things with their bodies—raise their body temperatures, alter their blood pressures and heart rate. Some people have been known to bleed on demand.

In spite of this information, mainstream contemporary medicine remains mired in a mind-body dualistic philosophy and persists in treating secondary symptoms of the body and mind as *causes of the disease,* while the primary cause of an illness may have other origins. What modern medicine labels "nonspecific" comes from beyond the halfmind . . . from spirit. The syndrome of a "broken heart" is one of these.

More attention must be paid to the will to existence; evidence exists that underlines its importance. One study, for instance, showed that "active" cancer patients do better than passive ones. Dr. Larry Dossey has observed: "The patient with the will to live frequently outlives his prognosis. He doesn't die on time."[10]

The will to existence and phenomena like the "broken heart syndrome" are not comprehensible in the light of first-order rational knowledge (except for a possible relationship to immunology). You may ask, "Isn't a 'broken heart' only a metaphor for a psychic wound?" An understandable question. I would answer that the psychic wound is a secondary effect of the primary spiritual wound and that the traditional way of viewing such a phenomenon limits itself only to the mind-body aspects of the event.

DISHARMONY WITHIN— DE-SPIRITMENT

The de-spirited self loses touch with spiritual imperatives and becomes mired in a first-order world. The self loses its uniqueness, becomes easily programmed by the everyday world and homogenized into the culture. The self joins the legion of the "faceless masses," losing its perspective. Its interests narrow, the self feels unhappy and "devitalized." Pessimistic attitudes are adopted, little joy or meaning in life is experienced. The will to existence is dimmed. This is the Scrooge syndrome that I described earlier.

Removed from the second order of things, the de-spirited mind formulates a narcissistic, existential philosophy of life: the here and now is "all there is."

This can end badly. Because the self has a need for a spirit connection, and since access to it is internally cut off, the self must satisfy what it perceives as "spirit hunger" elsewhere in order to feel alive.

Since it can't go inside to satisfy critical needs, it goes outside. When the self does this it becomes vulnerable to destructive forces. It does dangerous things because, although it doesn't "know" it, the will to existence is weak.

This is why people can't usually be talked out of doing destructive things.

One way de-spirited people feel "alive" is to seek out a pseudospiritual experience with substances like alcohol or other drugs. With these toxic substances, the body "feels" ecstatic, and the mind, in a poisoned state, is fooled. De-spirited people regard this as a "mystical" experience—a dangerous deception, in my view. Drugs of any type are active only in the mind-body complex. Drug-taking to achieve "higher" consciousness is a bogus and anti-spiritual experience, simply because poisoning the body is antithetical to spirit. And furthermore, it's too easy. Common sense tells us that.

This behavior is a reflection of a de-spirited state. People who don't care about themselves, who abuse their bodies, have a lowered will to existence. This is uncontestable. People smoke, eat too much, drink too much, and do other dangerous things to themselves because, in some way and in some part of their minds, they don't care that much about living. Otherwise they would curtail their destructive behavior and do the best they could to stay alive as long as possible.

Another way that de-spirited people stimulate ersatz pseudospiritual emotions is by short-term sensory overload: fun-seeking, multiple brief relationships that never evolve beyond infatuation, "casual sex," taking pleasure anarchically wherever it may be found. But this stimulation is short-lived. Remember, the halfmind is impressionable initially, but gets jaded very quickly. Physiology has shown that nerve or muscle tissue that is constantly stimulated needs progressively stronger stimulation to elicit the same response. Thus to keep the "high" going, de-spirited people seek more and more dangerous thrill-seeking, or behave more and more outrageously. It doesn't work.

A third way to attempt to reconnect with spirit within is by seeking to "find oneself"—looking for quick "answers." Thus people attach themselves to gurus or spend a great deal of their time in pursuit of faddish beliefs or psychological systems that offer to help them "get it together." But many are searching in the wrong place. All they are doing is dosing up on mind medicine. This potentially addictive alternative doesn't work, because the problem is not in mind but in spirit. The solutions are not intellectual but spiritual. Dropping out is no solution. Certainly a spirit quest under the direction of an ethical teacher is a laudable undertaking. But unfortunately, spirit questing has also become businessified—and the questers are easy marks. They would do better to start to look inside and focus their attention at home. People have not attained any spiritual growth at all unless they are applying spiritual wisdom to their everyday lives. Anything else and they are fooling themselves and wasting their time.

De-spiritedness is not an incurable condition. But one must go beyond the halfmind to repair things. There are those who have been able to reconnect within using religion, psychotherapy, or by dint of their own grit.

One ex-drug addict did it by becoming religious. An alcoholic stopped drinking because, in his words, "It was an effort of soul. I loved my family more than alcohol." A cocaine-addicted young mother "kicked the habit because I was hurting my children. Being a mother is more important. I love my kids more than drugs."

De-spirited people afficted with a weakened will to existence are vulnerable to illness, especially so if illness serves them by temporarily removing them from the mainstream of a de-spirited life. Our streets, hospitals, and prisons are full of people who have "dropped out" and settled for a vegetative existence, having burned out the energy of body and mind. The idea of "burn-out" itself signifies no less than a condition of spiritual depletion. Show me a person who hates his or her job and I'll show you a person who has either no spiritual element in work or whose job is so spiritually demanding that it has, in truth, burned the person out.

Two important factors influence vulnerability to de-spiritment and illness.

The first is luck.

Some people are better endowed than others with gifts of mind, body, and spirit.

Then there are those individuals who are born more or less de-spirited. There is nothing, short of a small miracle, that can change their destinies. Prisons are full of unfortunate people like this. No social program, no amount of love can help them because there is nothing within them to resonate to anything outside of them. As much as I regret to say this, because I would not like it to be, I have come to believe that these people are like the living dead—zombies.

How lucky do you think you have been?

A second factor is circumstance. The earlier a child becomes de-spirited, the more permanent the disconnection (except for those unusually gifted with an abundance of spirit who can endure in great adversity).

Except for those with a genius of spirit, people can give back only what they get. Love, as I have said before, is passed on, like a baton in a relay race. Children who lose touch with their own spirit become hard, adversarial, competitive, and deadened. They get sick easily, both because they are not properly cared for and because becoming sick is often the only way that they can get any semblance of love and attention from their disturbed or uninterested elders. Children who are overtly emotionally and physically abused become de-spirited very quickly. Children with parents who are unattentive and unloving become covertly de-spirited, even though they may appear to be happy and healthy.

Spiritually deprived children become spiritually deprived parents and spiritually deprived grandparents who in their turn raise their youngsters in the same way. Without spirit as a countervailing force, overtly abused people feel lonely, abandoned, angry, dependent, and pessimistic about life. Covertly abused people feel the same way but they hide it better; what they experience inside doesn't match the persona; they have the ability to put up a good front to the world. At the least they are lost, looking to others, as children do, to help them to reestablish and reintegrate themselves.

The unfortunate people who suffer from these conditions live lives of "quiet desperation." They live in a chronic state of anxiety and depression that may lead to psychosis. In some cases, especially when toxic substances are involved, they kill themselves. Removed from spirit there is no life.

This doesn't have to be. Except for the congenitally de-spirited, these people may be helped, they contain the solutions to their problems within themselves, in the area beyond their halfminds. Seeking help via psychotherapy, religion, artistic pursuits, other spiritually focused undertakings, or even all of them at the same time, coupled with lots of hard work, may help them begin to put the pieces of their mind together.

DISHARMONY WITHOUT— SPIRIT HAS NO ISSUE IN THE WORLD

The self that cannot express its spiritual imperatives in the world, although it can maintain its spiritual integrity "inside," becomes very frustrated in its dealings with the world. This frustration is expressed as anger, bitterness, and discontent. Eventually it affects the mind attitudinally and the body physically. Under enough pressure the individual may become de-spirited—"broken."

People who encounter frustration being themselves in the world, or are frustrated in fulfilling their potential or who are "offended" by their society understandably become unhappy. Their will to existence diminishes. They turn their frustration and anger inward and make themselves sick. Backaches, migraines, ulcers, hypertension, obesity, chronic anxiety, and mild depression are just some of the ailments that plague people when the self's expression in the world, whether it be home, work, or elsewhere, is stifled.

Jocelyn, a thirty-four-year-old lawyer, said, "I am eating myself alive" at her boss's refusal to promote her because she was a woman. Alex, forty-three, yearns to live on St. Thomas and be a "beach bum" instead of running the bond department at a Wall Street brokerage firm. Luis, thirty-two, works in the garment center and "can't get anywhere because I'm Hispanic." Many people who are in the wrong place, the wrong jobs, the wrong marriages, or frustrated with their lot because they made the wrong choices in life are in this category.

Sometimes people "choose," in a sense, to be in frustrating situations because they are too insecure to remove themselves from them. And sometimes they can't. Russian dissidents who have been sent to Siberia for their stand on human rights know this well. A price must always be paid so the self can express its spiritual imperatives within the world. It takes guts to pay that price.

But frustration can be overcome. Creative people find time for spirit. They find a way to balance their lives and express their spirituality whatever the conditions. It's not really an "either-or" situation, although many see it that way. A postman I knew told me that his job was indeed tedious but "it gives me an opportunity to be outside, and I always stop off in the school playground for a while every day and hang out with the kids." An assembly-line worker became active in his church in the evenings; an accountant who deals with figures all day jogs at lunchtime, takes karate and painting classes two nights a week, and teaches Sunday school. A multimillionaire businesswoman is a literacy volunteer one night a week.

Some people adapt to frustrating situations by making trade-offs concerning their priorities. John, thirty-nine, a car salesman, complained, "I guess I can't have everything I want when I want it. When I come home from work I want some love and attention—affection. What do I get? A peck on the

cheek. Or if I try to fool around—y'know, grab her—or something. I get an organ recital—y'know, like 'I have a headache,'
or 'it's that time,' or something else."

His wife, Agnes, is a neat, ordered, and compulsive person
who is emotionally austere and formal. She was raised in a
small Pennsylvania town, in a strict religious and social tradition
where duty and responsibility were portrayed as virtues while
intimacy and familiarity were discouraged. "Fun" was just not
important in her upbringing. That's one of the reasons that she
married John, an entertaining person. Unfortunately, the more
John tried to be intimate and romantic, the more she pushed
him away. She said that she "wasn't raised that way . . . to be
that close. I would like to be but I guess I can't, emotionally."
Without intimacy it was difficult for their spirits to connect.
This was most frustrating to John, but he willingly continued
the relationship. "It's a trade-off," he says. He loved Agnes, he
said, for her "loyalty, attractiveness—although I don't get much
of it, devotion, and all her other good qualities. She's an ideal
wife. So I am a little horny—it won't kill me. It's better than
having a sexpot who's sleeping with my neighbors for a wife."

When people can't find a way to balance their lives within
the context of their family and work, they may go beyond its
confines. This can be beneficial or catastrophic. John storms
out of the house when he gets "pissed" at Agnes but goes to a
nearby gym and plays basketball. No harm done.

A great deal of harm can occur when people can't trade
off. Felicia, a hotel manager, had an affair with her boss because, in her words: "I was angry at my husband and I wanted
to get even with him. He didn't like me working." Her husband
found out about her affair and reacted angrily. He called her a
"slut" to her children and family, and divorced her. She became distraught. From that point on her life went quickly
downhill. She sought solace for her pain in drugs and sex. She
made several suicide attempts until she was hospitalized and
finally she received help.

Felicia had no spiritual support to serve her as an emotional safety net after her affair was discovered. There was nothing and no one for her. The man with whom she had an affair shunned her completely because, as she said, "The S.O.B. was saving his own skin. But I fixed him. I told his wife."

Such a safety net could have served to limit the damage done. Her religion wasn't available to her because, according to its tenets, she had sinned, and felt too embarrassed to talk to her priest. She thus removed herself from the succor of spirit. Her priest never had a chance to help.

If she had access to the spiritual bedrock underneath her, she would not have "free-fallen" into increasingly difficult circumstances: drinkings, drugs, sleeping with hotel guests, and losing her job.

If she were aware of a spiritual alternative, she could have said something like, "Okay, I made a mistake. I am sorry. Let me try to put the pieces back together as well as possible. I am not going to surrender my self-respect, integrity, and honor for one mistake." With a spiritual option she could have avoided a great deal of pain, not only to herself but to her children. She could have tried to work it out with her husband. In fact, several months after their divorce he told me that he had "calmed down," still loved her, and would have considered a reconciliation if she hadn't gone "down the tubes."

Like Felicia, most people do not consider a spiritual perspective when adversity occurs. Adversity is perceived not as part of a greater "whole" in the broader light of spirit, but in an immediate first-order sense as *the* "whole." When this happens frustration is increased and more and more turmoil is caused. A spiritual view helps a person to tolerate frustration, to increase impulse control, and to contemplate, discuss, and get a perspective on the situation before action is taken. Impulsive action compromises the integrity, honor, and dignity of the self.

Everyone, willingly or unwillingly, makes mistakes. What is sometimes more important and more erosive to the self is not so much the mistake itself but rather how the mistake is handled. Mistakes that are not handled correctly become infinitely more serious when they infiltrate the spiritual plane of the person's self. Felicia, for example, compromised the elements of this spiritual plane: self-respect, self-esteem, honesty. She compromised her integrity, her marriage vow to be faithful to her husband, which was important to her, by having sexual relations with her boss. She could have avoided spiritual repercussions simply by getting help for her ailing marriage or separating from her husband before getting involved. Once separated, she would be free to do whatever she wished without compromising her integrity. Her self-esteem would have been unsullied. Indeed she might have been all the better for the experience. Certainly she would have maintained the respect of her children.

The will to existence can be affected positively. Love reinforces the will to live and to life. Babies make their parents and their relatives want to live.

People have been known to invoke spirit over mind over matter: using a strong will to existence to overcome severe illnesses; using humor, prayer, or attitudinal methods to overcome their conditions; all to the amazement of their doctors.

Have you ever, when you felt terrible and thought you were getting sick, told yourself: "I won't get sick!" and it worked?

A NEW PSYCHIATRY OF THE
HUMAN SPIRIT

I would like briefly to consider psychiatry. Of all today's *medical* disciplines, psychiatry* comes closest to recognizing and recruiting things beyond the halfmind in the service of patients—in my view, it comes closest to the most "spiritual-medical therapy." It touches the "will to existence" and is in a

---

* In this section I am talking specifically to medical doctors. My other comments are directed to all of the various healing professions.

position to assess the state of this "will," as all doctors would be well advised to do, in patients.

Psychiatry has a considerable shamanistic dimension. That's why psychiatrists may be lightheartedly referred to by some as "shrinks" or "spooks." At their best, psychiatrists have time and undivided attention to give their patients, something even the most spirited and altruistic physicians find difficult to do because of their busy schedules. In the contemporary world, one hour of undivided attention is a commodity that is hard to come by. It is easier to care and to listen if one is not in a rush.

Caring and listening were the main attributes of the old romanticized family doctor, who treated the family from cradle to grave and dispensed time and attention generously. He wore his shaman's mantle well.

A woman told me what her "old family doctor" meant to her family: "We lived on a farm and when I got sick, I got really sick. But when Doc came walking into the room, why, he just filled the room with himself. I felt better the moment I saw him and I knew everything was going to be okay. He had a magic touch."

When medicine men or modern physicians practice their art, whether they know it or not, or like it or not, they deal with the "unexplainable" and invoke this force in the healing process. Whether this is called morale, life force, spunk, the will to live, superstition, the supernatural, or whatever, it all boils down to spirit.

Psychotherapy is similar to shamanism in that it deals with the same factors: belief, hope, faith, and spirit. But it doesn't admit it, at least publicly. It prefers to stake its territory on the sounder foundation of medical knowledge.

How can psychiatry ignore the fact that the "therapeutic alliance"—the patient's belief that help is forthcoming, shared with the therapist's belief and sense of mission that he or she can be helpful—is really a "spiritual" alliance? Patients know well that the doctor's knowledge, added to the quality of the spirit of the doctor-patient relationship, is what patients use to heal themselves. Patients see through this farce—they know better than doctors that the therapists' "orientation" (if they have one) is just the flexible framework for a spiritual process to take place. Immature or ineffective therapists think the method and the medicine (although obviously helpful) does the trick. Effective therapists know that the process, coupled with knowledge and experience, opens the patient's mind to spirit and heals by creating harmony between patient and therapist, within the patient's self and between the patient's self and the world.

There is no essential difference between the *process* of psychotherapy today and what shamans did thousands of years ago. We just know a lot more. The *ethos* of psychotherapy—caring, nurturing, loving—hasn't changed. What any good psychotherapist offers is knowledge, love, commitment, and concern.

But today this process is fast becoming extinct. Only a few family doctors and private practice psychiatrists give undivided attention to patients for a protracted period of time. This is because a "businessified," modernized medical establishment, responding to governmental and private sector forces, halfmindedly promotes technology and downgrades the shamanistic aspects of medicine, and psychiatry with it. In spite of the years of medical training that it takes to become a psychiatrist, and because of the often nonmaterial nature of their work, psychiatrists have been relegated to the fringes of medicine. In fact, many insurance companies don't offer coverage for psychotherapy. Today's psychiatrists are finding that they have become, with their spirited colleagues, the last bastion of humanistic nonassembly-line medicine.

Some psychiatrists have surrendered the shamanistic side of their practice and choose instead to focus on technology and pharmacology, exclusively dispensing medications for illnesses that need not only medication but attention, time, caring, and involvement. Thus increasing numbers of patients are placing themselves in the care of less qualified people when their spirits are suffering, because more and more psychiatrists are becoming "technicians." By doing so, these patients become vulnerable to exploitation.

The truth is that there is no total pharmacological treatment for a suffering spirit. It takes a kindred spirit to help the healing process.

This serious situation must be corrected and quickly. Psychiatrists, instead of jumping on the biomolecular bandwagon, should pioneer the exploration of the world beyond the half-mind while keeping abreast of new knowledge. Psychiatry, in the light of new knowledge about spirit, should, with their non-medical colleagues, aspire to create a new therapeutic synergy between all of the mental health professions, and between hard science (especially the field of immunology) and shamanism that will make for more effective therapies than man has ever known.

The time to start is now.

·9·

THE SPIRITED
SELF

*A wise and wonderful woman told
me:*

*"I have a spirit that lives within
my mind and body. It is something
extra—something that I am lucky to
have, because, you see, it is a nice
spirit, kind and wonderful, and it is
in my care. The world makes my
mind unhappy at times, people act
terribly at times, my spirit sees this
and is sad. But I know that my task
is to care for this spirit and not let
things of the world hurt it, and that
things of the world are secondary to
this immortal spirit in my care. It is
more than me, I assure you."*

Let's get practical, and personal.

It is very useful for you to learn how spirit operates
within yourself.

It is very useful to know if you are de-spirited, because
something *can* be done about it. You can apply your
seventh sense to your everyday existence, and it has

the potential to help you to live a happier, more contented, and more fulfilled life.

But to do all these things you must first become spiritually intelligent.

If you are like most people, you have a lot to learn because no matter what you learned—intellectually and socially in school, physically on the athletic field, or emotionally during your lifetime or in psychotherapy—chances are that your spiritual education has been ignored. Even religion, mysticism, or whatever other experiences you might have had have probably not helped you become spirited.

But that's water under the bridge. If you want to learn, you can start now.

This chapter contains a curriculum for you to follow. Go through it in your own time and at your own pace. You've got the rest of your life.

The curriculum is divided into several parts. First, you'll see an example of how one spirited person uses his seventh sense in life. Then I list some of the qualities possessed by spirited people I've met during the course of this study. Their common characteristics will supply you with guidelines to help you assess the state of your own spirit as you answer the questions in the self-assessment section. That section contains questions that will challenge your halfmind, leading to raising your own spiritual awareness and assisting you to become spiritually minded. The goal is to be well beyond your halfmind by the time you have finished answering the questions for yourself. Finally I offer some guidelines on how to use your spiritedness in your daily life.

The rest is up to you.

USING YOUR SEVENTH SENSE

The basic premise to becoming spiritually intelligent is a belief that there is more to life than what you perceive through your five senses. You must acknowledge a personal awareness that an incomprehensible "something more" operates in life, whether you choose to pay attention to it or not, or have no inkling a notion of what it is. To do this, call upon your own seventh sense. Have you ever had any thoughts, feelings, or experiences that are consistent with a belief in "something more"?

This belief opens the door to becoming spirited. For example, learning works best if you recognize that something exists and are curious to learn about it. For instance, if you want to learn mathematics you will be motivated to do so. The same goes for spiritedness. You must recognize its existence and want to learn as much as you can about it in order to get that way.

Remember, what I am referring to is personal spiritedness, unrelated to any spiritual training (from the outside in) that you have ever had. As I have stated previously, such training could be a hindrance or a help.

Any difficulty you have in acknowledging the idea of "something more" will impair your ability to use spiritual knowledge. It will not necessarily impair the ability of exceptional people to live a spiritual life—nothing is absolute.

If you have trouble accepting this idea, consider this: With all of the vagaries surrounding the subject of spirit, two things are certain. The first is that people are born and people die. Death, as far as we know today, is irreversible, universal, and final (although "reanimationists" will dispute this statement).

In addition, it can be stated, with some certainty, that first-order life on earth is "real"—tangible (many mystics will dispute this statement).

Okay so far? On the whole, most people would agree with these assertions.

Now, a qualitative question logically follows: Since we are born, live a life, then die, is life on earth all there is, or is "something more" possible? I am not talking about an afterlife. One does not need a heaven or hell to acknowledge that there is "something more" to life than the everyday world. Most of the people I interviewed believed that there was "something more" and that life on earth wasn't all there is (some didn't know what it was; those who followed a traditional religion stated their religious beliefs).

A few dissenters adamantly claimed that nothing existed beyond earth life. "Life is all there is. Dead is dead," one sailor said. To these few, the prospect of becoming spiritually intelligent was as interesting as the prospect of growing palm trees is to an Eskimo. "Spiritually intelligent," said the same sailor, "here's my spirit." And he pointed to his genitals. A woman in Appalachia was irritated when I asked about spirit: "No money, six kids, and a sick husband. Spirit ain't gonna help me. I don't need that stuff. I need money. There ain't nuthin' more to life than this, and I don't like life. When I die I am gonna get a good rest."

· BEYOND 50/50 ·

Those who believe that everyday life is "all there is" have a 50 percent chance of being right. Maybe everyday life *is* all there is. Maybe it isn't. But there are no possibilities beyond this premise. Whether they are right or wrong, they are locked into the world of the halfmind. Their philosophic ballgame is over.

Those who consider that everyday life isn't all there is, whether or not this belief is based on logic, religious or other faith, a body of individual or shared experience, and/or identifiable knowledge, have infinite possibilities open to them. Their ballgame has just begun.

What has impressed me, and I cannot emphasize this strongly enough, is the positive benefits of having such a belief. Everyone I have met who believes that there is "something more" to their existence finds it highly beneficial and life enhancing. Thus there is proof in this illogical pudding. Just the belief in something more is a ticket to a world beyond the half-mind.

I talked this over with Carl, a strongly opinionated sixty-four-year-old engineer. He presented a good example of how a person who believes in "something more" can use this belief in a practical way. He was quite animated during our talk: "There is a fifty/fifty chance that life on earth is all there is. Maybe yes. Maybe no. Right? Now, if I had some experiences that can't be explained by what I see and hear then the odds aren't even anymore, right?"

"Not exactly," I answered. "What about magnetism, electricity? You can't see or hear them."

"Yeah, but that's scientific stuff," he interrupted. "Okay. Now let me tell you why I think the odds aren't really even, because I have had some weird experiences in my life. Once I dreamed about an accident before it happened. Now, can science explain that? And if it can, then science is getting over the fifty/fifty barrier. Here's another one. I swear that I knew my way around my family's hometown in Poland when I went to visit it recently, and I never was there before. Figure that out. And another time I heard my mother's voice tell me to stop on a corner when I was riding my bike and a car I wouldn't normally have seen came whizzing out of an alley. Weird things." He paused for a moment.

"This isn't electricity or magnetism. To me these things can't be explained by what I see and hear in the world around me, and won't be. There is more than meets the eye—'something more.' These weird happenings tip the scales from fifty/fifty to something like—maybe eighty/twenty for me. Believe me, it's not that I am bullshitting myself because I am afraid to die. I don't think there is a hereafter out there. I don't know what the hell is out there. You gotta understand that the things my rational mind can't explain reduce the odds supporting the idea that life on earth is all there is. Something more is going on, only I don't know what it is, and I am willing to accept my ignorance and believe that there is more to life than this . . ." He banged on a table.

"I am glad I think this way. It helps. Makes my life better. Makes me feel good. It's not only fascinating but interesting, even exciting. Believing there is something more than what I touch and feel and see around me gives me strength not to take things too seriously. It means that I shouldn't get too involved in things of the earth because this is not all there is. This . . ."

Then he paused for a moment. A sad expression came over his face.

"This—helps me through troubled times. When my son died I almost died, too. I couldn't stand it. I think I would have crawled in a hole and given up if I didn't think that there was something more than the fifty/fifty . . . even fifty-one/forty-nine. Maybe my son still exists, in some form or other, beyond my own memory. That is a comfort. If I believed that he existed no place, no more, well, then there would have been no point to go on, would there?

"This belief helps in other ways. It keeps me honest. I see others cheat, lie, carouse—all that stuff. I don't do it. What for? If there is something more, and not in the traditional religious sense, well, it's not worth anything in everyday life to compromise what is a permanent part of me. Integrity, you might call it. I want to leave this world with integrity, and no one has ever offered me a price high enough to give it over. I want to be proud of what I see in the mirror. Be open. Have nothing to hide." He continued. "I want you to understand that this isn't a church thing, although I went to Sunday school when I was a kid. It was boring. God is too big for religion. This is something that I have discovered myself. Step by step. Practically. And I fell on my face a lot. I'm no angel."

Carl, whether he knows it or not, lives according to a "cosmic accountability."

You may ask, "What's different between Carl and those who behave in the same manner according to a 'religious accountability'? Hasn't religion been saying the same thing for centuries? Isn't Carl a religious person by another name?"

The difference is that Carl came to these realizations by himself, from the inside out. There is no middleman between Carl and spirit. He is aware that he has a spirit and he is accountable to it. He doesn't relate to spirit out of fear of condemnation or damnation. That's the difference. Like Carl, everyone must find his or her own unique way to spirit. Following a traditional religion doesn't necessarily make anyone spiritually intelligent, although there are many spiritually intelligent people who adhere to traditional religions.

Here's another person who found his own way. A middle-aged businessman explained how his realization of the possibility that there was "something more" was enough to change his life for the better. He said: "A long time ago when I addressed the issue of life after death I always assumed that when you are dead you are dead. That was my hallmark belief. Then came Kübler-Ross. She made me think. Then I talked to Ray Moody, who collected near-death experiences. There could be other logical explanations to what he talked about, but survival after death became an issue to me. Before it was black and white—when you are dead, you're dead. Now something was different.

"What was I to do?

"Was I going to lead my life as if there was nothing, or as if there is something more? I decided to lead my life as if there is something more. Because it would enhance the present life that I lead—make it more useful, more productive.

"There is no advantage to me to assume that dead is dead. There is an advantage to me to make the assumption on the unknown, that there is something more—maybe life hereafter. So therefore I am going to make that choice. If it felt funny and alien to me, I couldn't do that. But it didn't feel funny at all. It felt like a belief. And this belief has affected my life for the good in many ways.

"I feel it's okay, and without scientific proof, to say that I resonate with this idea of spirit."

THE SPIRITED PERSON

What are spirited people like?

Spirited people live beyond their halfminds. They are wholeminded. What they do and how they do it serves as a good model for those who wish to become spirited as well.

Spirited individuals are credible, productive people. They possess, as one woman stated, a "reservoir" of spirit within, are happy with themselves, have "kindred" relationships, are helpful to others, endure adversity well, and live their lives according to spiritual imperatives. They say that their belief in "something more" enables them to be this way.

First, a warning.

Spirited people are very nice folks, but they are not perfect. Although they have their problems and conflicts like anyone else, one thing is noticeably different—their spirit shines through. A warning for the skeptical reader is in order: What follows will certainly seem romantic, idealistic, or sentimental to you . . . but that's what spirit is. Love is romantic, sentimental, and idealistic.

I just call it as I see it.

Following are some characteristics, attitudes, and beliefs of spirited people (I have placed quotation marks around comments that people offered during their interviews):

Spirited people place an emotional and spiritual priority on life decisions. They are aware of an "accountability" to the "best part of themselves"—*a cosmic accountability*. Their self-esteem is rooted elsewhere than in the everyday world. Thus, for the most part, they are honest, trustworthy, and responsible—mature. They consciously adhere to universal "virtues" that consistently surface in credos like the Hippocratic oath and the Boy and Girl Scout oath, as well as in art, literature, and religion. "Virtues," as I describe them, are not a product of my own biases. Rest assured that I have made a considerable effort to be as objective as possible in describing such characteristics.

One "virtue" that spirited people have in common is that they *don't want to hurt others*, for any reason. Tim, twenty-five, explains: "It's not so much that I do things to please anyone around me, it's that I do them because they are right and they don't hurt other people. I am not accountable to people but I am accountable to something I think is more enduring, and that is to be moral and to be the best that I can be. In one way it's the same thing I learned in the Boy Scouts and in church, but it's different because there is no coercion or fear. I am doing it because I feel, inside of me, that it's right, and it is something that I didn't learn from anyone else."

People who are spirited have a spiritual source of strength and possess a *powerful will to existence*. Lara, forty-three, uses this "power" in her daily life. "Since I believe that there is something more than what is apparent around me, I can pray for strength, compassion, patience. I can ask spirit to cleanse me—to wash bad thoughts and feelings out of me. I close my eyes and make believe that I am blowing all my bad thoughts and my bad feelings out of my mind, and that a clean light comes in. And it works. And I love life. And that means I love nature and people. And I try to act on this love in my community."

People who are spirited *feel part of something "bigger."* Marguerite, fifty-eight, explains: "If I thought that this [everyday life] is all there is I would be miserable, because then life is finite, limited. Sure, I could travel and do and experience it all, but that seems shallow to me. Life to me is like going to school, death is graduation, but to what I don't know." In painful circumstances this attitude confers a "spiritual immunity."

Debbie, thirty-three, said, "Things don't bother me so much because I know it's all part of a bigger picture." Rudy, a young farmer, said: "When something bad happens I say to myself that I am a flyspeck in the universe and there's something going on that's bigger than me. Then I ask myself 'How can I make things better for everyone?' instead of getting into a poor-me pity party. I know there is a big picture here in life. I see it, feel it when I look up at the sky on a clear night. This makes me feel like everything is not all my responsibility, that some things are out of my hands—and that's a relief. I can't say what it is, if it's God or something else. It's just the fact, at least to me, that there is something."

People who are spirited have *a sense of "dedication"* and a philosophy professing that life has meaning and should be dedicated to the expression of spiritual imperatives. Many use their work to express spiritual imperatives and create a sense of spiritual communion with fellow workers. "There is a reason for living," a seventy-two-year-old woman told me, "and that reason is to be kind and good to others. I have done that all my life, at home and at work, and have been rewarded with many friends. What is life about if not to feel love and spread it around? Why would anyone want to hurt anyone?" Allan, a sixty-two-year-old publisher, said: "There is a purpose to life but I don't know what it is exactly. Sometimes I feel that it's a test for something else. I feel that my magazine is a sacred trust and that its quality and honesty must meet this test in spite of the financial pressures to make it less than it is. It's sort of my report card."

People who are spirited are often loved and respected by others and sought out by them for emotional and spiritual help and solace. They easily put themselves in another person's shoes and identify with the oppressed. They lead humanistic social movements, often at their own peril. They make waves in society and often suffer for it.

People who are spirited *don't often sell out*, Faust-style— perhaps because they do not value the everyday life currency that people sell out for: status, wealth, sex, narcissism, and so on. They do their best not to cheat, betray their friends, break their word, or disappoint their children.

Of course these people aren't paragons of virtue. They have the same superficial human frailties as anyone else. Everyone gets grouchy, irritable, and ornery at one time or another. But what is different about the spirited person is that no matter how poorly their personal fortunes are faring, they can often maintain a semblance of integrity and consistency. They are deeply good: a self in harmony, a sound spirit with a sound mind in, ideally, a sound body. They live a balanced life; a harmony of love, people, work, play, creativity coursing back and forth, at different times, along a spectrum of human attributes. They live in both worlds. Their life, devoted to learning, spans a broad dimension of experience: emotional, spiritual, intellectual, social, physical. Since their life is consistent with teachings of most of the great prophets of all religions, East and West, they would be welcome in any religion.

• WHAT ABOUT YOU? •

How spirited are you?
Can you relate any of the above characteristics to yourself?
Are you rooted totally in the world around you? Do you

have a sense of "cosmic accountability"? How powerful is your own will to existence? Do you ever use your seventh sense? Do you ever hope, aspire, or pray for "cosmic" help, by whatever name you choose to call it? Are you totally involved in the everyday life you lead, or do you save time each day for spirit? How do you get rid of your problems or cleanse your mind when it is troubled?

What is the state of your own spirit? Are you "harmonious" within yourself? Are you aware of "spiritual imperatives"? Can you freely express them in the world?

Are you de-spirited? If you are, how did this come to pass?

Why not do a systematic self-assessment concerning the state of your spirit to see how spirit-intelligent or spirit-ignorant you actually are?

To do this you must go beyond your halfmind.

To go beyond your halfmind, you simply give time to spirit. The first thing to do is to spend some time by yourself, so you may reflect on these matters in solitude.

One simple thing you can do is to go into your bathroom when things are quiet in your home, shut the door, and take a long look at yourself in a mirror. Relax, make some faces at yourself if you feel uncomfortable. What do you feel and think about the person you see? Can you look deep into your own eyes? Does it make you uncomfortable? Keep trying until you can look long and hard. How bright is the light in your eyes? Are you proud and admiring of what you see? Do you feel love for what you see?

Another thing to do is to take a long walk, preferably in a natural setting like woods or a park, and start thinking about things. Take this book with you or write down some of these questions, and review them when you are alone.

Try to observe the way your mind works and what it thinks about.

Are your thoughts positive or negative? Optimistic or pessimistic? Enthusiastic or jaded? Do you have a tendency to obsess about negative things, to focus on the faults of other people, to fret and worry about how you are being "wronged," to want to be where you are not? If you do, this means you are de-spirited to some degree. If your thoughts are joyful, it is a sign that you are spirited.

Think about your "local" world and the people whose lives you touch every day. Who makes you happy? Who troubles you? Can you improve these relationships? Whom do you make happy? Do you even think about making others happy?

How harmonious are you within your self? Can you separate messages from your halfmind, your body, and your seventh sense?

Have you polarized your life? Do you allow yourself spiritual time? Have you attained a balance between love, work, play, creative endeavors, physical and artistic expression—or do you go through life automatically, halfmindedly numbed out? Can you have fun? Can you experience pleasure, savor your food, delight in relationships?

Did you see yourself in any of the people or descriptions (robot, Scrooge, Faust) in the preceding pages? Reflect carefully on your answers for they will supply you with an agenda for action.

Life is short—you only live once. Those spirited people who believe that this life isn't "all there is" have in their hands what they feel is a powerful and practical life philosophy, one that offers the possibility of collecting the fruits of both the first and second orders of existence, and of becoming spirited.

What is your life philosophy? Have you ever thought about this before? If not, here's a helpful hint: Think carefully about the answer to the following question: "How do you want to be remembered when you die?"

Your answer will reveal to you much of your own philosophy of life. By comparing how you are actually living with how you would like to be remembered, you will end up with an agenda for the future—something to strive for. For example,

Sheila, thirty-five, wants to be fondly remembered as a loving, caring person by her children (because she doesn't remember her own mother that way) but on examining her actual life she found that she is joyless, irritable, rigid, and critical with them. Resolved to change things, she now takes one hour a day to reflect upon these matters and has vowed to be less rigid, more spontaneous and humorous. One of the things she now does is to leave the children "love notes" in their school lunches and under their pillows, which delights them. She even plays on the floor with them—something that she would never do before. Although this doesn't sound like very much, it has totally altered her children's perception of her.

Make this comparison for yourself. Start by unpacking all of your dreams, past, present, and future. Examine them carefully. If it's helpful, make a list. How does your present life stack up against your early hopes and aspirations? Reviewing the subjects of your daydreams will give you some clues to what you are frustrated about. Remember, daydreams may be part of the ineffable language—the voice of your spirit urging for fulfillment of spiritual imperatives. Common daydreams of "trapped" people concern "dropping out"—for example, living a leisurely life somewhere as opposed to working at a hated job, adopting a new and exciting career, making up for lost time with the people they love, or finding the romance that has gone out of their lives, or never was there. Those who live in an unpleasant reality and daydream their lives away are afflicted with the "Someday syndrome." This is a sign of ongoing de-spiritment. Don't let this happen to you.

What is the meaning of your life? What do you stand for? What would you die for? Are you proud of the way you have lived? Is your integrity intact? What are the worst things that you have ever done? Have you sold out? Betrayed your friends? Cheated? And for what price? How have these acts affected you?

Do you have a sense of cosmic accountability? Do you think of yourself as an important member not only of your family and your culture but of the universe? Can you call on "something more" for strength and solace when you are hurting?

Are you aware of "spiritual currency" as a reward for doing something good, something spiritual? Our society places an inordinate emphasis on "show" rewards as a sign of accomplishment—material goods, paid in the currency of the realm. This has become perverted in our society. Those with the most good seem to be viewed as the "most important," at least as long as they possess these goods. But any act of kindness, caring, loving, consideration, or charity accrues a more durable although less evident "reward" to the doer. Doing good makes people feel good. Because it is often a private act, goodness not only doesn't enrich the doer materially but others are usually unaware of the act's having taken place at all. People don't get paid money for helping a disabled person across the street, or planting a beautiful garden, or taking in a stray animal, or giving the kids on the block milk and cookies. But what they do feels good and makes others feel good about them.

BECOMING SPIRITED

Is it so hard to become spirited? Is this too "ideal" an existence for all but a few saintly people to aspire to?

Not at all, because you contain all of the answers to this quest inside of you, at this very minute. All you have to do to become spirited is to think about your spirit and learn to identify spiritual imperatives within you. Simply put, to go beyond your halfmind. Once you do this conceptually, then you may live your life accordingly. I am not suggesting that you throw your present life to the winds or abandon your responsibilities. What I am suggesting is that you make a considered appraisal of where you currently are in your life, compare your findings with where you want to be, and devise a plan to attain a more balanced, wholeminded existence. Then make it happen.

Remember, the only obstacles that impede your becoming spirited are the de-spirited values, attitudes, and conditioning present in your halfmind. Once you get rid of them, almost anything is possible. There's a way to reconnect with spirit and to regain your seventh sense.

RECONNECTING

In most cases reconnecting is possible because spirit is always present, even when the S-Connection is shut down. It is very important for you to historically review the evolution of your spirit throughout your life and to identify what enhanced it and what led to de-spiritment; create your *spiritual history*, so to speak. The careful consideration of these factors will help you formulate a plan for re-spiriting yourself. It is good for everyone to review their spiritual history, one especially important for psychotherapists to do with their patients.

Keep pushing beyond your halfmind to answer the following questions. Take your time with each of them. It may take you days to dredge up the memories, dreams, aspirations, fantasies, and attendant thoughts and feelings that these questions may bring to mind.

• *How were you treated as a child?*

It is important to be aware of the age at which your spirit first came under pressure. When a young child is either deprived of love or devastated by cruel authority, or both, the S-Connection can be severely damaged. To be healthy and happy, a child needs to resonate with other "kindred" spirits, especially its parents, to feel love and to thrive. This is very important.

How did your mother and father relate to you? Were they de-spiriters or spirit "gardeners"? I firmly believe that *a child's spirit is joined, in a way that I am unable to explain, to the spirits of its parents, and especially its mother. I further believe that a channel of spiritual communication exists between kindred spirits and especially mothers and their children.*

My belief is based on clinical experience, from what I have witnessed with my own eyes. One event that occurred when I was a pediatric intern is typical. In the nursery there was a newborn who, when her mother approached within ten paces (not more), would consistently turn her head in the mother's direction. What astonished me was that the baby was in an incubator and the mother was outside of the enclosed nursery where nothing—no sight, sound, vibration, or odor—could signal her presence. I was skeptical about this phenomenon, as any young physician would be, but the experienced older nurses weren't. As one said, "It happens all the time. Sure, kids know their mothers." When I asked the baby's mother about this, she expressed no surprise at all. "Sure," she said, laughing, "my own mother and I can read each other's minds."

Plenty of anecdotal evidence exists to support this view. Ask your friends and relatives if any unexplained communication exists between them and their parents or children. Now pause for a moment to think this over.

To whom is your spirit joined?

As a child you were born spirited. Intellectual and social growth came afterward. As a child your spirit was at one with those of your parents and grandparents and perhaps with all to whom you are biologically connected—even perhaps to a cosmic oneness that unites all consciousness and matter in the universe. This spiritual "oneness" between people explains the abundant affection and devotion that parents and grandparents have for their offspring, and that your parents probably had for you. It explains why parents lay down their lives for their children, something the halfmind would never do. This love is so powerful and meaningful that it can spring only from spirit. When a baby is born the kindred spirits of three generations naturally resonate with one another. This process is experienced emotionally and expressed as behavior: holding, kissing, cuddling, breast-feeding. If things of the halfmind don't interfere closeness between grandparents, parents, and child brings joy and happiness, and illuminates their collective spirits. It is a spiritual dance of love. The S-Connection flourishes.

What kind of relationships did you have when you were a child? Were you adored, or were you treated like "furniture"? What is your current relationship to the children in your life? Are you spiritually at one with any kids?

When children are deprived of the attention of a devoted and loving spirit, or are subject to parental and grandparental neglect or cruelty, they suffer and become de-spirited early in life. The earlier a child's spirit is "broken," the less chance there is of it eventually reconnecting, unless the child is a "spiritual genius" with an abundance of spirit.

When the opportunity presents itself, find out about your infancy from your parents, relatives, or anyone that knew you as a child. Look at your baby pictures. What kind of child do you see? What was the state of your spirit and the spirits of those who cared for you?

• *How aware are you of spirit within yourself?*

How spiritually endowed are you? What is the "quantity" and "quality" of spirit within yourself? (Reread the quotation at the beginning of this chapter to understand this question more fully.)

Spiritual endowment is important. It is the reason why not all children who suffer end up "broken." The exceptional child, endowed with abundant spiritual strength, who is hurt early in life protects its connection to its spirit while appearing to comply with cruel authority. How is it possible that people survive the greatest difficulties and emerge unscathed, even the better for it? The only explanation can be that they possessed such an abundance of spiritual intelligence and strength that they could endure untold miseries.

A child may protect its spirit by "hiding" it from the outside world, all the while seemingly acquiescing to the powers that be. During this period the child secludes its spirit within an internal sanctuary. The spiritually strong or gifted child who copes with adversity in this way temporarily goes underground. The child's spirit awaits an opportunity to reemerge within the self and into the world another day. Lila, a nineteen-year-old singer, lived in a ghetto until she won a scholarship to a prestigious music school. "I lived in a slum. My home was a mess," she said. "I had no father to speak of. My mother was always bringing men home. I took care of my brothers and sisters. My only sanctuary was my music. I lived my life with earphones on. I always liked the sound of opera. It took me out of my house to a beautiful place far away, and I always knew—a little voice told me—that if I worked real hard, I would get there someday. My mother needed me to take care of the family. I got started singing in church. Would you believe it? I had to sneak out of the house to go to church. And I loved to sing to God. Church was a sanctuary for me, too. It showed me there was another life possible. Music and church saved my life."

Ernie, a youngster who had an abusive alcoholic father, told me that he used his garden for a sanctuary. "It was the only place where I felt peace. When I put my hands in the soil and I watched those vegetables come out of the ground, from nothing . . . and when my father tied one on and he came after all of us, I would hide in the garden and snuggle into the ground and dream of having my own farm one day."

What happened to your spirit when you were young? Was it "out there," or did you have to put it away?
• *Have you had a mentor?*

A third factor that helps people whose spirit is under stress is being fortunate enough to find a helper—a mentor, a helping hand to their spirit. A mentor may be an inspiring person or a person with an inspiring idea or belief. Many people who claim to have had a religious experience, to have "been saved," are eloquent in testifying how they were removed from a state of abject de-spiritedness, transformed for the better, and discovered a new and exciting reason for living—because of a mentor. Mentors come in many garb: friends, clergymen, loved ones, relatives, teachers, or even bosses.

What important people in your life have touched your spirit? Who has loved you and whom do you love? Are you a mentor for anyone?

• *Has your S-Connection been under stress?*

How long has your S-Connection been under stress? A brief de-spiriting encounter will have little enduring effect. A long-term de-spiriting relationship is more malignant.

What is currently stressing your own S-Connection? When did it start? How do you feel it? What can you do about it?

• *How "Faustian" are you?*

The "Faust syndrome" concerns your own responsibility for surrendering the S-Connection in the first place. Have you sold out? How? For what reward? How has this affected your self-esteem? How much would you allow people to read the book of your life openly? How much guilt and shame do you walk around with?

Tell yourself the truth. However grim your answers to these questions, even if you have "sold out," rest assured that you can make amends to yourself and start over. Reconnecting is not difficult once a person decides to make the effort. And you can start at any age. Today is the best time.

REORDERING PRIORITIES

Believe it or not, awareness of the fact that life on earth is finite and that everyone dies some day is a powerful piece of knowledge. Think about the implications of this idea. It makes things of the first order pale in importance.

There is an amusing story, adapted from Yiddish folklore (cited by Dr. Bernie Siegel in his excellent book *Love, Medicine and Miracles*),[1] that illustrates how easily people fail to recognize when spirit is operating. A patient is told by his physician that his disease is incurable and that he has one day to live. Distraught, he pleads with God to save him. God answers: "Don't worry, I will save you." "Thank you," the man says, sobbing. Then his doctor returns. "I've been thinking about you," he says. "If you take these pills, there's a chance that you will be saved." "No, thanks," says the patient. "God will do it." Shortly afterward a nurse arrives with a teaspoon full of medicine. "Take this and you'll be okay. It worked for my mother," she says. The patient sends her away. "God will do it for me," he tells her haughtily. He goes to sleep with a smile on his face. When he awakens the next morning he is flabbergasted to find himself in heaven. He finds God and runs up to him: "Hey, God!" he shouts. "Here I am dead and you said you would save me." God looks at him with an exasperated expression on his face and throws up his hands: "Don't yell at me, dummy, I sent you a doctor and a nurse, didn't I?"

That's what happens when people aren't tuned into the seventh sense—opportunities are missed.

The belief in "something more" than our brief passage on earth even though its workings are mysterious, helps people to put things in proper perspective, to take life on earth less seriously, and to live it a lot better. This belief, and its attendant curiosity, helps you to go beyond your halfmind, to be open to your seventh sense and make your everyday life infinitely richer. I hope you've answered the preceding questions for yourself and are now thinking about things in a more spiritual way. Following are some practical suggestions to help you use spirit in your life. Becoming spirited or not is solely up to you. If you want to do it you can. There is no earthly reason that can stop you.

Remember, you only live once. Your time on earth is limited; everyday life is finite. You are accountable to your spiritual imperatives first, before the "party line" of the culture in which you live. By reviewing your spiritual imperatives, you will be able to formulate a life philosophy. Then try to live according to your philosophy.

Travel light in life, stay out of ruts; be mobile and flexible, so you don't get bogged down in a meaningless existence where all of your energies have to be absorbed in maintaining the status quo. The more material possessions you acquire, the more vulnerable to the Faust syndrome you become. If you enjoy material possessions, all well and good, but just be aware of the emotional and spiritual price that you are paying for them. For example, a man who chooses to spend his life working to pay for a beautiful home, snazzy cars, and sending his children to the "best" schools isn't guaranteed happiness; in fact, after enough years he might become a stranger to his family, just because he has devoted his energies away from his home. Unless he can balance his life carefully, his wife and children won't really know him, and he easily might come to resent them for having fun spending his hard-earned money. Remember, the people that you love and who love you want *you*, not *things*. Especially kids. And if that's not the message you are getting, or the way they feel, then something is terribly wrong. It's time to sit down and talk this over with them. Find a healthy balance among love, work, and play, and do all three with spirit. If you and the people closest to you feel relatively happy, then most probably you are doing a pretty good balancing act. If not, change your priorities. Don't paint yourself into a "Faustian" corner.

If you are among the fortunate ones who have enough money to live the way they want to, change gears. Don't spend all of your time running after more and more money. Spend your days in more spiritual pursuits. Sure, if you are a businessperson you have learned that money is your "scorecard," but how much money do you need? Start a *spiritual* scorecard. Spend time with your family. Help other people. One high-powered businessman I know switched gears and spends two days a week baby-sitting his grandchildren. In fact, he is teaching them about the stock market. A woman I know started a historical society in her town and used it as a rallying point to get local youth involved in constructive projects. A businessman in New York pays the college tuition of local underprivileged youths if they make the necessary grades.

You need spiritual time. Don't make yourself miserable by overcommitting yourself. Our society demands too much of us; we have to be all things to all people: to be skinny, athletic, "brilliant," to work hard, love, play, to be always "on." Women have to be wives, mothers, children, workers; men have to be fathers, husbands, workers, community leaders, jocks. It's exhausting. These demands are beyond the abilities of most people to fulfill. There is too much to do and too little time to savor life. The curious thing is that the way we live is not etched in stone—we *choose* to live like this. Whose fault is it, for example, that children have to wait on a snowy cold street for a school bus at seven o'clock in the morning, that families don't have breakfast together, that commuters get home after their kids are asleep, and so on? *Ours.* We have created a society that doesn't fit our natural, biological needs. We have to adapt to *it* instead of *it* adapting to us. Ridiculous, isn't it?

Don't accept it without a fight. Think carefully before you make a commitment, whether it be to a job, or to a person. How will this commitment upset the spiritual balance you are trying to achieve? Is the commitment worth the emotional and spiritual price that you will inevitably pay to fulfill it?

This admonition is especially relevant for prospective parents. I have reached a point in my own thinking that I now believe that people who are by their characters *totally and permanently work-oriented* may spare themselves untold stress by remaining unmarried. And certainly, if they do get married, spare themselves by not having children. (I am not talking about a temporary "workaholic" situation that is time-limited and necessary.) This might seem to be a radical statement, but what's the sense of work-impassioned people drawing and quartering themselves between their work and family? Better not to have a family if they can't moderate their passion for their career. Surely they can compensate for their needs for intimacy and family in other ways, for example with an uncommitted romantic relationship or by nurturing other people's children. Saints have done it!

If certain responsibilities are unavoidable, then carefully plan what you can do to limit the emotional and spiritual damage that might result from fulfilling them. For example, mothers who have to work should demand to have a day-care center in the workplace. There is no logical reason why flex-time can't be "institutionalized" so parents can have the opportunity to balance their lives better. Fathers can demand time off to attend their kids' important school functions. Better yet, if it's possible, work at home or near your family so you can see them during the day. Opening a family business is one way of doing this. Use your own creativity to balance things.

Guard your integrity. It's a permanent part of you. It is a major ingredient of your own self-esteem and self-image; wear it on your sleeve for others to see. Integrity in a parent forms the basis of children's respect. Integrity in a marriage ensures the deepest sense of trust and commitment, the perfect soil for love to flourish in. Integrity in a friend assures a vital connection for life. Integrity at work insures permanent respect. So no matter how great the temptation, try not to sell out. Avoid dishonest dealings. I have previously explained the difference between guilt and shame. An assault on integrity results in shame, and that erodes spirit. Andy, forty, is the president of a large retail chain. But he has never been happy in his job because he "screwed" a friend to get there. "When we were competing for this job I put him down in front of the bosses and behind his back. He never had a fair chance. He was too loyal a friend and too good a person to retaliate. I hurt him terribly. Now when I see him he turns the other way."

If you are involved in a de-spirited system, be heroic and change it. If you can't change it, leave it, no matter the cost. Otherwise you might become de-spirited, too. Loretta, twenty-five-years old, got a job in the garment district. Her boss wanted to pay her a minimum wage but claim that he paid her a higher salary on his income tax form. For this he promised to give her some money "under the table." Loretta refused and two weeks later was fired. Although she was quite upset at the time, she eventually opened up her own button supply business and became quite successful. Maria, a young secretary, was fired because she "wouldn't sleep with my disgusting boss." She found a better job. Myron, thirty-five, sold his shares in a successful business because "both of my two partners wanted the other out and each tried to get me to give the other the shaft. I didn't want to do that, so I arranged to leave. Now they are killing each other."

Don't trap yourself in a one-track life that allows you no time for spirit, artistic expression, or physical exercise. These are the basic requirements for a balanced existence. Don't give them up. Remember the best way to prevent becoming robotlike is to be constantly involved in some type of artistic, creative process. What works for some people is pursuing an interest in art, music, crafts; for others it is noncompetitive solitary physical activities like walking, biking, or running. The relaxation response, as described by Benson (*The Relaxation Response, Your Maximum Mind*), is a simple, practical, and flexible method to focus your consciousness away from the everyday world for a short period of time.

And read, read, read. Read all of the great philosophers once again, and the novelists and playwrights and poets—read as much as you can, whenever you can. Keep a good book with you at all times. Books are an important source of enduring spiritual knowledge. Sure, if you need a soporific, watch your favorite TV program. Otherwise—read.

Pay special attention to the ongoing battle that constantly wages in your mind between first-order influence and the ineffable language of the spirit. Stay with your seventh sense as much as possible and insure that your relationships stay in that realm, too.

Reflect on this before you fall asleep. Review the events of the day, then review your feelings about them. Did you act according to spiritual imperatives? If you didn't, why not? If you think that you didn't do your best for yourself or others, make amends the next day. Al, a fifty-six-year-old publisher, while reviewing his day before he fell asleep realized that he "de-spirited" one of his young editors by harshly criticizing him during a staff meeting. He resolved to make amends. The next day he took the young woman out to lunch and had a personal talk with her. Jim, thirty-four, had a fight with his wife at breakfast and sent her flowers at lunchtime. Florence, forty-five, was madly in love with her husband but less interested in sex than he was, although she didn't dislike it. He was constantly complaining and unhappy about their infrequent lovemaking. She "made herself do something about it." One of the things she did was to get a hotel room one afternoon near where he worked and tell him to meet her there at lunchtime. "You'd think I gave him a million dollars," she said. "He's a great guy. If he's happy that's what is important. Then I am happy, too. It goes back and forth. He's good to me. I am good to him, in the things that we both like."

Be alert to the difference, so prevalent in our society, between conditional and unconditional love—love given for performance or for pleasure. Remember, the degree of spiritedness in a relationship, especially a romantic one, determines its quality. Don't let spirit disappear from your relationships.

This admonition is especially important as it concerns today's children, who are increasingly being looked upon as "products" by their parents and "consumers" by society. Let me give you an example of what I mean. Johnny, five years old, bangs away at the family piano one day and serendipitously produces a few pleasant sounds. He is having a great time in this pleasurable activity. But his mother, thoroughly conditioned into the first-order way, views her child's play not as a way for him to have fun, but as something to bring satisfaction to her and to make him famous. "My Beethoven!" she cries, and bundles a bewildered Johnny, now a prodigy, off to piano lessons, thus effectively stuffing his piano playing into a first-order cubbyhole. What was a delightful pastime for the child now becomes work—halfminded performance subject to rules and measurement. His mother doesn't get off scot free, either. What once delighted her now makes her miserable; she's the one who has to drag him screaming to his lessons and make sure that he practices. The fun is gone.

Understanding the differences between pleasurable activities and the pressures of performance will equip you to be a spiritual guide for children, a countervailing force to a society that is constantly "measuring" and "classifying" the poor kids. Allow children to experience as much appropriate pleasure as possible. Don't view them as products. Don't stuff them into a first-order blueprint. Guide them, don't push them, and above all listen to them—listen to the oracle in them. Let them know the essence of you. Read to them. Tell them your stories. In this way you will foster their spiritedness.

Balance your life. You can do it. It is amazing how so many people who feel trapped or are frightened about change learn that it is not reality impeding their growth but their attitudes. There are ways out. It may take a bit of ingenuity to integrate love and work, for example. But, with time, attention, and careful consideration, most people can do it. At the least things can always be improved. The ideal, of course, is to integrate both orders into one's existence. There is no excuse for not "spiriting" your personal relationships with a well-mannered and cheerful disposition. This might be more difficult in a grim work environment where a cheerful disposition may be looked upon negatively (some bosses think that if you are happy you are not working hard enough).

If you are the boss, tend to the spiritual well-being of your employees. Set a spirited example. For instance, how about giving them some time off to volunteer in a nursing home or day-care center for a short period every month or to teach one afternoon a week in a local school? Create an on-site day-care center. If you think that this will decrease their work performance, you are wrong.

Business doesn't have to be the death knell for spirit, but it often is. I have been told by many successful businesspeople that they feel trapped within the first order where they found success. They feared becoming permanently halfminded, infected by the ethic of "businessification," and incapable of freeing themselves of its influence, even if they wanted to do so. For them it's lonely at the top. If they don't shift gears all they have to look forward to is increasing de-spiritment. But there are always the exceptional few who have the ability, after their fortune is made, to proceed beyond their halfmind and rummage through their childhood dreams and endeavor to bring them to life once again. I know a person who did this. What he did was quite unique, and well illustrates how a compromise between the first order and the seventh sense can be achieved. His name is Martin. He is a successful entrepreneur who "just always has and always will love baseball."

To Martin, baseball is "a continuation of the dreams and games of my childhood that make me feel good. [Baseball] leaves me with a very good feeling all the time. It takes up a great deal of my daydreaming time. Sometimes in the middle of a stressful time I will daydream baseball situations—myself pitching to some of the great hitters and getting them to ground out. It's also relaxing. I will be thinking of a business situation and for one reason or another, that I am not conscious of, my mind will dream baseball."

Martin made his dreams come true, by integrating a first-order imperative—making a living—with his love for his beloved game. He did something that most people would not have the means to do—he bought a baseball team.

This move, for him, achieved an integration between the first and second orders of his life. An article he wrote stands as testimony to both sides of his stroke of genius. In the article, after explaining the financial pros and cons of owning a sports franchise, he added: "People ask why I want to do a fool thing like get involved in a baseball franchise. Here's my answer." And he wrote a poem that would stir the heart of any child of any age who ever loved or played baseball.[2] (See Appendix D.)

Like Martin, a multitude of others, whether they are mothers, laborers, professional people, or shopkeepers, have found ways to use their work as a vehicle for the expression of spiritual imperatives. People who are able to do this, no matter what kind of work they do, feel fulfilled and are most always given a great deal of respect by others.

Does your work allow you to express spiritual imperatives?

Remember, it makes no sense to work permanently at a job you dislike or to dream away your life wishing you were somewhere else. Plan to do something to change your situation as soon as you can appropriately do so.

But what if you are genuinely trapped in a job you don't like, or at least you have convinced yourself of that? Do you have to resign yourself to being an unhappy person? Not at all. You are not helpless. If you are *truly* trapped, plan either to change things at work or eventually leave. If not, start looking at another career. Use your spirit. If the place is unpleasant physically, then spruce it up. Remember, don't concern yourself about what other people think. Just do what you feel is right and use the power of your spirit. If people at work are unpleasant, if your boss is grouchy, don't get infected by their de-spirited state. You can still be cheerful, well mannered, attractively dressed, kind, considerate, and interested in your co-workers and their welfare no matter how they act—and you can call on your spirit to help. If you ignore the negative feedback you get from the "outside" and focus on the satisfaction you get from expressing spiritual imperatives, from making the world that you touch a better place, well, that's its own reward. You will also be surprised to find that by supplying a good example and not participating in the negative system, the place gets better. At the same time, look for other opportunities. Go to school if necessary, no matter how long it takes. Just knowing there is a way out will help you tolerate the daily drudgery much better. The secret is to keep a dream in the forefront of your mind, and work to make it come true. Learn to deal in spiritual currency. Be alert to the spiritual cost of your life decisions. Social imperatives often make it hard to do this. Our country is full of families that live thousands of miles from one another, grandparents who never see their grandchildren, parents who never see their children. Such a separation is not worth the money that a job in a distant city might bring. What is sad is that often people make these choices freely and unthinkingly because they weren't thinking about spirit when they made them. One of the most moving experiences in my life occurred while I was addressing a gathering of young parents in a western city on the subject of grandparents and grandchildren. Most of them were displaced easterners and Californians. At the end of my talk I noticed that several young women in the audience were weeping. The same young women showed up at an afternoon workshop that I held. About forty other men and women were there, too. It was an emotional meeting. After about a half hour of people venting feelings, complaining, agonizing, and sobbing about how much they missed their parents and how hard it was to be isolated from their families, there wasn't a dry eye in the room. I was as moved as my listeners. The experience graphically demonstrated how it feels to pay a spiritual price for a life decision; most of the people at that meeting had left their families to seek work or adventure.

Think about the spiritual implications of your acts. Good deeds will enhance your happiness and self-respect. You will benefit in other ways, too; recent studies in the emerging field of psychoneuroimmunology suggest a pay-off in better health. Boston University psychologist David McClelland and his colleagues showed college students a film of Mother Teresa tending to the sick and dying of Calcutta. The immune functions of the audience (measured by blood concentration of serum-immunoglobulin-AD) increased. This happened even in people that professed not to like Mother Teresa. McClelland noted this "Mother Teresa was contacting them in a part of their brains that they were unaware of and that was responding to the strength of her tender loving care."[3] Although Robert Ornstein, responding to McClelland's study, stated that McClelland "has gone beyond what the data support," he went on to ask: "Could attention to the larger group [of people], away from our biologically primary but primitive focus upon ourselves, and away from the hostile reaction to others, be something we are also organized to resound to?" He finishes this commentary with "we may well have to think differently about how closely we are related to others in order to understand ourselves . . ."[4]

Start to use your seventh sense in your relationships. Remember, don't allow people to make you act in a nonspiritual way. Of course this isn't easy to do. We are only human, still most of us can do better. A negative attitude, seeing the glass half empty instead of half full, is terribly destructive. Yet this kind of attitude pervades our society. A child brings home a B on his report card and his parents say "Why not an A?" A man brings home a new tool kit, joyously shows it to his wife, and she says "Why do you need that?" A woman happily shows her husband a new dress she just bought and he gives her a lecture about money. People go around with a grouchy expression totally ignoring how much what they do, or how they look, affects other people. We seem to be unaware of, or we consciously ignore, our ability to depress or illuminate the people we live with, and the places we inhabit. Be aware of making people smile, and making everything that you touch better, especially with children. They depend on you for their happiness.

You can do this. Don't be a slave to your fears. Don't be accountable to the world, be accountable to your spiritual imperatives and the world will follow. If you want better relationships with those close to you, tell them how you feel and get to work on it. Don't avoid the people that you have problems with, get rid of the problems. If you find yourself unable to do so, find a therapist who can help you change things in your character that you don't like.

Listen to what the people you love criticize you about. What they say is most probably true. Instead of getting angry at them for what they say, use it as an agenda for change—as learning.

Give time to your spirit in your love relationships. Remember, one of the most important and clearest things that emerged from this study is that relationships wither when spirit dies, and when unconditional love is removed. Don't let this happen to your loves. You must spend time alone, in a relaxed environment, to nurture love relationships. This is very important for married people to do. Make sure that you have at least one night during a week and some time on a weekend when you can get away with your spouse. If you have kids, ask your friends or relatives, especially grandparents, to pitch in and help. Get away with one another, alone, as often as possible, and don't "do" any business or other work on your vacation. If one of you can't sit still that long to enjoy some peaceful nonstructured time, get some help so that you can do it. During your time together don't criticize one another; bite your tongue if a critical thought comes into your mind. Make each other happy. Don't judge, measure, control, or be bossy. It kills romance.

Practice having fun. Be good to the people you love. Spend time with them. Care for them. Garden them. Spend time with them doing natural things, creative things. Keep your halfmind out of your love life.

And spend time with children. They will lift your spirits, realize that you are necessary to them. Most adults are unaware of how much children love them, need them, and respect them. Whether you are grandparent, parent, aunt, uncle, cousin, or friend, enjoy the children in your world by being warm, loving, kind, understanding, and noncritical toward children. You will gain a kindred spirit for life.

Here are some thoughts to consider daily.

Examine your schedule. If you haven't programmed enough spiritual time, then do it. Before you fall asleep each night, think. Did you nourish your self by spending some "spirit-time" during the day? Did you live the day exclusively in the first order? If you did, prescribe a spiritual day for yourself. Remember a simple equation: no spirit, no happiness.

Tune into the ineffable language. When you awaken in the morning, review your dreams. What are they telling you about the state of your spirit? Are they happy dreams? Are they tumultuous? Remember, tumultuous dreams mean that something is bothering you. Do some detective work and find out what it is. Then change things. Cynthia, twenty-two, had a recurring nightmare that she was falling, but she always woke up before she hit the ground. She realized that her terror represented the way she felt about her existence and "falling" represented her self-destructive attitudes, which resulted in her living from crisis to crisis. She sought therapy to change what she was doing to herself.

Review your daydreams, too. They can be converted to an agenda for action if you can decipher their meaning. What are the themes in your daydreams? How are they related to frustrated spiritual imperatives? Are you longing for love? Freedom? Creative expression? What's blocking you from expressing these imperatives—social imperatives, biological imperatives, your attitudes, fears, character structure? What else?

Once you have figured things out, reevaluate your priorities, discuss your plans with those whom your subsequent decisions might affect, and then act. Sure, it might be scary. Giving up a job you do not like or moving from a place where you'd rather not be or changing a "zombie-fied" life that's making you a lot of money is not easy. Although settling for a frustrated existence, out of fear or insecurity, may make sense to the halfmind, I assure you that what may seem to be the "practical" thing to do for the moment can be de-spiriting over the long term.

As you become spirited, spread it around, and be courageous in doing so. Adopt a spiritual attitude toward your community. If you see something wrong, do something about it. Help others. There is a lot to do out there. There is no reason why we have to live in filthy environments. Do what you can. If you live in an apartment building, don't worry about what others are doing, keep your area clean. After all, you live there. One woman I know in New York City sweeps her street every morning to the initial amazement of her neighbors, which soon changed to admiration. "I don't care what people think, or that keeping the streets clean is someone else's job. The point is that I live here. My baby plays on this street. I can wait for someone else to do it, or complain that it never gets done, like most people do . . . but that means that I have to continue living in filth. And I don't want to."

So make your community the type of place in which you want to live . . . and if you have to raise hell to do it, without physically hurting others, that's okay. It's part of our American tradition. Remember, if you are rooted in spiritual imperatives it doesn't matter what others think about you. It's what you think about yourself and how you fulfill your imperatives that matter. Remember Patrick Henry's example.

Fight for what's right . . . and what's right has to do with the expression of spiritual imperatives. Don't let the de-spiriters dominate you or your world. What have you got to lose?

You only live once, right?

What can the everyday world *really* do to you if you are rooted in your spirit?

Not much in the long run.

TOWARD A LONG VIEW OF LIFE AND A SENSE OF COSMIC ACCOUNTABILITY

We stand on the threshold of a golden opportunity to make things better than they ever were for all mankind here on earth. We must not step over that threshold as halfminded, de-spirited beings. I hope that this book will help in that regard.

I would like to end on a personal note. For me, doing the study, discussing the subject with my friends and colleagues, and writing this book has been an illuminating experience. By so doing I have myself become more spiritually knowledgeable. I see the workings of spirit where I was blind to it before. I see kindness, altruism, joy, giving, caring in a clearer light. On the other hand, pain and misery seem more apparent, too, especially as it concerns young children. I see people settling too easily for a first-order existence. And I feel sad for them, and especially because they are trapping themselves. I hope that this book will help them to improve their lot and in turn help *all* of our children.

I have emerged from this work knowing that indeed there is more to life than meets the eye. I can't realistically make a scientific case for this in light of the scarcity of "evidence." But I have learned that a long view of life is helpful in dealing with day-to-day living. I have learned that what is important are the outcomes of unfolding dramas, not the day-to-day ups and downs of things. I have learned that, in personal problems, what counts is commitment, which in its turn fosters the kindred relationship, a bond capable of absorbing many blows without breaking.

I have learned that we are ready to take a great leap forward in the helping professions, of relating spirit to our current knowledge. The medicine of the future will push beyond the boundaries of holistic theory to a place where spirit reigns over mind and matter, where the will to existence will be harnessed as an awesome force for good and its biochemical correlates will be well established. We will be able to do miraculous things with our bodies, not just by mentally willing it—mind alone is incapable of acting in this way—but by spirit supplying the vital force for mind and body to fulfill their potential. I plan to continue my own studies in this area, and I urge others to consider spirit in all aspects of the healing professions. Here's a brief example of how the concept of spirit can be applied in therapy.

JACKIE

Jackie, a tenth-grader, became increasingly depressed as she suffered together with her parents through their long and exceptionally stormy divorce. Her depression impaired her day-to-day functioning. In school her grades dropped and she became disorderly. At home she became angry and reclusive, socially she became, as suffering teenagers often do, "wilder and wilder." Her will to existence decreased. She said she didn't care if she lived or died. Her self-esteem and self-respect deteriorated as she became more and more involved in destructive behavior.

Her family brought her for help. Although she was unaware of her progressing dispiritment, once in therapy, Jackie began to express many of the "brokenhearted" feelings that she had kept from consciousness by creating a tumultuous "outside" world, which consisted of going from crisis to crisis. She said, "My parents are jerks for getting divorced. Why can't they work it out? Why do they have to destroy the family?"

I brought up the subject of spirit, saying that this was a wonderful part of her. How did the divorce affect this "part of her"? She sobbed and sobbed and talked about her pain.

"What part of you is doing all this destructive behavior? Surely it isn't your spirit?" We talked about the "computer" part reacting in an unthinking manner to what was happening in the everyday world. She began to realize how her halfmind was reacting and that there was indeed another part of her that was removed from the world. And it was a part of her that she had never paid much attention to, since she lived by her halfmind.

"How can you find a way to let your spirit run your life instead of your halfmind, which only reacts to 'outside' forces?"

She found a way. On that day, after four months in therapy, she sauntered into the office, report card in hand. She flipped it toward me in an offhand manner (I had told her the week before that I would like to see it). I smiled as I examined it. Her grades and behavior had markedly improved.

"That's great, Jackie, good for you," I said, unable to squelch my enthusiasm, and admiring the extraordinary effort she must have put forth in her studies.

"I got tired of getting bad marks," she said.

"All of a sudden?" I was taken aback. Up to several weeks before, she had ranted and raved against school.

"I wanted to do good, to be myself, not to hurt myself because I have been hurt. Not to repeat the same thing."

"What changed?"

"Something inside of me. I want to succeed."

"Why now?"

"I care more. And I was afraid that if I didn't do better I would get left back and that would be terrible."

"Terrible, how 'terrible'? In what way?"

"Embarrassing . . ."

"Embarrassing? But you knew that before. Why now?"

"I have more pride now. Getting left back is humiliating. The kids will laugh at me. I—I—would be embarrassed for myself."

"Pride, where does that come from? That's a new word for you."

"From inside of me, somewhere I never knew existed. I don't hurt any more. Before, my heart hurt like I was stabbed with a knife. Now it feels better since I am getting rid of my problems, so now I have pride and dignity and I can't make myself get left back. It's as simple as that. I decided to pay less attention to what was going on around me, having a good time, I mean, and more attention to my pride in myself. I did some bad things but I can forgive myself and start over. I'm only a kid.

"Well—" She paused, then laughed. "My spirit doesn't deserve to get left back—right?"

Jackie had connected with her spirit. This gave her another way of looking at things and removed her from her previous total immersion in the everyday world. Spirit gave her an alternative, while her material world remained the same. Since she now viewed the real-life authority figures in her life, her parents, as "jerks" because to her they seemed unable to handle their own lives, she had nowhere to turn for guidance and nurturing. So she went inside, to her spirit. Her remark about "paying less attention to what was going on around me" was an indication that she was focusing her attention inward and starting to reintegrate. She had found that the feelings related to "pride" helped her as a scorecard for her behavior. What swelled her pride was good, what diminished it was bad. Once the concept of pride was set in her mind, it initiated very positive behaviors; she was happier and she regained control. Once she turned toward herself, her difficult outside world diminished in importance. This is not a psychotic resolution to a problem, the kind that occurs when people remove themselves from reality. On the contrary, Jackie took over her life, with the aid of "pride," and changed it for the better.

She learned the profound meaning of the common saying "You only live once," and its implications—that life is a jewel in a larger setting and the best life is lived in terms of outcome, and her outcome was yet unwritten. This view conferred, for her, some immunity from the normal miseries of life. She found an internal authority, beyond her halfmind, and found this authority to be consistent, reliable, loving, respectful, predictable, and decent. And it was hers alone.

Like Jackie, I have learned that a direct relationship with spirit is nourishing and rationally helps to place things in their proper perspective. The idea that an individual can live in the world and know that it is only "part of the whole" is comforting in time of stress.

I have learned that we all have the capacity to throw a spiritual switch in one another and to make each other happy. A simple smile and a kind word go a long way in this world.

I have learned with more clarity than ever something I found time and again in clinical practice: that we are all the same deep inside, and our differences, which get most of the attention, are superficial. What is wrong with the world is that people meet one another with the worst part of themselves— their halfminds. If we meet wholemindedly, we would see that we are all one. Our differences lie in our halfminds.

As far as spirit and matter are concerned, we are all connected with one another. When this spiritual truth is realized, taught to our children, and acted upon, our world will change for the better in a short while.

Until humanity becomes wholeminded, we will not have a golden age on our planet.

Until we have a golden age on our planet, we should stay put and not infect the cosmos with our problems.

Never, never should we travel to the stars, until we have allowed the stars to fill our selves.

· EPILOGUE ·
Toward the Medicine of the Future

The study of spirit and its workings within the self has enormous implications for understanding and treating various forms of mental distress and illness. Considering spirit makes it necessary to proceed beyond contemporary biopsychosocial and mind-body models that are currently used in conceptualizing and treating mental disorders. A new spirituo-mind-body model that includes spirit will, in my opinion, be the basis for the medicine of the future. Let me give you a brief idea of how I currently envision this model as I proceed to investigate its potential clinically.

As a person matures and becomes increasingly involved with the everyday world, spirit's capacity for expression depends on the resources—both innate and learned—of body and mind. Reverberating circuits set up a resonance, internally among spirit, body, and mind, and externally between the self and the environment.

Internally, the condition of the body—its health, its talents, its abilities—interacts with mind and spirit. When an "equipment" failure makes it impossible for spirit to be expressed, it may not only be denied issue into the external world, it will also become isolated from the mind. This leads to a state of halfmindedness and de-spiritedness.

There are an infinite amount of types of "equipment" handicaps. Some are evident to the eye; they may be physical, like cerebral palsy, or mental, like retardation, or both. Others are not so easily identified. The physical package may look fine but conceal biochemical handicaps that may have physical or mental manifestations—diabetes, manic-depressive illness, alcoholism. Anyone who has known an alcoholic or suffered from alcoholism is aware of the considerable spiritual price that this disease exacts on the patient and his or her family. Furthermore, alcoholism serves as a prime example of how a physical addiction can profoundly affect the mind and transform the personality of the sufferer, blocking the person's spirit not only from issuing into the world but also from issuing within the self. It only takes a short walk down your local skid row to see this in its most severe form.

Even temperament, which is part of our inborn "equipment," as Chess and Thomas[1] have shown, can cause problems. Attentional deficit disorder is one such condition with severe effects on children. Even "normal" temperamental variations can lead to suffering if (as they often do) they lead to the child's being criticized for it or when the individual finds that his or her temperamental pattern leads to impaired functioning—rigidity, overemotionality, compulsive behavior. All these quirks and foibles that compose the spectrum of human personality may cause different degrees of trouble because they impair the individual's spiritual expression.

At the extreme, spirit may be barred from emerging altogether if the bodily "equipment" is severely damaged. Again, this happens for physical reasons—in a coma, for example. Or it may be acted out in cruel behavior. Psychiatry categorizes people with these kinds of problems as "sociopathic"—persons with no "conscience" and no empathy for others. Peck calls these individuals the "People of the Lie," explaining that they are afflicted by "evil."*2

We have to deal with our "equipment" every day. Everyone finds it necessary to do some fancy footwork in order to deal with the constantly accumulating baggage of de-spirited attitudes and behaviors that the mind soaks up every day as a result of having to deal with the "equipment" we have been issued by nature.

Structurally the self is composed of three parts: spirit, mind, and body. For spirit to manifest itself within the individual and via the individual in the everyday world, mind and body must work together in the service of spirit. When they don't, or can't, the individual becomes increasingly de-spirited, the destruction of the self is triggered, body and psyche wither, and the will to existence disintegrates. When spirit is served by mind and body, the self lives life according to spiritual imperatives, and the will to existence flourishes.

This knowledge opens a new door for society's healers. Knowing that the relationship within the vital triad of spirit, mind, and body profoundly affects mental and physical health, we must proceed beyond currently held mind-body formulations to include spirit. Ways must be found to apply this knowl-

---

*I do not agree that "evil" per se exists. For me "evil" is varying degrees of de-spiritedness. It is the absence of spirit, in essence a "short-circuited" mind and body running amok. This may occur in people of great mental or physical ability. The Nazi, Adolf Eichmann, an intellectually competent man surely, is one oft-cited example of the epitome of "evil." He was known to have proposed a toast to his "technical" triumph when he heard the news from Auschwitz that the executioners under his orders had attained his "production goal" by destroying 25,000 Jews in one day in the gas chambers.

edge practically to the alleviation of pain and suffering arising from pathological states of spirit, mind, and body, created by de-spiritment.

These pathological states can be divided into three groups.

The first includes mental problems that exist without hereditary "equipment" impairment. Experientially, they range from existential "angst" to mild depression arising from the inability of the self to express spiritual imperatives. This creates disharmony within the spirit-mind-body triad. In this group are such problems as neurotic conditions, unhappy relationships, and difficult work-related situations.

The second group includes conditions where "equipment" is mildly impaired and the person can't do much to improve things. Temperamental disorders fall into this category. For example, I once worked with a man with "emotional dyscontrol." He had little conscious control over how he experienced the intensity of his feelings or the volatility with which he expressed them. He perpetually felt angry and frustrated at himself because he couldn't "control" himself. In his words, "It's like I am riding on a roller coaster, which is my emotions, and all I can do is go along for the ride. I can't be the way I want to be at times. I come across like a son of a bitch, and I'm not. And there is nothing I can do about it."

In this group of conditions spirit can break through some of the time and not at others. Personality problems (such as the ones cited above), biochemical impairments, addictive disease, and many others all fall into this category.

In the third group, the body's "equipment" is so severely impaired that spirit has little issue at all. This is true in degenerative diseases like Alzheimer's, infantile autism, sociopathy, and the like.

Conditions within the first two groups result in varying states of "reversible" de-spiritment, and can be better treated when a dualistic traditional mind-body approach is expanded into a triadic spirit-mind-body orientation. Unfortunately the third category of conditions is hard to help in any significant way.

Treating the total spirit-mind-body triad makes sense. Why treat one or two parts of the self when the cause of the problems lies within *all* of the self?

Thus I have begun to explore this possibility in a way that logically proceeds beyond the current boundaries of psychotherapy to a new transcendent, yet practically applied, psychology of the human spirit. I have named this therapeutic approach *integrative therapy*. Just as the purpose of psychoanalysis is to help the individual to integrate the microscopic mind functions of ego, superego, and id, the purpose of integrative therapy is to help the patient integrate the macroscopic functions of mind, body, and spirit. The goals of this therapy are to:

- Learn how the different components of mind, body, and spirit operate within the self and then to integrate these functions of the self by attaining a vital balance that includes spirit.
- Balance the expression of spiritual imperatives with psychological, biological, and social ones.
- Go beyond the halfmind.
- Vitalize the will to existence.
- Develop a relationship to others and the cosmos that transcends the individuality of the self.

Put another way, to proceed full circle, beyond individuality, to the state of oneness with spirit in which one enters the world and attains the final stage of human development.

I have begun to use this approach in my clinical work and am so impressed with the early results that I would like to share what I am doing. Understand that this is all very new and that I am constantly revising my formulations with every patient.

Here is the way I am currently proceeding with adult patients.

After a new patient has expressed the reasons for seeking consultation, emptied his or her emotional reservoir as well as possible, and assuaged the sense of urgency about the situation, I obtain a detailed *life history*. I proceed chronologically through the patient's life, paying attention not only to events and how they "felt," and medical history, but with a special ear to learning about the evolution of the patient's spirit-mind-body relationship. I listen attentively with the hope of identifying de-spiriting forces that affect the patient. Along the way I ask myself what enhances spiritual expression in this person. What circumstances diminish it? What is the patient's assessment of his or her vitality and will to existence? At the appropriate time I explain the concept of integrative therapy to the patient and we discuss its implications in detail.

We then proceed to an *everyday life review*. This is a thorough physical, psychological, and spiritual assessment of the patient's existential state. It includes a mental status exam, a physical workup, and other evaluations. The complex dynamics of the interaction among spirit, mind, and body, as experienced by the patient in the present and past, is explored. The state of the patient's de-spiritedness is assessed in terms of the battle among spiritual, social, and biological imperatives and how it has affected the choices and the way of life the patient has chosen. A diagnosis—an explanation of the patient's condition and its causes—is offered in terms of traditional medicine and psychology (mind-body) as well as from an integrative (spirit-mind-body) point of view.

The *final diagnosis* identifies the degree of de-spiritment and describes how the individual parts of the triad are affected: de-spiritment, mental depression, physical exhaustion. We then proceed to formulate a treatment program that is specific for each aspect of the triad.

In the *treatment plan,* I present the *goal* to the patient: to help him or her achieve harmony among spirit, mind, and body and restore the vital balance within the triad.

As for the *technique,* I use the traditional patient-therapist diadic relationship.

Integrative therapy is essentially spiritual-emotional learning with the goal of returning the patient to a spirited state. It consists of teaching patients to be aware of the workings of each part of the triad within, and applying the philosophy and concepts set forth in this work to their lives. Spirit, mind, and body are explored and dealt with. For the spirit, the patient is urged to work on gaining access to spirit by increasing "spiritual time." Doing this also provides sanctuary from the everyday world and from constant halfmind programming. Each individual chooses whatever personal and specific practices he or she finds helpful. This may range from prayer or other traditional religious practices, "imaging," the "relaxation response," musical or artistic pursuits, communing with nature, or some other activity. I urge that patients spend at least two hours a day in the spiritual dimension of their existence.

Psychotherapy is the treatment of choice for the mind. This is of paramount importance, because it is the mind that negotiates the entrance of spirit into the world. Thus the patient is helped to "unpeel" the layers upon layers of negative psychological attitudes and behaviors learned from the everyday world, which block spirit's connection to the mind-body. To empty the halfmind, I use a traditional psychoanalytically oriented psychotherapeutic focus.

Destructive health habits kill, so the patient is taught to become aware of his or her body and learn how it resonates with spirit and mind. Healthful habits are encouraged. Attitudes and behaviors that are destructive to physical health are explored in light of how they contradict the patient's will to existence.

During this process I freely recruit other people—professionals or specialized groups—on the patient's behalf. Thus family, friends, clergymen, teachers, or others may be present at sessions. In addition, when indicated, I urge patients to attend groups like Parents Without Partners, Alcoholics Anonymous, Weight Watchers, or whatever is appropriate.

Integrative therapy is built on solid and diverse foundations of knowledge. It not only includes treatments and methodologies that are currently being practiced in the field of psychiatry—such as "talking" therapies, psychopharmacology, physical health practices, and so on—but brings spirit into the therapist's office. All it does is simply add a spiritual dimension to the treatment process, professing that happiness is related to the successful expression of spiritual imperatives (being "spirited") and misery to the frustration of their expression (being "de-spirited").

In the brief time that I have been practicing integrative therapy I have found that it is quickly effective, for the most part. Patients come to view themselves as a part of something much bigger, infinite. They move beyond the narcissistic developmental station of individuality, the "me," beyond the "I"—"thou," to the "we," the "one."

Conceiving of oneself as a vehicle of spirit transcends the perception of the self as an isolated entity and imparts a sense of responsibility that is not only personal, but cosmic. Conceiving of the self as a part of "something more" roots the person in another dimension of existence that offers the self a sanctuary beyond the turmoil of the everyday world. As perceived by the wholemind, this notion offers another reality, another rationale, for living. It necessitates a responsibility to, and for, something much larger than the self. Once accepted, this notion is immediately therapeutic—a powerful countervailing force to narcissistic implosion, which is the basic ingredient of all neurosis.

The idea that one's psyche and body are vehicles for the

expression of spiritual imperatives into the world, and that the expression of these imperatives makes for a stronger, happier, and fulfilled person, gives profound meaning to existence. Once the idea is accepted, a broader life view is possible and things of this world pale in importance and, because they are placed in a context of a larger reality, are more easily dealt with. Let me emphasize that accepting a cosmic and spiritual reality is an active and assertive process, unlike the experience of some religious converts who just passively "surrender" their problems to a higher force. Often this "conversion" is only a rationalization for throwing in the towel in life.

Integrative therapy does not lead to a passive relinquishment of the responsibilities of existence by placing the self in another's hands. On the contrary. With this new therapy patients have evolved to a point where they live with one foot in the everyday world and the other in the cosmos. They learn how to slug it out with everyday life because they are not totally immersed in it. Their ethical, moral roots are in another place, so that they become resistant to de-spiriting situations.

All this is good.

And it's only the beginning.

· APPENDIX A ·
A Short History of Spirit

In contemporary society, religion holds domain over spirit. Although not deigning to "prove" scientifically that spirit exists, every religion believes in its existence in some way. Faith aside, religion supplies "soft data" for spirit's existence. Its universality, man's universal belief in a creative force is either a collective delusion or "soft" evidence that a force really exists in one form or another. (Everyone who saw the movie *Star Wars* responded emotionally to the line, "May the Force be with us.") Religious practices, the powerful argument propounding a world by grand design (which is now actually being flirted with by proponents of the "new physics"), and personal religious experience must also be taken into account. Aphorisms like "You can't fool all of the people all of the time" or "If it looks like a duck, walks like a duck, and quacks like a duck, it must be a duck" at least bring attention to the unprovable.

Of course there is well-founded opposition to this "soft data." Science attempts to explain the genesis of grand design in its own terms—dwarf stars, supernovas, and so on. For even the most skeptical, the religious argument cannot be totally and irrevocably discounted; although we may agree that consensus doesn't make for reality, we can as easily agree that where there is smoke there is fire.

Spirit is mentioned in the Bible: "And the spirit of God moved upon the face of the waters" (Genesis 1:1–3), and Jesus said, "Father, into thy hands I commend my spirit" (Luke 23:46). For William James, religion and spirit were one and the same. He wrote: "Religion . . . shall mean for us the feelings, acts and experiences of individual men in their solitude."[1]

Spirit is considered and talked about in religious circles. Religion proposes other dimensions to life, including another existence—a hereafter emphasizing the important point that perhaps there is existence, whether conscious or not, beyond what we know in everyday life. Certainly religion can extend consciousness beyond the halfmind and inspire, as religious art and music will testify.

Because the *practice* of religion is carried out by the halfmind, religion becomes instrumental—otherwise spirit could be well left in its care. The relationship of religion to spirit may be adversely affected by proprietary interest. Spirit, after all, does keep religious institutions in business. The possibilities for exploitation are infinite. An exploitative religion, a salespitch for the hereafter, can profit unscrupulously because it dispels the fear—that we label "God"—of the unknown.

When religion stands between the individual and creation it serves as a middleman. When this position is abused (some unscrupulous TV evangelists have created empires by exploiting religion), an organized religious institution can sequester the personal spirit and dominate it. Too many people already have willingly tethered their personal spirit to a communal religious flagpole and subsequently have lost intimate contact with its cosmic root. On the other hand, an ethical and moral religion can nurture the spirit, especially when people use religion as a foundation for living a spiritual life. At its best religion offers the self personal validation, a sanctuary for the spirit, spiritual communion with others, a meaning to existence, and a belief concerning the hereafter. These are sorely needed in a society that ignores the human spirit.

Whatever its assets and liabilities, religion has recognized spirit and offers a lot of "soft" support that spirit exists—impressive even if religion has a vested interest in that existence. Religion materializes what would be ignored by many. Right now, it is the main proponent of, and a safe place for, spirit on earth.

Philosophers, scientists, and cosmologists have heatedly argued over matters of spirit. Some dispute aspects of the relationship between spirit and matter. There are those who say that spirit and matter can't be divided. Others say they can. Some scientists have "de-materialized matter from objects to processes, fields and wholes."[2] Yet others claim that the argument is spurious and that spirit and matter do not really exist at all— that everything is pure consciousness. In *The Seth Material*, for example, Seth states, "We are individualized portions of energy, materialized within physical existence, to learn to form ideas from energy, and make them physical. We project ideas onto an object so that we can deal with it. But the object is thought, materialized . . . The entity is the basic self, immortal and non-physical. It communicates on an energy level with other entities, and has an almost inexhaustible supply of energy at its command."[3]

The philosopher George Santayana agreed with this view. He viewed spirit as "simply pure transcendental consciousness that must be distinguished from its physical basis."[4] Aristotle disagreed, professing that the soul is "a form . . . beginning with and ceasing to be with the body . . . nor can it in any way operate or exist without the body."[5] The soul, in Aristotle's view, stands to the stuff of the particular body as "the configuration of the statue to the material of which it is made, as vision to the eye capable of seeing, as cutting power to the serviceable ax."[6] Plato disagreed with Aristotle, equating the notion of soul with the principle of life. For Plato the idea of life is deathless and eternal, therefore "the immortal part of us is not destroyed by death . . . our souls will exist somewhere in another world."[7]

Plato's ideas have developed into a basis for themes that maintain that "soul is a substance, in the sense that it could be said to exist alone and disembodied."[8] Aristotle maintained in *De Anima* that the soul was not distinct, so the demise of the body meant the demise of the soul. He felt, however, that since no organ existed for the intellect, it was possible it could survive after the death of the body. St. Thomas Aquinas attempted to reconcile everyone's viewpoints in *Summa Theologica* by diplomatically stating that everyone is right and that the soul is both corporeal and subsistent. Santayana felt that a spirit existed, and although unable to intervene in the world it could achieve a freedom that represented the "highest and purest good."[9] Hegel also mentioned spirit, but in historical and cultural rather than personal terms. The Greeks held a unitary view of the universe, believing that there was no separation between spirit and matter. To them, matter was alive and endowed with *physis*. Descartes, building on this idea, proclaimed a dualist view. He divided the world into mind and matter, proclaiming *Cogito, ergo sum*—"I think, therefore I am." From the study of "matter" came Sir Isaac Newton's mechanistic worldview and the emergence of physics as a field of study. Today physicists are reconsidering a unitary view of the universe, basing their thesis on their observation that the universe shares a molecular commonality.

The great deal of controversy that surrounds matters of the spirit should make you confident that your own opinion on the subject is probably as valid as anyone else's.

Man has always sought a meaning—"a wholeness beyond

the self"[10] and thus has always been interested in spirit. Animism, for example, the belief in the existence of supernatural beings—spirits, ghosts—that interact with people, has been with us since the beginning of time. Native Americans view all things in the world as inhabited by spirits, creating an interconnected universe—a living, spiritual organic matrix overseen by a "Creator." In animistic cultures spirits were feared and had to be controlled. Thus the position of "controller" was created to intercede between man and spirit. The shaman became the first middleman. Shamans are also the "keepers of mythology, geneaology, belief systems, and the secret language of the tribe."[11] Religious clergy may also function as shamans. Most religions contain a mystic sect where this activity is sanctioned; the practice of exorcism is an example.

Eastern religions have approached the issue of spirit from a cosmic viewpoint, claiming that divinity may assume the shape of many-armed gods and goddesses answering to various names: Allah, Jehovah, Krishna, Brahman, Buddha or "I am that I am." For the Hindus God is widespread, a resident within everyone, universally connecting all as "one." Clergy function as teachers, wise men who point the way to cosmic "oneness."

Prescientific medicine has always been linked to the spirit. The ability of the mind and spirit to affect the body has generated cures linked to belief systems. The shaman started out as a religious healer and evolved into a scientist when religion and science parted ways. Contemporary psychiatry still uses, to the patient's advantage, some of the "art" of medicine based on techniques shamans have used over the centuries (suggestion, hypnosis, feedback, belief systems). Ideas of illness attributed to evil spirits are an integral part of primitive belief systems including voodoo (people actually can die when "cursed") and contemporary interest in the "placebo response" and the interaction between immunology and psychology.

The scientific method dispelled much of the "evil spirit" theory of disease causation. Of epilepsy, attributed to demonic possession, Hippocrates said, "They who first referred this disease to the gods appear to me to have been just such persons as the conjurors, purificators, mountebanks, and charlatans now who claim great piety and superior knowledge."[12] Hippocrates believed in a vital force that acted independently through the body but was bound to it. Galen (A.D. 130–200) believed that "natural spirits" were innate in all things. In his view, when natural spirits combined with vital spirits, animal spirits were created. This produced the rational soul, seated in the brain. Maimonides put forth a neo-Platonic notion of the "world intellect" arising in the Godhead and actualizing the soul and intellect in human beings. At death the actualized intellect remained as a collective emanation, a physical force, that influenced subsequent generations. During the Dark Ages, superstition, ignorance, and religious fanaticism ruled. The fledgling disciplines of science and medicine were outlawed. Aristotle's works were burned. After the Dark Ages, medical science came into its own, slowly detaching itself from religion. A dualistic view emerged. Contemporary medicine for the most part still adheres to this view. The separation of mind and body has caused medicine to become mired in an intellectual and mechanistic view of illness.

In the early 1800s natural scientists spoke of a "life force." This was "thought of as though supplementing in the living body the physical substances and forces as the magnetic force supplements the mere iron on the magnet."[13] Rudolph Steiner, a "spiritual scientist" who wrote in the early 1900s and who has left a considerable legacy, called the spirit the "hidden in all things,"[14] developed a comprehensive (including Eastern and Western theories and constructs) and complex theoretical system and devised a curriculum for spiritual learning that persists today. He believed that the spiritual man matured in the physical self just as the child matured in the mother's womb.

The arts are very much concerned with spirit. Spirit resonates to universals and to beauty—the nuts and bolts of artistic experience. "It is characteristic of the greatest art," writes Sullivan, "that the attitude it communicates to us is felt by us to be valid, to be a more subtle and comprehensive contact with reality than we can normally make."[15]

The arts deal in beauty and wonder and feed the spirit. "By viewing Nature," wrote Dryden, "Nature's handmaid Art Makes mighty things from small beginnings grow."[16] "Art is an expressive pathway for the creative aspects of the spirit . . . a way of one spirit reaching another, through its sensory voice. Inspiration is the pathway from the spirit to the mind and body of the artist." Artists know this, but again it is hard to prove—it is still only "soft data." Artist Ralph Fasenella said of his subjects, "The person breathes into me and I breathe into him. Then it [the artistic impression] comes out through me. If I dig deep enough, I touch other people."[17] Art, passing through the senses to the relay of the mind and then to the spirit, is subjectively perceived. What illuminates one spirit may do nothing for another. The only consensus to be found here is in the almost universal admiration people have for the great works of art.

Spirit has been addressed by writers and poets. William Faulkner wrote: "By artist I mean of course everyone who has tried to create that which was not here before him, with no other tools and materials than the uncommerciable one of the human spirit; who has tried to carve, no matter how crudely, on the wall of that final oblivion, in the tongue of the human spirit, 'Kilroy was here.'"[18]

Aristotle was aware of the spiritual universality that literature and poetry express. "Poetry is something more philosophic and of graver import than history, since its statements are in the nature of universals, whereas those of history are singulars."[19]

Examination of other cultures reveals a great deal about how man deals with the mysterious "something else." Those whom we in the West call "primitive" people (in the technological sense) can be more spirit "intelligent"—closely connected and sensitive to this dimension of existence. Descriptions of the nature of the primitives' relationship to spirit are to be found in anthropological and social science literature. I have already dealt with the history of psychology and the spirit in the body of this work.

· APPENDIX B ·
Altered States of Consciousness

In the bibliography and additonal references section, I have listed some excellent books that deal with the subject of altered mind-body perception. Obviously there is a great deal of controversy in this area, and justifiedly so, since it offers a field day to charlatans. Ersatz "spiritual" experience can easily be mimicked by toxic states, psychological aberrations, drugs, self-hypnosis, and in other ways. In spite of these drawbacks, which are often cited by skeptics, the fact remains that the timeless universality of these experiences makes them worthy, at the least, of discussion.

Altered mind-body perception refers to a group of phenomena that have in common an altered state of consciousness. In that state, the normal spatial relationship between the mind and the body is subjectively perceived as distorted. This altered consciousness spans a broad functional spectrum from mild depersonalization to frank mental illness. Although spiritual scientists like Rudolf Steiner alleged that these states are related to a different kind of cognition, allowing an individual knowledge of other dimensions of existence, the data used to support these premises is primarily anecdotal. No one really knows. Some of the most commonly reported states are:

- Out-of-body experience: A person's awareness seems to be separated from the physical body and the feeling seems more vivid than a dream. The sensation is one of floating out of the body, and is experienced as a pleasant one.[1]
- Depersonalization: The person feels separated and detached from the self, observing him or herself from the "outside." There appears to be a division into an "observing ego" and an "experiencing ego."
- Autoscopy. The experience is of the presence of a double— the existence of an illusory phantom of the self.
- Body-boundary disturbances in mental illness. All sorts of distortions in time and space are experienced by the person who is diagnosed as definitely mental ill according to currently accepted categories.
- Near-death experience. An experience often reported in many different cultures. It describes the feeling of rising out of one's body at the moment of death and traveling down a long corridor toward a brilliant light. There a "being of light" questions and reevaluates the person's life. Subjects return to the physical body with a sense of love and peace and the realization that they have undergone a profound emotional experience.

· APPENDIX C ·
A Healing Force

The self possesses a will to existence and a commitment to life that is rooted beyond the halfmind. When this will to live is strong, it recruits a healing force that originates, I believe, in spirit. This healing force activates the physiological "equipment" of the body not only to combat illness but to facilitate wellness.

Throughout the centuries shamans and religious healers have recognized a connection between nonmaterial genesis of physical and mental illness. To the modern mind, primitive man's "diagnostic system," which includes anthropomorphisizing spirit and attributing it to plants and animals as individualized "spirits" or ghosts seems childlike and naive. Such healers, by activating the spiritual consciousness of their passive and trusting patients and interceding for them with the "spirit world" (thus recruiting this "force" on their behalf), have achieved documented cures that baffle modern science. So, even if modern man believes that primitives are deluded in their beliefs, their cures are evidence that they are (and were) doing some things right.

One example of shamanistic medicine is the practice of sorcery in the Kuru tribe of the New Guinea highlands. The tribe recognizes two categories of illness: maladies due to malicious acts of men (acts of sorcery, curses, and spells) and diseases attributed to the assaults of various less malign sources (natural spirits and ghosts of the recently dead). Illness is inflicted by supernatural forces upon individuals who transgress tribal rules. Life-threatening diseases, such as liver disorders and serious respiratory infections, are caused by the malicious acts of men. Less malign sources cause minor afflictions or temporary illness.

In their belief system, "spirits," not "spirit" as I mean it, cause ailments when they aren't respected, as when sacred places are invaded. Illness allegedly caused by these forces are manifested by clear-cut disease syndromes. Such illness is cured by tribal healing methods—and the clinical syndromes really disappear. Healing is achieved by "placating spirits" and re-establishing harmony between man and nature. For example, a man awakening one morning with a stiff neck may gain relief by placating, with a gift of food, a "sacred" tree that he imagines he offended. Preventive medicine is practiced, too; when people die their possessions must be equally distributed, and in the prescribed fashion, or an angered "ghost" will return to wreak havoc on the offenders. If the distribution is done correctly misfortune is avoided.

When a person falls ill and can't attribute it to any cause, the shaman is called on. His role is to diagnose the illness, discover the cause (what spirit was offended and how), and intercede with and placate the offended "ghosts" or "sorcerers" to "heal" the sufferer's ailments.

And they do.

Lately the tribe has come to recognize another group of illnesses that are congruent with western medicine: nonsorcery-caused illness like epidemics, colds, headaches, and the infirmities of old age. These conditions have come to have "evident causes" and are excluded from the category of sorcery.

Western medicine may attribute the healing to hysteria, autosuggestion, or some other psychological factor, but the fact remains that these clinically evident illnesses appear and disappear. The healing abilities of shamans have been amply demonstrated in strict scientific studies. To date we cannot, within the context of western medicine, understand what is going on any more than we can understand the ability of people to submit to lengthy operations under acupuncture anesthesia.

But these things happen. That fact in itself is enough to stimulate further interest and inquiry into this fascinating subject. Dr. Jerome Frank has stated that the success of healing methods based on various ideologies and methods compels us to conclude that the healing power of faith resides in the person's state of mind.[1] I would add that healing power extends beyond the mind to spirit.

Obviously the shamanistic system of healing has its drawbacks for it leaves suffering people open to unethical charlatans, quacks, and zealots who ignore, or even deride, the abundant store of knowledge accumulated by modern medical science. Some religions that advocate "faith healing" are also guilty of this. Nevertheless, however mysterious its workings, the efficacy of what may be called "spiritual" healing (or, as I prefer, healing with the seventh sense) *has been established*.

A further mystery, unexplained by modern rational ideology, is that sometimes what cures the patient is not so much what the healer does; rather some force *within* the healer is responsible for the cure. Certain people are *gifted* with healing powers. The success they achieve with their patients arises not only from their worldly learning and experience but from this special talent. They seem to be able to influence the "life force" for good. Evidence supports Dr. Frank's observation that "Some healers serve as a conduit for a healing force in the universe, often called the life force, that for want of a better term, must be called supernatural. That is, [it] cannot be conceptually incorporated into the secular cosmology that dominates western scientific thinking."[2]

Most modern western medical healers have narrowed their interest to the mind-body dimensions of the self and for the most part ignore the possible role of "the healing force" in the universe. This notion doesn't match what they have been taught. Most learned, in their technologically polarized (half-minded) training, that if something can't be materialized and measured, *"ça n'existe pas"*—it doesn't exist. But since the possibility that a "life force" exists is so evident, medicine can't shove it completely under the rug. Thus the subject has been exiled to the back of the medical school classroom, its existence validated by being labeled as a "nonspecific factor" affecting healing (that is, the "placebo response") and relegated to the aegis of the medical school chaplains, psychiatrists, and those who work with dying patients.

Gifted physicians freely dispense "nonspecific factors" in the form of the wholeminded art of medicine known as "bedside manner" besides using the scientific knowledge lodged in their intellectual halfmind. They do it naturally, and many would be hard put to answer what role the "art of medicine" played in their success as healers. But their patients know the answer.

The primitives, nonscientific as they are, know this better than we do and accept it as part of the way things are. Many "modern" people I spoke with believe the same thing. "Proving" this notion is, of course, difficult if we stick to the tenets of "hard" science; it is easier if we trust anecdotes, emotions, and human experience. Establishing that spirit affects illness is not impossible as long as "scientific proof" is not required. What about emotional proof, spiritual proof, experiential proof, human testimony? At the least this must be considered.

INFLUENCE OF SPIRIT AT DIFFERENT
STAGES OF ILLNESS

Spirit may influence the process and nature of illness at different times and at successive stages. It is important here to reemphasize that spirit doesn't "get ill," it is the mind-body "equipment"—the vehicle of spirit—that does. Nevertheless, spirit has a crucial role to play in preventing and determining the course and severity of illness. For clarity's sake I have divided the course of illness into four broad stages. The first stage, vulnerability, occurs before the onset of the illness. The stressed individual is more vulnerable to illness. Medical science has confirmed that anyone who is exhausted, unhappy, or "run down," or whose mind-body is fatigued, is vulnerable to many different ailments: bacterial or viral infection, mental exhaustion, or varied other forms of disease. As an aside, it is important to mention that spirit is not the only factor affecting vulnerability. The body, for example, has its own vulnerability in the form of inherited characteristics that predispose to certain illness, such as Huntington's chorea, sickle cell anemia, and others.

The degree of harmony within the self is directly related to the state of the self's vulnerability. A harmonious self has a strong "will to existence" and the best chance of resisting any noxious assault on its integrity, whatever form the assault may take, from fracture to leukemia.

Recent studies have shown that "optimists"—people who may be classified as "charismatic" and possessing an abundance of spirit—are happier and healthier than the general population. Optimism, as an attitude, "pays dividends as wide-ranging as health, longevity, job success and higher scores on achievement tests."[3]

A de-spirited self, with low vitality and a diminished will to existence, is a breeding ground for misery. De-spiritedness leads to a pessimistic, "Scrooge-like," outlook. According to studies, pessimists make a mess of their lives; more bad things befall them, like marital breakups, family troubles, and troubles in school. They are also more lonely and estranged from people; talking gloom and doom is a turn-off. In an ongoing study of ninety-nine members of the Harvard graduating class of the four years between 1939 to 1944 reported by Dr. George Valliant, it is becoming apparent that "around the age of 45 the health of the pessimists started to deteriorate more quickly."[4]

In a short second stage, illness appears. The form it takes becomes evident (strep throat, flu, depression, malignant disease, chronic illness). The illness process is triggered and starts to unfold. It is now three-dimensional. Spirit, mind, and body are involved.

In the third stage, the illness becomes manifest. Symptoms appear. The disease takes on a life of its own, and the self becomes consumed by the illness. The will to exist serves as a countervailing force to the illness.

In the fourth, or resolution, stage, the illness is resolved in one of several ways: the patient is healed, dies, or has to learn to live with the illness forever—it becomes chronic.

· APPENDIX D ·
Poem[1]

It seems extremely stupid
To buy a baseball team these days.
Most lose a lot of money,
You've got to pay to play.
So why, you ask, do you want one?
Is there some secret that you know?
Well, the secret's here inside me.
It's been here fifty years or more.
Have you ever picked a grounder
On a makeshift field of rocks?
Or slid into second base
On a blacktop parking lot?
Have you hung in against Wild Willy
And his ninety miles of heat?
Did you just keep coming back

And wouldn't let yourself be beat?
You could run like Pepper Martin
And pitch like Dizzy Dean.
At school you might be striking out
But you'd be winning in your dreams.
You knew twenty years of averages
And you snuck in all the games.
A lot of years have passed,
And you still know all the names.
You've married, worked and fathered.
Your hair has turned all gray.
But there's still the same excitement
At the ballpark every day.
If all the future holds for me
Is a lot more of the same,
Then I'm long in extra innings,
It's a never-ending game.
It's time to start a new one.
The seasons come and go.
It's always, "Wait till next year,"
When we'll strike the winning blow.
I wish I'd been good enough
To make it on the field.
But Casey said it best of all
And to his words I'll yield:
"A struggling few got up to go, leaving there the rest
With that hope that springs eternal
within the human breast."

· NOTES ·

INTRODUCTION

1. William James, *The Varieties of Religious Experience* (New York: Viking Penguin, 1983), 31.

CHAPTER 1

1. Sigmund Freud, private conversation reported in *Psychiatric News*, March 1987.

CHAPTER 2

1. Carl Jung, *Man and His Symbols* (New York: Doubleday, 1964), 330.

2. Ernest Becker, *The Denial of Death* (New York: Free Press), 193.
3. James Gleick, "Science on the Track of God," *New York Times*, Jan. 11, 1987, 22.

CHAPTER 3

1. R. M. Bucke, *Cosmic Consciousness and the Evolution of the Human Mind* (New York: Citadel, 1984).
2. M. Sharaf, *Fury on Earth* (New York: St. Martin's Press, 1983).
3. Loren H. Crabtree, Jr., in *Psychiatric Times*, December 1986, 22.
4. P. Webbink, *Power of the Eyes* (New York: Springer Publishing Co., 1986), 85.
5. F. A. Mesmer, *Mesmerism*, trans. George Bloch (Los Altos, CA: William Kaufman, Inc., 1980), 35.
6. Larry Dossey, *Space Time and Medicine* (Boulder, CO: Shambala Publications, 1982), 100.
7. Ibid.
8. R. Spitz, "Anaclitic Depression," *Psychoanalytic Study of the Child*, vol. 6 (New York: International Universities Press, 1946), 113–117.
9. R. Spitz in *Manual of Child Psychopathology*, Benjamin Wolman, ed. (New York: McGraw-Hill, 1972), 498.
10. Rudolf Steiner, *An Outline of Occult Science* (Spring Valley, NY: Anthroposophic Press, 1984), 15.
11. Robert Ornstein, *Multimind* (Boston: Houghton Mifflin, 1986), 83.
12. Ibid., 68.
13. Ibid., 64.
14. Ibid., 68.
15. K. Eric Drexler, *Engines of Creation* (New York: Anchor/Doubleday, 1986), summary statement, flyleaf.

16. William James, *The Varieties of Religious Experience* (New York: Viking Penguin, 1983), 55.
17. Steiner, *An Outline of Occult Science*, 13.
18. A. M. Greeley, *Ecstasy: A Way of Knowing* (Englewood Cliffs, NJ: Prentice-Hall, 1974), 61.
19. Rudolph Otto in *The Encyclopedia of Philosophy*, Paul Edwards, ed., vol. V (New York: Macmillan Publishing Co., The Free Press, 1967), 15.
20. Silvano Arieti, *Creativity: The Magic Synthesis* (New York: Basic Books, 1976), 61.
21. J.W.N. Sullivan, *Beethoven, His Spiritual Development* (New York: Vintage, 1960), 3.
22. Will Durant, *The Story of Philosophy* (New York: Pocket Books, 1961), 271.
23. A. Storr, *Jung* (Glasgow: William Collins & Sons, 1973), 60.
24. J. Mishlove, *The Roots of Consciousness* (New York: Random House, 1975), 25.

• CHAPTER 4 •

1. Whit Burnet, ed., *The Spirit of Man* (New York: Hawthorn Books, 1958), 356.
2. Paul Edwards, *Encyclopedia of Philosophy* (New York: Macmillan/Free Press, 1967), 147.
3. R. W. Emerson, "Essay on Heroism" (New York: the Peter Pauper Press).
4. J.W.N. Sullivan, *Beethoven, His Spiritual Development* (New York: Vintage, 1960), 30.
5. C. G. Jung, *Memories, Dreams and Reflections* (New York: Vintage Books, 1961), 303.
6. Speech in Va. Convention, March 23, 1775, from William Wirt, *Patrick Henry*, 1818.

7. Charles Dickens, *The Old Curiosity Shop* (N.Y. Books Inc., 1807), 38.
8. L. LeShan, *The Medium, the Mystic and the Physicist* (New York: Ballantine, 1975), 126.
9. NBC *Vermont Morning News*, December 18, 1986.
10. Edgar Cayce, *Edgar Cayce's Story of the Origin and Destiny of Man* (New York: Berkeley Books, 1972).
11. Anna Freud, *The Ego and the Mechanisms of Defense* (New York: International Universities Press, 1946).
12. H. Smith, *The Religions of Man* (New York: Harper & Row/Perennial Library, 1956), 86.
13. Edwards, *Encyclopedia of Philosophy*, 519.

CHAPTER 5

1. H. Smith, *The Religions of Man* (New York: Harper & Row/Perennial Library, 1959), 8.

CHAPTER 6

1. Charles Dickens, *A Christmas Carol* (New York: Washington Square Press, 1963), 18.
2. J. W. von Goethe, *Faust* (New York: W. W. Norton, 1976), 452.

CHAPTER 8

1. J. D. Frank, *Persuasion and Healing* (New York: Schocken, 1973), 74.
2. H. Benson, *The Mind-Body Effect* (New York: Berkeley, 1980).

3. L. LeShan, *How to Meditate* (Boston: Little, Brown, 1974).
4. S. Locke and D. Colligan, *The Healer Within* (New York: E. P. Dutton, 1987).
5. J. Borysenko, *Minding the Body, Minding the Mind* (New York: Addison-Wesley, 1987).
6. G. Jampolosky, *Teach Only Love* (New York: Bantam, 1983), 36.
7. C. Peterson, Interview in the *New York Times*, February 3, 1987, C5.
8. J. Strachey, ed., *The Complete Psychological Works of Sigmund Freud*, vol. 7 (London: Hogarth Press, 1959), 289.
9. Frank, *Persuasion and Healing*, 138.
10. L. Dossey, *Space, Time and Medicine* (Boulder, CO: Shambala Publications, 1982), 210.

•CHAPTER 9•

1. B. S. Siegel, *Love, Medicine and Miracles* (New York: Harper & Row, 1986).
2. M. Stone, "Batting for Dollars," *California Business*, November 1986, 48.
3. R. Ornstein and D. Sobel, "The Healing Brain," *Psychology Today*, March 1987, 52.
4. Ibid.

•EPILOGUE•

1. A. Thomas, S. Chess, and H.G. Birch, *Temperament and Behavior Disorders in Children* (New York: New York University Press, 1968).
2. M. S. Peck, *People of the Lie* (New York: Simon & Schuster, 1983).

APPENDIX A
•————————•

1. William James, *The Varieties of Religious Experience* (New York: Viking Penguin, 1983), p. 72.
2. L. Dossey, *Space, Time and Medicine* (Boulder, CO: Shambala Publications, 1982), 223.
3. J. Roberts, *The Seth Material* (New York: Bantam, 1970), 13.
4. Paul Edwards, *Encyclopedia of Philosophy* (New York: Macmillan/Free Press, 1967), 287.
5. Ibid., 140.
6. Ibid.
7. Ibid., 139.
8. Ibid., 140.
9. J. Mishlove, *The Roots of Consciousness* (New York: Random House, 1975), 5.
10. Paul Edwards, *Encyclopedia of Philosophy* (New York: Macmillan, The Free Press, 1967), 146.
11. Viktor E. Frankl, *The Doctor and the Soul* (New York: Alfred E. Knopf, 1955), xvi.
12. G. A. Zilboorg, *A History of Medical Psychology* (New York: W. W. Norton, 1960), 44.
13. Rudolf Steiner, *An Outline of Occult Science* (Spring Valley, NY: Anthroposophic Press, 1984), 25.
14. Ibid.
15. J.W.N. Sullivan, *Beethoven, His Spiritual Development* (New York: Vintage, 1960), 16.
16. J. Dryden, *Annus Mirabilis*, 1667, st. 155 (New York: Little, Brown and Co., 1968).
17. R. Fassenella, Interview on CBS TV, October 5, 1986.
18. William Faulkner, quotation from an acceptance speech on the occasion of the American Book Awards, 1955.
19. Edwards, *Encyclopedia of Philosophy*, 143.

APPENDIX B

1. R. A. Monroe, *Journeys Out of the Body* (New York: Doubleday, 1971).

APPENDIX C

1. J. D. Frank, *Persuasion and Healing* (New York: Schocken, 1973), 327.
2. Ibid., 75.
3. C. Peterson, Interview in the *New York Times*, February 3, 1987, C5.
4. George E. Valliant, *Adaptation to Life* (Boston: Little, Brown and Co., 1977).

APPENDIX D

1. M. Stone, "Poem: Untitled," *California Business Magazine*, November 1986, 48.

ADDITIONAL
· REFERENCES ·

Bateson, Gregory. *Mind and Nature*. New York: E.P. Dutton, 1979.

Brantl, George, ed. *Catholicism*. New York: George Braziller, 1962.

Capra, Fritjof. *The Tao of Physics*. Berkeley, CA: Shambala Publications, 1975.

Castaneda, Carlos. *The Teachings of Don Juan: A Yaqui Way of Knowledge*. New York: Pocket Books, 1974.

Cavendish, Richard, ed. *Man, Myth, and Magic*. Freeport, NY: Marshall Cavendish Corp., 1983.

Clark, Ronald. *Einstein: The Life and Times*. New York: World Publishing Company, 1971.

Cornford, Francis, trans. *The Republic of Plato*. New York: Oxford University Press, 1945.

Davies, Paul. *God and the New Physics.* New York: Simon & Schuster, 1983.

Frankl, Victor. *Man's Search for Meaning.* New York: Pocket Books, 1959/63.

Fromm, Erich. *Beyond the Chains of Illusion.* New York: Pocket Books, 1963.

Gardner, Howard. *Frames of Mind.* New York: Basic Books, 1985.

Hawken, Paul. *The Magic of Findhorn.* New York: Harper & Row, 1975.

Hesse, Herman. *Siddhartha.* New York: Bantam, 1971.

Hicks, David. *Tetum Ghosts and Kin/Fieldwork in an Indonesian Community.* Palo Alto, CA: Mayfield Publishing Co., 1976.

Hoff, Benjamin. *The Tao of Pooh.* New York: E. P. Dutton, 1982.

Hooper, Judith and Teresi, Dick. *The Three Pound Universe.* New York: Macmillan, 1986.

Josephy, Alvin M., Jr. *The Indian Heritage of America.* New York: Bantam, 1976.

Jowett, B., trans. *The Works of Plato.* New York: Dial Press, 1936.

Jung, Carl. *Memories, Dreams, and Reflections.* Great Britain: Random House, 1961, 1962, 1963.

———. *Man and His Symbols.* Garden City, NY: Doubleday, 1964.

Lilly, John. *The Deep Self.* New York: Warner Books, 1977.

Lindenbaum, Shirley. *Kuru Society—Disease and Danger in the New Guinea Highlands.* Palo Alto, CA: Mayfield Publishing Co., 1979.

Lowen, Alexander. *The Betrayal of the Body.* New York: Macmillan, 1967.

Neihardt, John G. *Black Elk Speaks.* New York: Pocket Books, 1932.

Parrinder, Geoffrey, ed. *World Religions*. New York: Facts on File, 1971.

Peck, Scott. *People of the Lie*. New York: Simon & Schuster, 1983.

Pirsig, Robert. *Zen and the Art of Motorcycle Maintenance*. New York: Bantam, 1975.

Radin, Paul. *Primitive Man as Philosopher*. New York: Dover, 1957.

Renou, Louis, ed. *Hinduism*. New York: George Braziller, 1962.

Sartre, Jean-Paul. *Existentialism and Human Emotions*. New York: Wisdom Library/Philosophical Library, 1957.

Satbrem. *Sri Aurobindo, or The Adventure of Consciousness*. New York: Harper & Row, 1968.

Schwartz, Joseph, and McGuiness, Michael. *Einstein for Beginners*. New York: Pantheon Books, 1979.

Shawn, Wallace, and Andre, Gregory. *My Dinner with Andre*. New York: Grove Press, 1981.

Staniforth, Maxwell, trans. *Meditations (Marcus Aurelius)*. New York: Penguin Books, 1964.

Stevenson, Ian. *Children who Remember Previous Lives*. Charlottesville, VA.: The University of Virginia Press, 1987.

Taylor, Richard. *Metaphysics*. Englewood Cliffs, NJ: Prentice-Hall Foundations of Philosophy, 1983.

Tober, Bob, and Wolf, Fred Alan. *Space-Time and Beyond*. New York: Bantam New Age Books, 1983.

Tredennick, Hugh, trans. *The Last Days of Socrates (Plato)*. New York: Penguin Books, 1954.

Twitchell, Paul. *Spiritual Notebook*. Menlo Park, CA: IWP Publishing, 1982.

Wei, Henry, trans. *The Guiding Light of Lao Tzu*. Wheaton, IL: Theosophical Publishing House, 1982.

Wilber, Ken. *The Spectrum of Consciousness*. Wheaton, IL: Theosophical Publishing House, 1977.

· INDEX ·